International Me(
The Art of Business Diplomacy

Second Edition

Picture on cover: Hommage à Berthe Morisot (fragment) by Ken Wood, 1962.

Permission has been granted by Mr Kenwood for reproduction of his painting Hommage à Berthe Morisot, 1962, on the cover of the book.

International Mediation – The Art of Business Diplomacy

Second Edition

With a Foreword by

Lord Hurd of Westwell

A CIP Catalogue record for this book is available from the Library of Congress.

ISBN 1 84592 346 4 (Tottel Publishing Ltd)
ISBN 90 411 2579 5 (Kluwer Law International)

Published by

Kluwer Law International
P.O. Box 316
2400 AH Alpen aan den Rijn
The Netherlands

Tottel Publishing Ltd
Maxwelton House
41–43 Boltro Road
Haywards Heath
West Sussex
RH16 1BJ
United Kingdom

Sold and distributed in the United Kingdom and Ireland by
Tottel Publishing Ltd

Sold and distributed in North, Central and South America by
Aspen Publishers, Inc
7201 McKinney Circle
Frederick, MD 21704
United States of America

Sold and distributed in all other countries by
Turpin Distribution Services Ltd
Stratton Business Park
Pegasus Drive
Biggleswade
Bedfordshire SG18 8TQ
United Kingdom

Typeset by Kerrypress Ltd, Luton, Beds
Printed and bound in Great Britain by Antony Rowe, Chippenham, Wilts

Contents

Acknowledgements

We should like to recognise the work and support of many colleagues and friends over the years who have helped to bring about a change of knowledge and support for mediation.

We particularly wish to acknowledge the hard work of our co-directors at CEDR, our chairmen, Sir Alex Jarratt, Lord Hurd and Sir Peter Middleton, our Trustees and all the staff, past and present, who have been key to the development of CEDR as a centre of excellence for international mediations.

In addition to those who contributed to our first edition, for the second edition we are also grateful to Jo Zoricich and Rachel James, our PA's, to Ranse Howell and Graham Massie for their comments on the book, to Alice Tapfield for research on the cases and materials and to Lisa Drake for her support on work with the publishers.

A number of senior in-house Counsel from multinational companies gave freely of their time to tell us of their experience, perceptions and expectations for the future. Particular thanks are due to Jan Eijsbouts, Hans Peter Frick, Martin Hayman, Michael Leathes, Dr Singhvi, Hans Stucki, Robert Webb QC and Sir Laurence Street.

We also wish to thank our publishers, Tottel Publishing and Kluwer Law International, for their support.

Last, but not least, we owe a debt to the many parties from around the world and their lawyers who have given us the opportunity of working in the dynamic and evolving process of mediation in their many business settings.

Eileen Carroll

Karl Mackie

September 2006

Foreword

I am pleased that my closing question to the first edition of this book, proved to be a timely one. I know that since that work was written, the authors and CEDR have worked in various ways with major international institutions – the UN, NATO, OECD, and World Trade Organisation. Mediation is of increasing interest as a technique of independent intervention in the evolving political order of global trade. Equally I am happy to record that commercial companies are using it to a much greater extent than when this book was first published, as the authors describe only too clearly. It is a tribute to them and to CEDR that their work has proved to have such a powerful potential to enhance our management of conflict, and I am sure that the next edition will be able to describe a further leap forward.

The Rt Hon Lord Hurd of Westwell CH CBE

British Foreign Secretary from 1989–1995

Foreword to First Edition

Many years of government and international diplomacy have taught me the importance of standing back from conflict in order to resolve it. It is interesting to see the techniques of international diplomacy being adopted by lawyers, judges and other professionals to solve business problems.

The field of international diplomacy teaches many lessons in human interaction – and the authors have recognised the need to acknowledge all elements of conflict and not to narrow the focus to one discipline.

The work of the mediator is very important – and necessarily an understated activity. Mediators require energy, patience, persistence and a willingness to act as a neutral agent of all parties – total commitment is important.

This work should be an encouragement to international business and their advisers. The arrival of this approach is very promising for the fast moving, ever expanding global business community. It is impressive too, to see the speed with which CEDR as a non-profit organisation has established its influence on the international arena. The authors, both closely involved in founding CEDR, deserve credit for helping to create this momentum.

Although the international business world now appears to be borrowing from the arts of the political diplomat, who knows – political diplomats may have something to learn in turn from the systematic and rigorous professionalism being applied to international business conflicts?

The Rt Hon Lord Hurd of Westwell CH CBE

British Foreign Secretary from 1989–1995

Authors' Introduction

We firmly believe that the business community and those representing them are interested in effective and economic resolution of conflict. Our research with in-house lawyers in multinational companies revealed that there is a lack of knowledge about the workings of mediation as a resolution tool for international disputes – our purpose in writing this book was to inform those involved in resolving international disputes of the current practice and experience of international mediation. One leading Dutch lawyer controlling a global legal team predicted that mediation has a significant role to play in the future that surpasses the traditional approaches available.

Our faith in the concept of mediation in the 1980s led us to work for the launch of CEDR, Centre for Effective Dispute Resolution, created to provide institutional support for mediation internationally and domestically. Since then CEDR's growth and involvement in international mediation and training has been remarkable and inspiring for us and for many observers.

CEDR's training and track record of projects has given credibility to the use of mediation. CEDR's contract clauses (Part 2.2) have been incorporated into international contracts worldwide and have been upheld by the London Commercial Court. CEDR employs a multilingual staff (over eighteen languages including Mandarin are spoken), and provides mediators from around the world through its global network (MEDAL, see Part 2.4)

Equally we have personally mediated many and diverse international and commercial matters. Despite the strength of CEDR's development, international mediation is still in its infancy. We therefore wish to share with international lawyers and managers this practical experience to inform and encourage others; to provide a real picture of what happens in international mediation and how it is structured; to give practical guidance to allow parties to make the best of the process. We also see the potential to develop this approach in order to transform conflict management creativity and capability, and we touch on that also in this book.

This experience is filtering across the globe. In recent years we have seen a significant increase in international mediations with parties from many countries including the United States, Canada, Chile, Germany, the Netherlands, Cyprus, Denmark, Italy, Portugal, Spain, Ireland, Norway, France, Italy, Luxembourg, United Kingdom, China, Hong Kong, Bangladesh, Nigeria, Pakistan, Turkey, Lebanon, Saudi Arabia, Israel, Sri Lanka, Malawi, Guatemala, Uzbekistan, Venezuela and many others.

Most telling in terms of mediation's future scale of impact, the range of case values is wide – $200,000 to $1bn, the average length of mediation just under two days. The sectors involved are also broad, international trade, intellectual property, IT, maritime, insurance, mergers and acquisitions, telecommunications, construction, engineering and pharmaceuticals and virtually every area of legal practice. And we are engaged in a range of new international projects which is bringing mediation and better conflict management to more corporate, civil justice and global practice.

Above all we hope that our work will encourage greater use of mediation. Experience, more than any theory, has already proved it a highly effective tool to assist global business and its advisers in resolving business conflict. That is why in the Second Edition we have given more prominence to the Cases section of the book – we hope some of these will reflect your own experience, or encourage you to engage in greater use of this pragmatic but creative process.

Eileen Carroll

Karl Mackie

London 2006

PART ONE. **Mediating International Business Disputes: The Process, the Practice and the Potential**

Chapter 1. The Potential for International Mediation in Business Conflict

'Someone who hails from the business world – with its emphasis on "let's get the deal done", on behaving constructively, on finding ways to resolve impasse – simply isn't prepared for the ambivalence over whether or not to settle that seems ingrained in the typical dispute. One minute, the client appears interested in what can be worked out; the next, he's ready to go back to war. An atmosphere of mistrust hangs over the proceedings, poisoning the climate for successful negotiations. The sense of solubility that pervades the deal context – awareness that to reach a mutually satisfactory arrangement you may have to help the other guy solve his problems – is notably absent where a dispute is concerned. And too often the players stand around shuffling their feet, afraid to initiate talks and thereby convey weakness, while waiting in vain for the other side to blink.'

James Freund, The Neutral Negotiator, New York.

'In litigation you lose control. With mediation you keep control of the process, particularly on costs. Mediation clearly has a significant role to play in international disputes.'

Hans Peter Frick, General Counsel, Nestlé Switzerland.

'Mediation is a flexible process conducted confidentially in which a neutral person actively assists parties in working towards a negotiated agreement of a dispute or difference, with the parties in ultimate control of the decision to settle and the terms of resolution.'

(CEDR, 2005)

Managers caught in the conflict web

In this book we want to open the window on a dramatic, yet profoundly simple, new legal approach and management tool for handling international business conflicts more effectively. International mediation may have an ancient history, but as a practised professional approach, it is still relatively recent. Only in the last ten to twenty years has it grown significantly in scale or been incorporated into standard commercial contract clauses. As two mediators who have been consciously engaged in promoting the growth of this global phenomenon, we want to share our experience and the methodology with the widest possible business and legal audience. All our practice tells us that the value of this approach is both profound, and yet still under-utilised. Apart from the fact that the technique is still registering with international managers, there is also some inherent management and legal resistance to the approach which we want to address in this first chapter.

Managers meet conflicts and disputes in 101 different ways in organisational life – failures of suppliers to provide or customers to pay, employee grievances or non-performance, inter-departmental territorial arguments, breaches of intellectual or physical property rights, disagreements over corporate policy and practice either internally or with joint venture and alliance partners, disputed allocation of risk and reward in projects, personality clashes, divergence of expectations and understandings, regulatory supervision creating economic threat, and on and on. In many ways the miracle is that overt conflicts do not break out more often, given the complexity and competitive market of most business projects.

Managers may be sufficiently aware of cultural differences and risks to take even more care with cross-border business dealings, but they face an environment which is also significantly more capable of creating or exacerbating conflict. They have to deal with differences in cultural expectation and standards, problems of communication, divergence of decision-making styles and assumptions, differences in legal and regulatory treatment, mismatched business goals, economic or political upheavals. These create a heady brew of factors which increase the volatility of business practice in an international context. Given this backcloth of complexity and the competitive nature of the business world, it is surprising that overt conflict is not more apparent as a topic of business school curricula. Yet 'conflict management' as a term of art, is more often used in a political setting than in management meetings or business school programmes.

Conflict and creativity theorists might spin the story of how conflict can lead to renewed energy, catharsis, or to lateral solutions to problems. However, this theoretical approach hits up against a very simple fact of management life that is globally evident – managers usually do not like conflicts or anticipated conflicts. They typically perceive them as bad news, likely to interrupt careful business plans or agreements, likely to threaten the business bottom line or the manager's personal situation or career. A primitive response then kicks in, generally described by biological psychologists as the 'fight or flight' reaction. Managers are most likely either to become more aggressive and worsen the communication loop with the other party ('fight'), or they will seek ways to avoid recognising the conflict and will delay dealing with it or pretend it does not exist until it becomes a crisis ('flight'). Studies of managers in conflict confirm that their decision-making capabilities suffer in the process, whichever of the two modes is adopted. 'Working through' the conflict in a balanced way becomes more difficult.

As a result, in many business disputes, managers need help but often fail to call on it while they try the assertive or aggressive route out, or attempt to avoid confronting the issue. These methods may by chance work for them in many cases, albeit probably not achieving the full value from the conflict that another approach may have. Where they don't work and the 'difficulty' becomes a dispute, then what?

Traditionally at this point, where other economic or personal pressures have not worked, managers resort to a further professional route, they 'call in the lawyers'. This is commonly seen as a stage of escalation, thereby increasing the fight reaction, while giving managers the comfort of letting go of the issue as a management problem – thus fight and flight are achieved simultaneously. How the lawyers react will depend on the nature of the issues but, in international commercial dealings, they will typically and traditionally have two choices: (a) to go to a national court for litigation relief; or (b) to resort to international arbitration if provided for in the contract or otherwise agreed on an ad hoc basis. The conflict moves from being a commercial question, to being part of the 'legal business' and its methodologies and applicable principles.

The lawyer route

Mediation is a powerful art and structure bringing together into an open dialogue the architects and implementers of the commercial process that is in crisis. When disputes are left entirely to the legal community to resolve, it is like asking structural engineers to fix a major defect on a suspension bridge without letting them see the design plans and talk to mechanical engineers to help them to understand the options available for them to investigate and come up with solutions. Fixing a fault on a suspension bridge would obviously involve a number of disciplines and the solutions would not focus solely on the defect but also on consequences of action and non-action. Equally, when commercial companies 'fall out' because there is a defect in their relationship – for example, if they have not been paid or there is a conflict over services offered – they will, having failed to resolve it, often hand it to a legal team to find a legal solution based on entitlement and rights. Others who have responsibility and value to add to the resolution of the problem step back or are excluded from the process. The result is that the problem tends to be only viewed from one expert's view, applying a legal analysis. Commercial, technical, or people expertise may be excluded from the approach to the problem or are certainly not central to it. With this approach the whole 'bridge' between the parties may effectively be closed, without the commercial community ever then finding an effective and fair route to resolution.

Yet companies that fail to address conflict effectively, that are not – in the words of a study by the American Arbitration Association – 'dispute-wise', may lose significant value from their business. We have referred, at the beginning of this chapter, to the enormous range and variety of areas where managers confront conflicts. Our experiences and surveys confirm that few are well trained or feel adept at managing such conflicts, or are skilled in mediation.

The experience of the authors too in being trusted to intervene in corporate conflict, is that resolution of complex commercial problems requires not only better approaches to conflict management, but also many layers of understanding and approach. The more complex the problem, the greater the need for a broader and flexible approach to solutions. In international disputes, problems are compounded by geographical and cultural distance, different cultural understandings, political interference, changing commercial agendas and the many other potential hazards that can 'drive' on to our metaphoric bridge.

Given the difficulties that are particularly present in international disputes, it is not surprising that to adopt a wholly legal approach to their resolution often brings enormous frustrations and disappointment to all parties. These include:
– the time taken to achieve a workable result;
– the result not meeting expectations or predictions;
– the time and costs involved exceeding initial expectations;
– frustration of the client at the lack of commercial and technical understanding;
– diversion of the team from mainstream opportunities while they play the legal game.

Ironically, lawyers often share the frustration on behalf of those involved. However, like their clients, they may be caught in what negotiation specialists have described as the ''negotiator's dilemma' – open dialogue and conciliatory approaches may tempt the other side to greater demands. The main legal tools traditionally at their disposal are geared up to be complex and high-risk, relying on international arbitration or resorting to national courts for a decision. Thus until the growth of commercial mediation practice, lawyers lacked a systematic professional technique to address the problem. There is, however, now a realisation by some very experienced jurists that mediation has much to offer all those engaged in assisting international corporations solve their conflicts.

'... and in the same way as I have had my mind changed about litigation in favour of arbitration, my long devotion to arbitration is now being eroded by the realisation that the future will belong to ADR'[1].

Sir Michael Kerr, past President of the London Court of International Arbitration.

Mediation: bridging the gap

Getting back to our metaphor of the bridge, mediation – intervention of an independent third party to assist negotiations – itself provides a new form of a conceptual suspension bridge between managers or advisers in conflict. The mediation process offers an interim structure to open up a traffic of dialogue, marks out lanes over which communications can pass with less risk of head-on collision, adjusts the traffic flow to give users a sense of managed risk, and provides both momentum and relative safety from which to explore the various views from the bridge and the routes across it. To create an effective bridge the good mediator needs the skills of the project manager, the vision and maps of the bridge designer, yet also inherent respect for the creativity of principals, experts and advisers once the mediation process unleashes an effective flow of communication.

In its combination of flexibility alongside a degree of disciplined form, mediation is especially suited to the diversity—cultural, managerial, technical – of global business traffic. It renews time honoured ancient processes of community tribal adjustment at a 21st Century level.

Of course mediation is not a panacea. It cannot on its own overcome deeply-rooted intransigence or irreconcilable differences between businesses or other organisations in the global community. The alternatives to mediation however – arbitration, litigation, economic sanctions – are much blunter and costlier in approach and outcome. They create an opportunity for mediation as a complementary 'fast lane' when traffic conditions allow.

The more businesses experience the unique qualities and commercial benefits of mediation, the greater will be the pressure on managers to opt for this alternative fast-track process.

Those who have experienced mediation in international disputes attest to its effectiveness across a diverse range of international conflicts. A mediator can smooth out the process of managing difficult or tough communications, for example between joint venture partners who have been unable to agree on resolution of a critical commercial issue between themselves. The mediation process can also provide a formal structure and mode of operation for crystallising, debating and resolving intractable legal battles. These arguments often involve complex legal issues between two or more corporations – who may have invested millions in the formal process of law or arbitration and are close to (sometimes even beyond) the court door before they seek the assistance of the mediator. The case summaries reported throughout this book are all real cases, most were mediated by the authors or by other CEDR mediators. All but one reached successful outcomes agreed by the parties despite earlier impasse between sophisticated managers and advisers.

The challenge is to increase the extent of mediation's use so that there is more experience and therefore a greater body of managers and lawyers to support its growth. For this to be achieved, more advisers and businesses need to test its potential. Alongside this, the international mediation community has the responsibility to research mediation experience objectively or work with academics and others to do so and to use the results to advance training, scholarship and practice. We hope that this text will form a groundbreaking foundation on which further experience can build to enhance global business diplomacy in the 21st Century.

Mediation know-how

The potential and power of successful mediation interventions, along with recent growth trends in the use of this technique, suggest that it is likely to emerge as a key mechanism within the activities of new generations of international managers and professional advisers. In this book we aim to demonstrate clearly international mediation in practice, we will explore when and how it is best used, and provide the beginnings of a practical theory to explain why mediation adds value to business negotiations on the one hand and legal negotiations on the other.

Two special interests have motivated our writing of this book. First, to share our growing experience – as international mediators who also act as advisers, trainers and campaigners for international mediation. Even though business and legal mediation is now a more common part of legal education, there has been little attention paid to the special characteristics of international mediation practice. We seek to share our experience in order to encourage a broader use of this technique and to provide a benchmark against which future experience can be tested.

Second, we wish not just to describe the mediation process but also outline how and why it works. Because of the inherent flexibility of the process, particularly in the complex context of international work, it is vital that mediators and advisers understand how to adapt mediation to the specific circumstances of a case. John Kenneth Galbraith, the late celebrated economist once said that 'there is nothing so practical as a good theory'. We hope to provide in this work concepts about mediation practice which can assist as guides to advisers and managers so that they can adapt the mediation option to suit their specific needs and the circumstances of particular cases.

International commercial mediation practice has developed out of the work of creative lawyers who seek to avoid, for their clients, the costs and expense of formal, traditional processes. However, knowledge of how and why mediation works can also allow business managers to improve how they deal directly with difficult negotiations with their business partners, suppliers, customers and others. In this book we will endeavour to unravel the mystique sometimes associated with mediation practice. We also aim to help managers avoid the pitfalls of crude fight or flight approaches to difficult disputes, negotiations or conflicts and thereby bring mediation into the mainstream of management know-how and action. Many of the case studies in this book reflect disputes where business managers had attempted to negotiate resolution but had reached a total deadlock. Mediation broke the deadlock. Some at least could have been resolved much earlier.

The recent growth of international mediation

Global business diplomacy by professional mediators owes its growth to two great converging forces – creative lawyering and the expansion of cross-border trading. The essential ingredient of this innovation in negotiation process is that business managers reclaim control and can fashion solutions that meet business needs. The client/customer is back in the driving seat and can escape both from a legal quagmire and from the fight or flight dilemma.

Creative lawyering

'Let's kill all the lawyers' as a simple commercial slogan goes back to Shakespearean times. Businesses which find themselves in difficult conflict need lawyers. But lawyers, as with all service professionals, need to adapt and innovate to survive. International mediation owes its growth to lawyers searching for alternative, systematic approaches which will streamline and simplify the management and resolution of conflict.

Promotion of the process and culture change to reduce adherence to traditional adversarial methods—are prerequisites to mediation finding an effective place in the lawyer's toolkit for resolution of conflict. Campaigning for such a process change can only be effective if other advisers and clients learn the techniques and if legal systems can also adapt. The promotion of mediation for 'domestic' disputes has therefore been a vital foundation for mediation growth, later extended to international business lawyering.

Ironically, mediation has its origins in time-honoured practices in many different parts of the globe. The *wassit* as facilitator in Arab business relations, the community elder as mediator in Chinese society, the judge with a duty to promote settlement in Swiss, German, Danish, Japanese and other judicial practice – all of these attest to the long recognised benefits of third-party facilitation as an alternative to adjudication in defusing unnecessary conflict and overcoming deadlock.

However these practices have generally not transferred into modern 'professional' lawyering. In addition, in our experience these methods rarely represent professional mediation in the modern format so much as 'primitive' informal settlement practices. They rely on encouraging settlement either by way of exhortation to the parties or by giving an early indication to the parties of the way the adjudicator is inclined to decide the case, should it proceed.

Such techniques have been overtaken by a more comprehensive array of recognised skills and tactics which are available to the mediator to assist in negotiations. These are techniques which are closer to the arts of international political diplomacy than to legal culture. Much has been learnt over the last 25 years for example of 'shuttle diplomacy', first made famous by US Secretary of State, Henry Kissinger.

The process is also informed by more sophisticated modern knowledge now available on negotiation, group dynamics and decision-making. Most importantly, however, within the last two decades, particularly in the common law jurisdictions, parties seeking to avoid the costs and delay of the adversarial legal system, have developed a significant core of practical experiences in the successful mediation of commercial and civil litigation actions. This experience has provided the basis for more advanced training of mediators and of advisers which is also gradually extending into international practice.

Alongside and contributing to this has been the emergence of significant non-profit organisations promoting mediation internationally such as the organisation we helped found, CEDR (Centre for Effective Dispute Resolution) and the International Institute for Conflict Prevention and Resolution (CPR). Responding to this, international arbitration centres have been increasingly willing to extend their service offerings to include mediation and other ADR techniques. Leading international law firms in turn are recognising the need to adapt their professional practice to incorporate mediation contract clauses, advice and advocacy.

The pace of professional adjustment to new service technology is often slow. However, it has been speeded up in those jurisdictions where the courts have begun to direct cases into out-of-court mediation efforts – 'court-annexed' or 'court-referred' ADR. In directing cases into mediation, judges are recognising the potential value of mediation to achieve faster and sometimes better settlements than the courts can offer by traditional methods. For example by 1996 the Commercial Court in London, 60% of whose cases are international, had adopted robust Practice Directions which gave its judges the power to direct litigants into ADR proceedings. It has increasingly done so, fuelling the growth of international mediations and mediation awareness in London professional services. By 1999, ADR directions were part of the entire English civil justice system and by 2006 were extended to cover how parties should behave before they issued legal proceedings.

This development has not been limited to the English system or even common law jurisdictions spawned by the English system. By the end of the 20th Century, similar directions towards the encouragement and use of ADR were in place in countries such as Argentina, Australia, Canada, France, Greece, Hong Kong, Israel, New Zealand, Singapore and the USA. And the European Union had begun a debate on how to harmonise European legal systems if it treated mediation as a parallel track to the litigation system. The support for mediation was also marked in the legal developments and standard setting in those countries of Central and Eastern Europe who sought accession to the EU (see *The EU Mediation Atlas*, Further Reading).

Initially, mediators and creative lawyers were by and large seeking to tackle only domestic challenges—logjams in national courts and a crisis of confidence in the effectiveness of the adjudication/professional lawyering process. However, inevitably, international legal specialists have been drawn into this exploration. In addition, this movement to oil the wheels of national systems has been caught up in an evolution of even more profound social consequence-globalisation.

The global economy

The late 20th Century saw an exponential growth in the internationalisation of products and services, with not only the multinationals but also tradition- ally domestic companies exporting regularly, or providing insurance or financial or other services across borders. Alongside and related to this, is the increasing impact of new technology facilitating global production, distribution, services and culture. Even in the first years of the 21st century following the first edition of this book, there have been further develop- ments in global interconnectedness – with growth in the new economies of China, India, South America and Eastern Europe. And there has been marked growth in the powers of media and new technology around the Internet and mobile telecommunications. Global energy and climate chal- lenges (themselves part of a conflictual agenda) add to the further sense of an interconnected, yet rapidly changing, world.

In its turn this global marketplace drives the need for flexibility and responsiveness in business and consumer relations. The global economy throws down a challenge to governments and legal systems equally to offer matching flexibility and responsiveness in their legal systems, institutions, and dispute resolution mechanisms. The trend towards a growth in media- tion is part of a deeper and broader rethinking of the role of international law, legal systems and corporate governance in a world in flux. With improvements in technology, 'online' dispute resolution (ODR) also becomes a possible (and in cases such as consumer and domain name disputes, a real) part of the regular disputes landscape.

These changes in the global economy are reflected in the need to find, or train, more 'international managers' to service international business or business relationships. Such relationships are underpinned by legal struc- tures, particularly contractual mechanisms, which in themselves have to be revisited.

Traditionally, international contracts have provided for negotiation (or in the case of employment grievances, a hearing) by senior executives as a final negotiation stage to resolve disputes in joint ventures, distribution, licensing and similar long-term arrangements. If the negotiation mechanism is ineffective, international contracts have attempted to find a way around the difficulty of national courts and legal systems by a referral to international arbitration—judgment of the issues by a party-appointed tribunal of one or three persons.

In international arbitration too, the pressure to respond to the needs of international businesses has been apparent. National governments have increasingly given recognition to the importance of this privatised alternative to national justice systems, both by restricting in national laws the ability of parties to overturn the arbitration clause in national courts, and by signing up to international conventions to ease the enforcement of international arbitration awards in national courts. Refinements of these processes are still continuing in the development of international arbitration practice.

However, arbitration itself has largely mimicked lawyer litigation habits of formalism and adversarialism. Its core purpose of resolution by a process of external investigation and judgment, has tended to clash with the need for flexibility and speed required in the global economy. Contract draftsmen therefore increasingly resort to a mediation procedure to 'fill the gap' between negotiation and arbitration contractual mechanisms.

Finally, the demand for flexible legal processes extends beyond the needs of individual businesses. The global economy has also spawned global trading and economic and political blocs to smooth the path of international trade. Mediation is also increasingly finding its way into the legal structures and practice of these organisations. Today, the European Union and other regional trade blocs have included or proposed mediation process requirements in at least some elements of their practice and regulations. At a global level the World Trade Organisation's dispute settlement procedures which now almost transcend national sovereignty, include a mediation potential for disputes on economic issues and principles. Further proposals for reform of these, to meet the needs of international trade negotiation and to trigger greater use of mediation, are currently under discussion. The OECD (Organisation for Economic Co-operation and Development) has encouraged use of mediation in its guidelines for the conduct of multinational enterprises

Global mediation practice

This convergence of creative lawyering and global economy is by no means an obvious or even development. There is still a significant mismatch between the development in national legal systems of mediation services and skills and the needs of the global business and global politico-legal community. We hope this book will assist in the profound developments still to take place.

We wanted this work to be intensely practical, so we have asked lawyers and managers from a number of international companies to share their experiences with us, both in interviews and in a questionnaire survey. Their views and experiences are incorporated throughout this work, in addition to the experiences and views of those with whom we have mediated at an international level.

In addition we have tried to answer typical questions posed about mediation. We intend to distil and present the best of practical experience of international commercial mediation. We hope this will encourage greater use of mediation by international business and its advisers, but also provide a platform from which all of those engaged in international disputes can enhance their practice and enter the debate with us on how best to continually improve that practice.

The most frequently asked questions in the field of international mediation are:

- How does it work?
- How can it work for an effective, enforceable outcome if it is a non-binding process?
- How does it differ from international arbitration?
- What is the practical experience?
- What are the skills of the international mediator?
- What is the role of the lawyer and the commercial manager?
- How long will it take?
- How much will it cost?
- What is the likelihood of success?
- What can executives learn from mediation experience?

We develop around these questions our own analysis of how and why mediation works, and how best to work with it. It is a process that is at once simple in concept, yet complex and multifaceted in its application – a science in its elements, an art in its workings. We have also found that executives and lawyers typically respond well to the mediation process because it restores control to them. Yet they can also gain enormously in their personal capabilities by learning the techniques of how to make it easy to 'step into the other's shoes', which is at the heart of mediation's effectiveness.

A note on culture and conflict

It is of course natural in a book on international mediation and international business to consider the question of the impact of cultural differences and their relevance to the process of mediation, the reactions to it, and to the skills underlying it. Cross-cultural scholars have identified a range of traits by which cultural diversity can be categorised. All of them have relevance to mediation effectiveness. Categories normally highlighted cover areas such as:

Thinking patterns and belief systems

Some scholars have suggested that it is possible to distinguish cultures which predominantly use a 'linear' or analytical thinking style, versus those where specific experiences or a more intuitive or philosophical approach are more highly valued as a basis for setting forth arguments or beliefs. Equally there can be diversity of beliefs as to appropriate behaviour, including assumptions about conflict and negotiation and what is appropriate behaviour in these contexts. Or there can be different belief systems about time perspectives, or of 'success', or of the basis for effective decision-making. 'Stories' and 'humour' are significantly diverse across cultures, which can influence the pattern of any process of dialogue.

Behaviour

Cultural considerations also influence what behaviour is accepted as normal or appropriate, such as displays of emotion, use of silence, physical contact or distance. Behavioural differences are often the first obvious signal of cultural variations, including matters of personal expression, 'manners' and social etiquette, listening orientation, etc. Working with different 'paces' or protocols of negotiation or decision-making, is another common difference between cultures.

Relationship patterns and social norms

Cultures may also differ along the dimension of how 'individualist' they are versus 'collectivist' (i.e. refer to individual or group authority for decisions and support), or how consensus-based they are in approach compared to autocratic or meritocratic; how much they value principles versus social status; attitudes to time, or to business objectives, etc. These, like the earlier cultural characteristics or cultural identity, are often deeply embedded from childhood as well as subject to current social practice.

Corporate, political and legal system variations

There can be of course significant diversity between countries or cultures in terms of how companies are organised or the way the legal or political system interfaces with corporate and individual behaviour. Some cultures have greater consensual or facilitative management, in others decision-making may be more autocratic or pyramidal in style, or subject to greater regulation or political control. Some cultures value legal input more highly. Legal systems may differ widely, even within the broad umbrella framework descriptions of 'common law' (think of the US/England/Nigeria), or 'civil law' (compare Germany and Italy) or 'Asian law' (compare China with many of its neighbours). Even within the small island of the UK, there are significant differences in dealing with English or Scots Law.

The above list shows fairly simply how often and potentially how deeply cultural complexity will form a backdrop to any international mediation, apart from being itself a source of conflict or impasse in the first place in business relationships. Equally cultural complexity can be overplayed as a difficulty at times. Globalisation of business and communications have given larger groups of managers exposure to cultural diversity and an ability to adapt to it (including mediators working on international cases). This can lead to levels of sophistication and even the ability to play games with cultural stereotypes – in one of our cases at one point when the mediator was questioning a Chinese manager as to whether it was appropriate to take an offer to the next room, the manager said – 'But you must – I am Chinese and I will therefore lose face with all my team if you do not!' Second, in many commercial conflicts, there are already a diversity of nationalities even within the same corporate team. One of the authors handled a case involving an Indonesian company, for example, where there were three separate Scandinavian country nationals – all with their own strong sense of cultural identity – represented in the management teams around the table. Experienced mediators are also aware that even within a national culture, differences in a 'domestic' mediation can be just as dramatic as in an international case. One may be dealing with significant differences between different industry sectors, or between cultural norms of a state body versus a private enterprise, or between an unsophisticated personal injury claimant and an experienced claims manager negotiating on behalf of an insurance company.

16

A note on culture and conflict

While cultural complexity can be over-emphasised at times, it is still a regular and intrinsic feature of international mediation, and something to be acknowledged and worked with. The benefit mediation, compared to other processes, brings to this particular element (developed more fully in the next chapter) is threefold. First, good mediators are trained to empathise with party concerns and reactions, so should begin with a greater sensitivity to the people they are dealing with, including any cultural aspects. Second, mediators have to search for positive means of communicating with parties and must therefore engage with cultural norms. Third, their neutrality should allow them to take a more objective view of what is working and not working between the teams, and how problems might be addressed in order to find a way forward.

In other words, many benefits that we will outline about the process, and how it works in very diverse individual circumstances in conflicts, apply with equal force to how it deals with cultural diversity in negotiating. It gives dynamism to communications, by means of a skilled neutral communicator and project manager who is charged by all parties to seek to win 'buy-in' to a settlement from all the parties around the table and to find the best means to get there. It has to address each party's needs, as well as stretch their negotiation capabilities, and to do so the mediator must engage with whatever the cultural mix around the table. This is one of the 'layers of understanding' which contribute to mediation successfully bridging any gap between the parties. We expand on these capabilities of the process in the following chapters.

1   ADR = Alternative Dispute Resolution. Mediation is the most common ADR Technique.

Chapter 2. Breaking Deadlock: The Power of Mediation

'Mediation allows you to keep control of a dispute and to aim at a commercial solution rather than legal remedies. It can turn your dispute from a business threat into a business opportunity. ADR is a first option – arbitration and litigation are alternatives.'

Jan Eijsbouts, General Counsel, Akzo Nobel, Netherlands.

Mediation power and benefits: overview

International settings multiply the potential for insecurity, misunderstanding, miscommunication in corporate negotiations which break down. Positive efforts at building a bridge of dialogue against such a background can seem threatening or time-wasting. For these reasons too, mediation as a process is often initially seen by inexperienced advisers and managers as either likely to be ineffective or as a last resort – when pain on all sides leaves it as the only alternative – rather than as the sophisticated generic management and professional tool that it can be. 'Mediation is great in theory, but not for this case' is still an all too common response from managers or advisers tasked with preparing attack or defence manoeuvres in the heat of commercial conflicts.

Advisers and managers seeking to adopt mediation for a particular case therefore need to recognise that there is an important first stage of in-client advocacy and persuasion before the process can get off the ground. However, it has been interesting to witness a change of attitude to mediation, which we have experienced in the international cases we have mediated in the recent past, where parties are entering the process more readily and earlier. It is still a common feature, however, of many of these disputes, that there have often been several failed attempts to break commercial deadlock before resort to mediation.

Here is an example of this type of case. It involved two multinational chemical companies based in Europe. There had been a disposal of assets from one entity to the other. Post the completion, the purchasing company alleged that there had been a number of significant breaches of the Sale and Purchase Agreement (SPA) affecting the net asset value of the acquired company, and they claimed for payment of twenty million Euros. The claim was governed by Italian law and an arbitration clause. Nothing very remarkable, until you know that the Italian corporate lawyers agreed at the time of dispute to insert a mediation provision. The mediation was scheduled for two days with a very small team, with two members on each side. Some of the pre-mediation conversations to set up the process were conducted in Italian with linguistically able case managers at CEDR. Each team prepared mediation submissions setting out the background together with schedules of calculations and relevant documents. The venue for the mediation was a Merchant Bank in Portugal. The mediation was conducted in English and had a similar flexible structure to most commercial mediations. There were few surprises because of good preparation by all concerned. The mediator, experienced in international practice and commercial law, was able to evaluate elements of both the damages claim and the SPA, and to assist the commercial parties to reach a commercially viable deal which they had not achieved in several previous attempts. The focus and commitment of both teams enabled the mediator to work well with them and allowed for an appropriate reappraisal of the risks. The commitment of the financial director of the purchaser was also very important.

Sophisticated international business managers are well able to break through the deadlock if given the right environment, time commitment and proper analysis of the issues. Mediation makes such an environment much more likely. Another example involved a claim brought by an individual in the Californian Courts against shareholders in a UK corporation who were researching and developing media technology. The allegations included, amongst others, breach of copyright and wrongful trading. Venture capitalists were heavily involved and tried to broker a deal between the protagonists – and at an early stage of the complaint recommended mediation. California was the birthplace of commercial mediation as we know it, so a mediation in London was quickly agreed. The dispute was resolved in a day although the style and techniques of the parties were very different. An important element in this international case was the English mediator, who had practised in California, managing the different expectations of the English lawyer and the experienced Californian legal advisor. Mediation practice does have difficult nuances and, in international practice, it is very important to avoid assumptions about commonality of approach.

The trend in the last several years is therefore for sophisticated lawyers and their clients to recognise the real opportunities that professional mediation offers to break deadlock in negotiation, whether lawyer or client negotiations. Such recognition is not limited to common law or Anglo-Saxon jurisdictions, but is spreading to other continents and regions that can be equally receptive to the opportunities it offers.

To analyse why mediation was able to assist the commercial clients resolve their previous deadlock, it is worth pausing to recognise why we often reach deadlock in our negotiations. Reasons include:
– genuine disagreement on fundamental issues;
– positional entrenchment;
– lack of confidence in the other party;
– team dynamics and environment; and
– ineffective negotiation or communications.

In the mediation environment the parties are helped by the mediation process and the mediator's skill to:
– Step back – to analyse and understand the different viewpoints on the commercial breakdown. It is very common to reframe financial or legal analysis to bring a different perspective.
– Be creative. Changing the physical environment or the team dynamics or the communication methods can have an energising effect and be a force for change. In one international case a simple drawing of the dispute on a flip chart demonstrating overlap of two corporate vehicles, brought the moment of insight and breakthrough for one client's understanding.
– Build confidence. In preparing for mediation and spending a day or two looking at the issues, a solid foundation of key facts and understanding can emerge. In one case involving a failed power plant in Central America, the mediation process enabled both teams to work through complex calculations and understand the background to the dispute much better than they had before, so that it could be resolved without litigation or arbitration. The issues involved potentially four jurisdictions and multiple legal and commercial complexities.
– Engage in 'Real Listening' – A well managed mediation process ensures that the obstacles to negotiation progress are identified and bridges built.

The mediation process requires structured thinking, communication/process management, and often legal review, but leaves the commercial decision makers in control. It has many of the benefits of formal legal process without the risk and length. As the French philosopher Blaise Pascal said:

'People are usually more convinced by reasons they discover themselves than those found by others ...'

In summary, mediation can be very effective because it offers the following:
(1) A framework for proactive managed engagement.
(2) A commitment to engage for a defined but limited time period – one to two days.
(3) Senior managers are involved.
(4) A skilled experienced mediator can really help move the dialogue forward with energy and commitment.
(5) The mediator and the parties, through preparation and engagement, share information, perceptions and understandings which develop clarity on the reasons for deadlock – or move the focus to a different place.
(6) Mediation has a very high rate of success – over 80% of clients who use it, resolve their dispute.

We are witnessing a change of attitude amongst sophisticated lawyers and advisers, to the effect that serious deadlock should not automatically tip you into protracted litigation or arbitration. There is an earlier process that will allow a proper *strategic* approach to making progress. Our experience has demonstrated that the mediation process, properly conducted and engaged in, breaks negotiation deadlock. However, enough scepticism remains to make it worthwhile to spell out the benefits fully in this chapter, so that advocates can reinforce their case in persuading clients or managers in a particular situation. Ultimately, understanding where mediation brings power to conflict will help to improve its detailed practical adoption. The benefits of mediation can be considered both at a *process* level and in terms of *outcomes*. Deciding which of the many benefits to emphasise will vary with the circumstances of each deadlock and of the parties.

1   Mediation process benefits for negotiation

'Turbo-charged' negotiation – concentrated negotiating focus

The power of a professional mediation approach is essentially that it offers a highly focused 'pressure-chamber' for negotiations. The involvement of a third party in a disciplined structure and time frame, concentrates attention on settlement and encourages higher-level management involvement.

Thus mediation is particularly suitable for business/legal circumstances where parties want to put optimal effort into achieving a settlement rather than entering or continuing formal legal proceedings such as:

- Where business relationships make it essential that the parties negotiate a mutually acceptable outcome or amicable 'divorce';
- Where executives need to be assured that they have given their 'best shot' at trying to settle a case;
- Where it would be helpful to have a last effort at negotiating settlement before triggering litigation/arbitration proceedings or going into trial;
- Where sensitivity and complexity of a case or its commercial context calls for problem solving to be approached in a structured and measured way that will give weight to mutual sensitivities and the difficulty of conversations;
- Where parties need to find creative and better solutions to a current impasse.

The particular problems in international business of distance, fragmented communications, separation of management layers – give greater justification to the adoption of a formal *'negotiating summit'*. Mediation creates the appropriate conditions for this more than any other approach.

- Brings all the key players together.
- Focuses the parties minds.
- Signals that the parties have reached a critical choice point in their decision-making.
- Communicates the strength of feeling of each team and their perspective.
- By coaching, the mediator can produce further effort that stretches the parties' negotiating creativity.
- Communicates effectively the alternatives if there is no movement in the negotiation – thus ensures the parties do proper risk analysis.
- Parties maintain final decision-making authority which will often provide a catalyst for a deal and ownership of the deal.

'Oiling the wheels – renegotiating the agreement'
A group of eight international oil companies had entered into a joint venture agreement some 20 years earlier, which governed the management and cost/return allocation from an oil pipeline asset. Relations on the management committee overseeing the joint venture had become strained. Some of the companies claimed that others were unfairly exploiting literal aspects of the agreement which were not intended, they claimed, to have had such an effect. Also the commercial context of the industry and of some of the participants had changed dramatically, so that some participants were gaining perhaps more from the agreement than was originally envisaged. The only mechanism in the agreement for

revision of its terms required the involvement of the chief executives of all the companies. One of the 'losing' companies was threatening to withhold its share of the cost allocation. The other members of the management committee were faced with the prospect of bringing in all their chief executives, or opting for litigation. A suggestion of mediation by one of the manager's in-house lawyers led to four days of assisted negotiation over a three-month period. At the end of the mediation the parties had achieved a new formula for pricing and cost allocation. Discussions also led to the foundation being laid for the group to go on to update the entire legal agreement on the joint venture.

A fresh mind/objectivity

Managers and their advisers can easily lose their objectivity about an intense and difficult situation of conflict. Senior managers may find it difficult to disagree with their team, to get at the facts, or to communicate objectively with the other organisation's senior managers who may also be caught in the 'groupthink' loyalty trap. Mediation provides a third-party neutral who can:
– clarify the facts;
– help the parties share information and educate each other;
– provide a forum where senior executives can hear the issues set out by both their own team and that of the other side;
– bring together principals for direct discussions;
– safely explore sensitive matters in private meetings;
– neutrally offer suggestions for problem-solving and for resolution; and
– challenge assumptions and set ways of thinking.

French with tears – eight years of deadlock resolved
A UK health supplies company brought a claim of negligence and breach of contract against their accountant. Already a financial adviser to the company, the accountant had become involved on a friendly basis with their acquisition of the assets/business of a French company. He eventually became an equal investor with the UK company. After a year, following his decision to retire, the accountant transferred his invest-ment to the UK company's managing director in consideration for a personal loan. Six months later, serious fraud by two employees was discovered in the French company. The managing director injected more capital into the business but within six months he had to sell. Ultimately the losses led the UK operation to close, leaving him in serious debt. The managing director claimed the accountant should have advised on

the need for French professional advice regarding ongoing financial control systems, and that he had used undue influence to transform his equity stake into a personal loan. The managing director claimed $480,000 and the accountant counterclaimed $144,000 for unpaid loans and interest. After one day of mediation and concluding eight years of litigation, the managing director agreed to pay the accountant's costs in order to settle the court action.

The view from the US – a vehicle for risk assessment
A mediation was held to try to settle a litigation action between a US engineering company and an association of small manufacturers claiming restraint of trade under European competition law. The one-day mediation was attended for the US company by its European lawyers, the US-based General Counsel, and managers from several European branches of the US company. After the settlement had been signed, the US counsel told the mediator that one of the reasons he had agreed to mediation was that he had been unsure of how strong his European team's case was. He had wanted to hear it debated in an informal setting, both with an independent lawyer mediator and with the other side's lawyers before deciding whether to commit to further defence costs and risks in the action.

In other words mediation offers the best feature of litigation or arbitration – an independent third party; but does so within a framework of greater flexibility for the neutral, and greater safety and control for the parties.

Holistic approach

The reference framework for understanding the parameters of a dispute may have many starting points – contractual, commercial, technical, cultural etc. The reference points lead to different emphases in how the situation may be characterised or handled. Effective negotiation or mediation practice requires giving attention explicitly or intuitively to *all* of the dimensions – conducting a *'dispute diagnosis'* is an essential tool for mediators then to help the parties move on to find a remedy. There are always a number of elements that need to be reviewed but which can overlap or be weighted differently in a particular case. Taking the example of a dispute involving the failures of a power plant in Guatemala:

Contract

In this dispute there were a number of contractual documents which included the warranties under the Supply Agreement, the project financing documentation, and the insurance coverage for property and business interruption. The documents provided a starting point for analysis, a matrix of overlapping legal arrangements, with various rights and responsibilities. The governing law was not uniform, nor were the responsibilities of the many parties involved. A legal adviser presented with a dispute will almost certainly wish to use the contractual framework as a starting point or at least fundamental 'measuring instrument' of the character of the problem and possible remedies. However a commercial principal might place greater emphasis on risk and potential outcomes, in order to determine negotiating parameters.

Technical specifications

In this dispute there were complex computations regarding power outages and their financial consequences. These provided an idea as to why expectations, for example performance criteria, were not met. Technical failures are frequently a real starting point for disputes but quickly gather in their wake associated reference points which serve to 'muddy the waters' in terms of dispute dynamics and relationships.

Commercial

The financial data surrounding the project financing and the issues of production and its consequences, were critical in this dispute. The method-ology for calculation of losses was also vital in searching for areas of compromise. The mediation process over two days allowed for a better understanding of these to be achieved. The financial calculations and financial targets in a project are often at the heart of many international disputes and reasons for deadlock. An appreciation of the impact of these pressures on individuals, divisions or organisations and group structures, is essential to creative problem solving.

External change

In this dispute, as in many international cases, there were also external forces that influence, such as currency fluctuations and the effect on a local community of job losses due to the potential for plant closure. These external issues can all lead to changes of direction and emphasis in a project or joint venture. They often affect communications and relationships as well as sometimes impacting on the commercial dimensions and risks of the project.

Internal change

In this dispute there could have been a serious threat to community job security because there were clashes between the expectations of the local culture and the culture and background of the project financial backers. Whatever other factors are involved in a dispute, internal dynamics are almost invariably playing a role, if not when the dispute began, certainly by the time it has escalated to become an organisational issue. Changes in management personnel can be particularly high impact – frequent casualties of such changes are the non-contractual, personal understandings and give-and-take which made previous relationships work. However, change of personnel for the purpose of engaging in the mediation process in itself can equally at times be a factor in unlocking deadlock.

Communications

In this dispute communications were necessary between Central America, New York, London and the Netherlands and across a number of disciplines – law, insurance, commercial, engineering. There were also internal and external influences and communications. However, effective communications can be particularly difficult in international disputes. Even the ever-changing methods of communication technology – e-mail, phone, memo, video conference – all have their own downsides and experience problems in creating the appropriate impact. But the process that physically brings all interested personnel together in mediation, whilst expensive, has the potential to be very efficient and cost effective, compared to the fragmented and ad hoc efforts of typical direct negotiation at a distance.

Culture

In this dispute there were, understandably, various cultural attitudes and expectations to be considered. The English and Americans have been characterised as divided by a common language. There was a melting pot of Central American managers, New York managers and financiers, London lawyers, insurers and other State-side insurers, creating a great mix of possibilities. Dutch engineers were a missing but important ingredient of the mix of factors. The importance of working well with cultural differences has long been recognised in international business. Clashes as a result of cultural differences, or inability to recognise and adapt to cultural difference, can lead to relationship and performance breakdown. 'Cultural' differences may arise from business sectors as much as from geographic or ideological distinctions. Such differences can range from the various aspects of language, social custom and non-verbal behaviour, through to complex patterns of behaviour and perception. For example, some cultures emphasise social hierarchy and networks more than contract or individual rights; building relationships rather than 'straight talking'; adjusting to change rather than implementing contract formalities.

The mediator's training and approach emphasises how to reconvert legal/technical disputes into a human and commercial perspective. Resolution of commercial crises requires not only legal and technical principles but also calls for a neutral third party. A skilled mediator can help the parties address the many layers which underpin conflict, obstacles to settlement and settlement interests. Good mediators, who are well prepared and have been patient enough to ensure they understand the difficult issues affecting the parties' analysis, will effectively manage the process. They will ensure that the right level of communication and understanding takes place to allow the decision makers to make a breakthrough in their negotiations. It is the style and structure of the process, the effectiveness of the participants, and the skill of the mediators, which together present a unique opportunity to make real headway through deadlock and towards workable settlement.

A complementary tool

The flexibility of mediation means that parties are not restricted in how they choose to use the process. In particular, this means mediation can be woven into other dispute resolution approaches. It can be used to assist existing negotiations; it can act as an early 'trial run' of a potential arbitration or litigation case; or it can be used as a parallel process alongside existing arbitration or litigation proceedings and in fact at any stage of the proceedings – even beyond.

Mediation therefore not only provides a communication bridge between the parties. It also provides a bridge between the traditional alternatives for international disputes, negotiation and legal process, harnessing some of the best features of each into a single structure while leaving the other processes intact as real alternatives. Mediation enlarges the options and therefore increases the capability and effectiveness of managers caught in a dispute trap.

It is definitely, however, more productive to engage in mediation early, before there are significant costs sunk into formal conflict. Current trends, and the case studies we have cited, demonstrate an increased willingness by parties to engage in mediation after reaching stalemate or deadlock in negotiations, and not merely as an exit from protracted litigation.

Why mediation is more likely to break the deadlock

It is very common for parties to have had multiple attempts to resolve their differences and then participate in the mediation process and get results they did not expect.

I never believed this case would settle. (One of the most common remarks by first time users of the mediation process.)

Mediation achieves results in over 80 per cent of cases even where experienced commercial or legal negotiators have previously been unsuccessful. The clue to this success arises from the nature of the process and the role of the mediator. Some of the earlier headings in this chapter touch on this, but the essential ingredients in this equation can be summarised as:

1   Focus;
2   Neutrality;
3   Energy;
4   Neutral Project Management – of communications, dispute diagnosis and problem solving negotiations;
5   Mediation Melting Pot.

The mediator's personal qualities may intensify the impact of one or more of these factors, but to a great extent they are inherent in the process itself. Commercial managers, and their engagement and decision-making authority, are equally important catalysts for the success of the mediation process.

1   Focus

When parties resort even to what is only a quasi-formal third-party process such as mediation, the very fact of seeking outside intervention still helps 'raise the stakes'. The parties therefore are more likely to:
–   feel committed to the process because they requested the outside mediator's assistance (even if a requirement of the contract);
–   involve more senior managers or outside advisers as a gesture of respect

to the neutral mediator (with a greater tendency to do so the more credible or high-profile the neutral individual or institution);
- apply more organisation, energy and resources to reviewing the problem;
- recognise that they need to 'grasp the nettle' in a way they may not previously have done through more fragmented management contacts.

Commercial mediation has the character of a *'pressure chamber'* to concentrate energy and attention in a way only achieved otherwise by formal legal proceedings. It creates a similar momentum and expectation of outcome as achieved when going into an arbitration or judicial proceeding. All parties must direct their attention to the case and do so simultaneously and in the knowledge that the objective is to achieve a resolution of the problem.

Issues of distance, both geographical and between corporate or management layers, can become more critical in international cases, despite all the potential contributions of new telecommunications technology. Negotiations may be fragmented or lose momentum as a result of this distancing effect. This is even more apparent if the dispute has been passed to professional advisers in each jurisdiction to manage, multiplying the communication layers and principal-agent problems before decision-making can proceed. This effect will be multiplied by the common experience not only that different parties in a negotiation have a different sense of urgency but also by the fact that in an international case there are likely to be differing cultural attitudes to time and urgency of decision-making.

Mediation forces into focus, better than internal negotiation dynamics, the need to grapple with an international problem. It achieves this because of its third party involvement, hence introducing a quasi-formality and quasi-public decision process for the companies involved. Court-referred mediation, where a court requires the parties to try mediation before proceeding with litigation, may intensify this element:

'The major benefit of the process was that senior people from the [Japanese financial services company] were persuaded to travel to a neutral place and to address the problem at a very early stage when otherwise I suspect they would not have addressed it until just before or during the trial. The upshot was that we managed to resolve in 5 months a matter that would probably have led to a couple of years of expensive and management time-intensive litigation.'

Mark Yeadon, Slaughter and May, Hong Kong.

2 Neutrality

The key to achieving a helpful change of energy and attention, is the fact of introducing a neutral third party figure into the negotiations. By this means, the negotiation dynamic is altered. The mediator, being neutral, can:

-   bring freshness and flexibility to problem-solving;
-   facilitate difficult communications;
-   win respect and trust compared to that possible with partisan negotiators on the other side;
-   apply more leverage to encourage movement and flexibility in negotiations;
-   challenge without appearing to do so for partisan reasons;
-   help each party reality-test with a detached outsider (who brings either common sense or business experience or other expertise, as well as process skills); and
-   lead the parties on process because of the mediator's perceived lack of bias.

Neutrality can mean different things in any situation – for example perceived impartiality, lack of previous knowledge or business dealings with the parties, or lack of cultural association with any of the negotiating parties. What is important is to find someone whom the parties regard as sufficiently neutral to be an effective mediator between them (so long as they have been fully informed of any potential areas of conflict). For example, in some cases even a former senior business figure from one of the parties may still be sufficiently respected as an individual so as to be regarded as neutral. More often neutrality will only be achieved through lack of prior dealings with any party.

The normal sensitivities of parties in negotiation may be multiplied at an international level by an additional layer of cross-cultural suspicions or misunderstandings. Mediator neutrality is therefore an even more valuable commodity, although this may also be more difficult to achieve in international cases. The mediator and parties may also have to allow more time (in keeping with cultural norms) to build up respect and trust of the mediator's impartiality. We would stress that we do not believe that neutrality is only achieved by selecting from other nationalities – the key question is whether the parties respect the individual's capability of being impartial. Protection is inbuilt into the process by the parties' own power to agree or to reject a resolution.

3   Energy, patience and persistence

The mediator has been given the assignment to assist the parties to resolve the dispute. The mediator therefore:

–   will be less distracted by the substantive issues which concern each party;
–   will be free from political, group or commercial dynamics that are influencing the decision-making processes and attention of each party; and
–   should bring, because of the nature of the role and prior experience, more energy, optimism, patience and persistence to the question of joint problem-solving, than more partisan and sceptical or adversarial parties.

Mediator energy is very obviously a personal quality. However, we believe that in adopting the role (assuming some degree of knowledge and training), any individual's energy and attention will be more focused on joint problem-solving than if they were a member of a particular negotiating team. Additional individual qualities in this area are of course still required if international mediations are to be successful but, energy, patience and persistence in our view are particularly vital personal ingredients for mediator effectiveness. These essential qualities can be found in some of our most influential public role models such as Nelson Mandela.

'Mr Mandela has walked a long road and now stands at the top of the hill. A traveller would sit down and admire the view, but a man of destiny knows that beyond this hill lies another and another. The journey is never complete.'

FW de Klerk.

End of the road – working through deadlock
A construction contractor and an African government department (assisted by a project finance aid agency) had agreed to a five-day mediation to resolve outstanding claims from a major road building programme. At the mediation it became apparent that the government and project finance representatives had little authority to negotiate a deal. Most of the five days were spent on information-gathering and exchange of views. After the mediation had ended without resolution, the mediators persisted with one-to-one contacts with the parties. As a result they gained access to higher levels of the funding agency. Further mediation meetings were held over the next twelve months which led to

a request that the mediators provide a report to the parties recommending 'reasonable' terms of settlement. The parties were finally able to do a deal on the terms recommended which included an additional contribution from the aid agency.

4   Neutral project management of communications

The last case above is also an example of the particular value of mediation in international negotiations. Companies who do business internationally put a great deal of effort into effective project management in planning for infrastructure development or the technical delivery of a product or process. (For how to enhance such efforts by integrating mediation into project practice, see Chapter 10). However, at the level of relationship breakdown and negotiation stalemate, the same business discipline is normally not applied. Nor can it be applied so easily where parties are sensitive or even distrustful regarding other parties' negotiating intentions. International disputes are no different from other disputes in the sense that they arise out of a breakdown of relationships and a clash of interests and expectations. However, as we have already noted, but to re-emphasise, they are likely to be inherently more complex because of:

- geographical distance between relevant participants;
- language;
- culture;
- political and government control;
- international monetary factors;
- ideological and cultural diversity;
- heightened potential for change;
- more varied commercial circumstances;
- communication difficulty; and
- 'dispute drift' – loss of momentum in management of dialogue.

Because of this inherent complexity, negotiation in the international context lends itself more readily to the concept of a *project management approach,* rather than the simple 'communication and decision-making' framework which is more typically associated with traditional 'domestic' negotiation theory. Mediation is therefore particularly helpful because of the inherent project manager role which mediators must adopt in order to structure progress towards settlement.

Project management thinking requires one to analyse the different aspects of any dispute situation and to draw up a programme to manage the situation by creating a disciplined timetable, process structure and roles, and commercial objectives. Where the mediator adds value is that he:

– takes on the role of a joint project manager who treats the whole problem as a joint project of the parties with his leadership;

– encourages each team to get more focused in terms of their own internal project management and cross-party needs;

– usually works to a given timescale to help achieve disciplined analysis of the real obstacles and the range of options for resolving the problem;

– assists the parties to evolve a dialogue and education process around problems, options and settlement proposals;

– engages in, and assists the parties to conduct, a dispute diagnosis, and not just a dispute history, thus helping parties to understand the root causes of a commercial difference, and the potential remedies;

– helps the parties assess alternatives to settlement and critical obstacles to making progress in negotiation, for example information or people who should be at the table;

– helps build a bridge,of communication and dialogue through a range of 'neutral negotiator' tactics, for example joint and private meetings, sub-group meetings, outside contacts, guidance on submissions, proposals and negotiating options;

– helps the pace and quality of negotiations—parties have more time and safety to disclose their interests, concerns, constraints to or through a neutral third party, compared to more intense and unpredictable face-to-face negotiations; and

– provides a programme which is flexible enough both to accommodate commercial concerns and to take into account legal issues and predictions between the parties.

Overall mediation offers a tool to bring effective project management to bear on tough communications in difficult circumstances. The mediation process draws parties from the 'heat of the fray' onto a neutral bridge. Parties may initially look in different directions and focus on different horizons but, over time with patience and perseverance, the mediator may achieve a situation where the disputants see the problem with greater commonality, at least, and ultimately, to focus on the one horizon and solution when parties will then begin to sense what is more realistic as an all-round resolution option. Parties who take the opportunity of time and space on the metaphoric bridge with a neutral communication project manager, possess the ability to discover what will unite their communication efforts into a potentially successful joint problem-solving focus. Even where unsuccessful in resolution, greater clarity will be achieved of the nature and size of the deadlock.

5 Mediation melting pot

Mediators will travel to neutral locations or to the location of one party, but in pre-mediation preparation should ensure that appropriate personnel are going to be engaged in the mediation dialogue wherever it is held. The outcome is a 'mediation melting pot', blending the best of the commercial, financial, legal, cultural and technical brains in each organisation.

The commercial people have the opportunity to be briefed not only by their own team but by those representing the other teams so that they get a full picture of the issues in the context of solving the dispute. It is relatively rare otherwise that the decision makers necessarily get a complete picture of all the issues involved in a dispute even from their own teams. It is also extremely unusual, particularly once the matter becomes adversarial, for a commercial party to get a full understanding of all the different levels of the dispute from the other team.

2　Mediation Outcome Benefits

Business relationships

Mediation is ideally suited for situations where continuing dialogue or broad 'fairness' in relationships is essential, such as joint ventures or business alliances. Litigation and arbitration have a greater tendency to drive a wedge between parties. They can undermine effective communication as parties descend into case arguments and self-protectionism while conflict escalates. Mediation offers the openness and flexibility of commercial negotiations whereas negotiations 'in the shadow of the law' are of necessity more narrowly focused on legal rights, historic evidence and 'best case', rather than taking into account current commercial circumstances, objectives and opportunities. Mediation also offers the opportunity to legitimise different points of view by creating the right climate and an effective approach to dialogue.

Market collapse – a relationship on the brink
A major telecommunications equipment supplier was in dispute with its Middle East distributor. The distributor claimed that a major promotional launch went wrong because the supplier had failed to meet the

high demand generated, and the products which did arrive frequently proved to be defective, thus damaging the distributor's reputation in the country. The supplier claimed that it dealt with all defects under its standard warranty procedure and refused to pay any additional compensation for reputation loss. The distributor was the sole access point of the supplier to one country. He refused to take further supplies until compensation was paid. The supplier was, by the time of the mediation, ready to launch a new product. The dispute was holding back all sales in an important market. To pay compensation however would breach the supplier's core warranty compensation policy. At the end of a two-day mediation between lawyers and senior executives flown in for the process, the parties agreed to a sum of money which was classified, not as compensation but as a promotional budget for launch of the new product. Relations were restarted and the country opened up again for sales of the new item.

Business reputation

Mediation provides confidentiality and can lead to agreements which define the terms of future publicity about the dispute. Litigation by contrast is public, and both litigation and arbitration pronounce on 'fault', thus potentially damaging reputation and in an unpredictable way.

In the mediation case described above, the distributor was left feeling some vindication because of the sums of money paid for promotion. On the other hand, the supplier was able to avoid obvious breach of its standard warranty system which might have influenced other distributors' attitudes to future problems. In some cultures such as the Asian or the Middle Eastern, avoiding loss of face is a strongly prevalent cultural goal. Mediators do not pronounce on fault or conduct cross-examination of witnesses, thus facilitating face-saving outcomes and process. Cultural sensitivity is in fact more likely to be present throughout the process than in more formal dispute proceedings.

Savings on transaction costs

By turbo-charging the process of negotiation, reducing the time allocated to the dispute project, mediation therefore cuts transaction costs for its parties. In addition to direct costs of advisers and experts, indirect costs also need to be factored into any estimates of the costs of litigation or arbitration compared to mediation. These would include management time and expense on investigation, identifying local counsellor agents, as well as contribution to witness statements, case analysis and strategy implementation. Indirect costs can be at least as much as direct, and often much more. Direct and indirect costs are multiplied by a factor of at least 1.5 in international cases. In many companies however, the financial impact of transaction costs is easily ignored, or hidden as operating expenses under corporate accounting practice, compared to the outcome of a substantive award or settlement. Uncertainty of costs or outcome may severely damage a company's budget predictions.

The costs of conflict can be even more damaging if one includes such risks as – effects on company or manager morale, stress and health effects, and not least the diversion of attention by managers away from other business opportunities – whether with the other side in the conflict, or other business contacts.

> *Wood waste – getting out of a jam*
> *A Scandinavian company supplied conveyor belts, cutting and process-ing equipment to an Asian wood pulp producer. Within a year of the supply, the processor claimed major damages and loss of profit ($38m) because of regular machine breakdowns or damaged wood. In turn the equipment suppliers claimed that the wood pulp mill failed to train its staff in the proper handling of the equipment, breached warranty requirements by using makeshift local replacement parts rather than manufacturer parts, and exceeded the capacity of the equipment both by excessive running and by feed of wood types that were outside the proper specifications of the machinery supplied. Discussions on rem-edying the situation broke down. Soon after, the plant was closed down and awaited repair. The contract between the parties contained a simple provision for resolution of disputes – 'Arbitration in London'. The parties separately estimated that the arbitration could take one to two years and cost over a million pounds sterling each. They opted instead for a three-day mediation. Agreement was achieved on a basis of a modest cash sum in settlement together with additional replacement parts, maintenance and training programmes, thus keeping the relation-ship intact and ongoing support provided for the mill's operations.*

> *'My clients were very impressed by the effectiveness of the mediation process ...[They] are delighted that the matter has been finally resolved not least so they can now concentrate on their core business without this unwanted distraction. And for my part the main benefit is having a satisfied client.'*

'We avoided twelve weeks of an arbitration hearing. What more do I need to say?'

The power and benefits of mediation

The flexibility of the mediation process together with its inherent culture of effective neutral project management, produces a mix of ingredients that create a powerful momentum towards resolution. It is a mix which works surprisingly often and undoubtedly is responsible for that sense of 'magic' which is sometimes associated with mediation outcomes.

The approach concentrates on resolving disputes by allowing commercial parties to maintain decision making power in the context of a highly effective managed mediation process. These negotiating techniques are not soft options but involve a change of emphasis towards a *business* rather than legal rules model. In summary, mediation's benefits may be described under the acronym, ' FOCUS'.

The process enables the parties to engage in:

Forward thinking

Open dialogue

Commercial dialogue

Understanding the reasons for deadlock in respect of all parties

Strategic, multifaceted approach to solutions.

Mediation tends to appeal to commercial executives because it is results-driven, has a high success rate, and it gives them a sense of control and return to familiar commercial considerations. It converts loose negotiations into project-managed negotiations and it reconverts a legal dispute into a commercial dispute. It also tends to appeal to those professionals from a legal background who enjoy the highly charged atmosphere of mediation and its sense that a result is possible. Professionals too enjoy the opportunity to work in a slightly more free-ranging environment giving them a greater opportunity for creativity than they are normally permitted in the context of adversarial proceedings. Yet mediation also allows them to air in negotiations some of the key arguments and evidence that they may have put forward in formal legal proceedings. It can be a powerful win-win process with outcomes as good or, more often, much better than other alternatives of dealing with deadlock.

'Nothing that is complex is worthwhile if it is not anchored in common sense; much that is highly sophisticated can be built on an edifice of common sense. We believe that ADR has struck a chord and is succeeding precisely because it has gone back to

basics, has asked some simple questions, and has constructed some new approaches on a widely shared foundation. In this complex age we can all use a few simplicities that work.'

Henry & Lieberman, *The Manager's Guide to Resolving Legal Disputes.*

Chapter 3. The Decision to Mediate – How to Get Started

'*I have always seen mediation as "Pick yourself up, dust yourself down and start all over again".*'

Elizabeth Wall, Former Member of the Board of Directors, American Corporate Counsel Association.

'*I am inclined to mediate. Pragmatism is the reason. Mediation's benefits are magnified where parties have different cultural backgrounds. It is common sense, it is right-brain application, and it works!*'

Michael Leathes, Head of Intellectual Property, British American Tobacco.

Selection of cases

How does one select a case that is suitable for mediation? This question is often asked. In fact mediation has been used in most types of case which one could identify. The best rule of thumb is to ask: (a) Why have your current attempts to resolve matters failed? Do they include genuine disagreement, wrong personnel, inadequate focus and/or preparation or confusion about what the other side wants? If so: (b) is a legal battle likely to bring the best outcome, and do you need to win at all costs? If yes to the first, and no or some uncertainty about the second question, surprising progress to break the deadlock can be possible with a well-prepared mediation process and skilful, experienced mediator. Essentially any case can be mediated that could in theory have a negotiated outcome; whether it does settle will depend on factors peculiar to the parties in the case.

Mediating early in a conflict has the distinct advantage that you are investing in a process where corporate negotiations can, and do, control the outcome. Time and money is spent on a process that nearly always adds value, if not resolution. Mediation may help avoid litigation or arbitration and, at the same time, may achieve a similar or better result, certainly one that is more a controlled outcome. Also in many cases legal proceedings are either not an option, or have too much potential to damage a continuing relationship between the parties.

To the surprise of many lawyers new to mediation, in broad terms the more difficult the dispute, the more suitable it may be for mediation. This is because such difficulty or complexity will: (a) impact on the time and expense of formal proceedings; (b) will make a third party award more of a 'lottery' in terms of outcome; and (c) often provide greater potential for trade-offs and redesign of settlement packages. 'Difficulty' may be defined on several levels, including:

– multiple parties;
– multiple witnesses of fact;
– complex and/or multiple issues of law, fact and technical interpretation;
– uncertainties of forum or of enforceability of outcome; and
– complex commercial background (past, present or future).

Similarly, the greater the difficulty, the greater the potential benefits to the parties in involving an experienced mediator. As neutral project manager the mediator can work with the complexities and sensitivities involved to help parties design a settlement that optimises value to all.

Some of the most difficult and protracted cases have been mediated.

A last appeal – mediating against a complex legal background
A Dutch reinsurance company acquired an English reinsurance subsidiary. The acquisition went disastrously wrong because of an unexpected upsurge in natural disaster claims in the period just before acquisition. The terms of the acquisition prevented a legal claim against the vendor company. The Dutch company sued three of its professional advisers, a merchant bank, a firm of accountants and a firm of actuaries. Two years later the legal action was substantially lost after a 12-month trial leading to a 400-page judgment from the English Commercial Court. The Dutch company lodged an appeal against the actuaries. A two-week trial in the Court of Appeal was planned. The parties agreed to a one-day mediation as a last effort at settlement, one day before the appeal trial was due to begin. An agreement between the parties was reached by 7pm on the evening before the trial, followed by telephone calls to counsel and the court to withdraw the action. This brought down the curtain on a battle that had raged for seven years.

Corporate raiding – employment mediation
A dispute between financial products companies involved allegations of wrongful 'poaching' of personnel and significant financial losses

alleged to have been suffered. It was subject to arbitration in New York with parties from New York, Chicago, Dublin, London, Zurich and Paris. The dispute was mediated by the authors, in two days, in London. In the course of mediation it emerged that there was a second, unconnected pending arbitration between the two parties. This was also resolved as part of an overall settlement.

It is often thought that where there are allegations of fraud the matter will be unsuitable for mediation. However, a number of reinsurance disputes have been mediated where fraud and misrepresentation have been often central, as have many financial services cases or large project cases where suspicions of fraud have been in the background.

Lack of good faith
A claim for many million dollars brought into conflict insurers/ reinsurers from North America and Europe. A key allegation of the claim to void the cover was fraud. The parties had been involved in litigation on many issues for many years and matters were no nearer to resolution. They decided to mediate. The authors as a co-mediation team were with the parties for three long days which led to a part resolution. After a short gap of a few weeks, the remaining issues were resolved in a final meeting with the mediators partly because the insurers agreed to include some other issues that were subject to separate disputes between the parties.

The greatest impediment to the use of mediation is not so much getting a result as getting parties to the mediation table. Once the mediation process is in flow the opportunities to find an effective outcome are very high. Where experienced mediators are used, typically over 80 per cent of international cases are settled in mediation and most of the rest within a few months afterwards. In the last few years we have experienced a great willingness to mediate earlier and clients have been surprised at this ability to solve what appear intractable problems.

Routes into mediation – timing and approach

Practical experience suggests that mediation may be applied successfully at many different stages of a dispute. Mediation has been used successfully in cases where litigation is still not in prospect, through to cases even where judgment has been handed down but the parties wish to avoid the time and cost of appellate proceedings. If we consider as an example of how and when international cases have been referred for mediation in the last 12 months, the following types emerge:

Court-referred. There is an increasing trend globally towards court-referred or 'court-annexed' mediation. We have a great deal of international cases mediated in London due to the pioneering work of our Commercial Court and its judges. ADR 'Orders' are usually made early in the proceedings when parties first seek directions from the court. This has applied to a wide range of mercantile cases dealt with by the court, including financial services institutions in dispute over trading contract failures, insurance and reinsurance coverage, shipping and charter party disputes, professional negligence, etc. In 1999 ADR, and mediation particularly, became part of the English judicial system with the introduction of the new Civil Procedure Rules. The new rules permitted judges to encourage the parties to use an ADR procedure if the court considers that appropriate. Since the introduction of the new procedures there have been over 40 amendments and the 'pre-action protocols' now place even greater emphasis on early use of mediation, before the issue of proceedings. In other countries such as Argentina there is statutory provision for mandatory mediation before filing a lawsuit. In Indonesia the Supreme Court regulations require judges to order parties in any civil suit to attempt to mediate before the full hearing can be held in court. In some parts of the US, Canada and Australia there are mandatory regulations that impose mediation. The provisions vary from state to state, some allowing timing and detail to be decided by counsel – whilst maintaining the mandatory requirement.

Court-locked. At the other extreme parties have come to mediation where they have found themselves bogged down in what appear to be interminable court (or arbitration) proceedings (at first level, although often accompanied by multiple appeal hearings on preliminary points of substance or procedure). By this stage parties recognise that they are not going to get a conclusive court outcome and all parties have commercial reasons for wishing to extricate themselves from the case. For example, a reinsurance coverage/fraud case which had been through several layers of US courts without conclusion, was referred to mediation when the current judge showed herself disinclined to hear the action. Parties came to London because of prior knowledge of the mediators and the involvement of a number of European reinsurers in the case.

Imminent hearing. Even in situations where a case has progressed through the court or arbitration system, and parties have full information, parties often wish to avoid the risks of ultimate trial yet have been unable to negotiate settlement because of fundamental differences in their view of the case. Mediation is seen as a last resort to test each party's 'bottom-line' regarding settlement rather than to evaluate a case which has already had exhaustive evaluations on each side. For example, a disputed employee fraud claim in Asia, with US reinsurance coverage, was to be tried in the London Commercial Court. The case was due for trial on the day after mediation. Counsel attended the mediation not only to provide summary arguments for the mediator but also to write opening speeches for the trial during breaks in negotiation just in case the matter did not settle, although it did settle.

Preventive procedural lawyering. In cases where the courts do issue ADR directions, lawyers often come to anticipate the directions by negotiation with advisers on the other side. Thus they arrive at court with an appointed mediator and ADR procedure in place, merely asking the court to make a formal Order for the purpose of a future costs award should the procedure be unsuccessful. The same may happen for less positive reasons if parties find themselves before a judge/arbitrator they regard as ineffective or if they are in a jurisdiction with long delays to hearing and both parties want to extricate themselves.

Breaking deadlock. At the end of exhaustive negotiations, parties on all sides may still be reluctant to enter legal proceedings because (a) they do not wish to become involved in arbitration expense or (b) they wish to avoid litigation publicity, or have other commercial reasons which make proceedings unattractive, eg continuing business relations with the other side. In these cases parties are recognising the power of mediation to represent a *last, best shot at settlement* before more serious formal proceedings are invoked. As mediation gains authority and respect, this is a trend that is growing.

North Sea – a final storm
Eight international oil companies chose mediation over the terms of a long-standing joint venture agreement in the North Sea. This occurred because one of their number showed they were serious about going to court over the terms of the agreement if the group could not come up with a better offer on variation of the agreement due to changed commercial circumstances.

Chemical reaction – a catalyst for resolving deadlock
Two international chemical companies came to mediation when their negotiation, over five heads of claim under a Sale and Purchase

Agreement, ran into trouble. The claim involved allegations of incorrect management information, incorrect sales/capacity forecasts and environmental non-compliance. The mediator helped the parties review the heads of claim and helped simplify issues including the loss of profit claims – the matter settled in two intensive days. One party said:

> 'We fully appreciate your understanding of both the case and the party psychology which was a key factor in unlocking the negotiations every time we risk to blow the whole thing up – forgive us for the aggressive approach ...'
> *Italian Lawyer.*

Contract and scheme cases. An increasing number of commercial contracts now provide for mediation as a preliminary step before arbitration or court proceedings (see *Part 2* for model clauses). In *Cable and Wireless v IBM Ltd* October 2002, the English Commercial Court supported the enforceability of a properly drafted ADR clause with a clear referral to an institutional procedure, in this case CEDR, London. These types of clauses have been upheld by decisions in Australia, Austria, France, Canada, Sweden and the United States. The position in Europe is detailed in the *EU Mediation Atlas* (see *Further Reading*). We have also seen sophisticated counsel agree to amend their contractual arrangements or make ad hoc arrangements to make provision for mediations. Another trend in a number of jurisdictions but particularly the United States and England is the increased institutionalisation of mediation in industry schemes and government policy directives. These initiatives have led to mediation of disputes with clear international dimensions. The next example illustrates one such case – with parties from New York, Chicago and Europe.

> *Security concerns – location in mediation*
> *The National Association of Security Dealers in the USA launched a mediation scheme in the mid-1990s as an additional option to their traditional arbitration scheme. The scheme attracted several thousand cases within the first few years. Two NASD members chose to mediate one case in Europe because it had European financial connections and the parties also wished to avoid rumours about the case in the US market.*

Business relationship-driven. Sometimes commercial parties find themselves locked in deadlock but would never consider litigating because of strong commercial ties, eg because they are part of a joint venture or the same parent company or a family company. They see mediation as a halfway house that provides the formality and objectivity of third party intervention, without the inappropriate stigma of litigation. In such cases, parties may also be more prepared to consider a non-binding evaluation by the mediator as an aid to ending the deadlock.

Bottleneck – Restoring relationships through mediation
A household name multinational company was in dispute with a packaging company based in Europe over the technical failure of a new container. The parties had been unable to agree the allocation of losses and costs on the project. Mediation led to agreement on the figures and to a reopening of technical discussions on how to remedy the problem between the two companies' engineers.

Lights off – Corporate social responsibility
A power plant goes down due to equipment failure. Project finance and joint venture parties are threatening to withdraw. The lack of solution will have an immediate impact on the local community in relation to jobs and electricity supplies. Multiple parties including insurers are involved. A mediated solution restores stability all round.

Ad hoc. There are cases in litigation proceedings which fall into none of the above categories, but personal links between advisers or managers have led them to explore the concept of mediation as an alternative to continued warfare. Referral in such cases usually arises either because legal advisers have sufficient in-depth knowledge of mediation to put the case forcefully to their clients, or because one of the business people happens to hear of another businessman's experience or one of the in-house lawyers opens discussions about it on hearing the client complain about the mess of the case.

Brokered cases. Frequently parties have lost an effective route to communicate with the other side even about the question of entering negotiations. An independent broker, such as an ADR organisation, can make a range of contacts and exploratory meetings with all parties to mediate a procedural agreement, ie designing the final mediation process in terms to which all parties can consent, including appointment of the mediator. This can be particularly vital in large multi-party cases.

Brokering/consensus-building – The 'talks about talks' role
CEDR is often approached in both domestic and international disputes
to help get parties to the table, to have 'Talks about Talks'. A typical
example is a request from an in-house counsel of a major US Corpora-
tion asking us to advise on getting joint venture parties from Eastern
Europe to the table in an energy production dispute. We hosted several
meetings and successfully persuaded all parties to agree to an agenda,
schedule, mediator and process. A key element in these projects is
identifying who the interested parties are, and how to get them to agree
to 'come to the table'. As the field becomes more mature and interna-
tionally accepted, this is not as difficult as it once was. However,
experience in such messy situations suggests that there can nearly
always be value added by the independent broker facilitating set-up of
the process.

A Fresh Mind. Sometimes businesses or advisers cannot explain satisfacto-
rily why a particular negotiation is making no progress or there is a history
of bad feeling getting in the way of progress. They turn to a mediator to
change the dynamic and to help them understand what are the real
blockages to settlement on the other side, or to create a process and solution
that will rid the parties of historical baggage.

Venture Capitalists – The power of independent intervention
The Board of a private international company had been subject to a
long-running conflict between two respected senior directors and a
Chief Executive. The non-executive Chairman approached CEDR for a
mediator after his own informal efforts had not managed to end the
conflict. Agreement was reached in one day's mediation, with one of the
directors agreeing to take early retirement and the other taking on a
new role.

Guidelines to maximise potential use of mediation

The very flexibility of mediation can make it more difficult for managers or
advisers to decide when and how best to use it, in the absence of a contract
or industry scheme. Early in a case, they may feel that there is still plenty of
scope for direct discussions or threat of proceedings to produce results.
Later in the dispute, they may doubt the bona fides of the other party or
doubt that there is much more that a mediator can bring which has not been
already explored. Alongside this is the common perception (generally

misguided adversarialism in our view) that in deadlock an offer to negotiate is seen as a sign of weakness or concession to the other party/parties. Either way the result is limited use of mediation and unrealised potential for negotiation outcomes.

We recommend therefore that advisers and managers work to the following simple guidelines in assessing cases for suitability and timing of mediation offers. These guidelines should be used at the outset of awareness of a dispute, then revisited at regular intervals of no more than six months. *An effective record should be kept of previous advice from lawyers on their predictions of case progress and cost, and of comments by advisers or managers on problems in resorting to negotiation or mediation.*

– In organisational policy terms, do we have much to lose by stating that it is our corporate policy to seek where possible to settle cases at their appropriate level with minimal external cost or damage to business relations?

– Are negotiations constructive and making progress or are they blocked or unsatisfactory? If the latter, what is the most critical leverage to improve negotiations which an independent third party process could provide?

– Would we benefit from convening a forum for a 'without obligation' exploration of the core issues in the case and the negotiating positions of all parties, before taking further steps in the proceedings?

– What practical damage would be caused if we, or a neutral ADR organisation, were to explore the idea of mediation with the other party and they refused? How could we offset any risk?

– Do we lack certain information or data which weakens our ability to negotiate effectively? Is the adversarial process necessary to retrieve information or can we agree disclosure and exchange as part of a negotiation strategy?

– What are the likely forward costs, direct and indirect, in pursuing legal proceedings compared to the best and worst outcomes of the proceedings? What would be added to the cost or risks in future proceedings if we went to an unsuccessful mediation in the near future? How would we reduce such cost or such risk?

There are few cases of stalled negotiations where there is not an important case for mediation to at least be attempted. We believe it is likely to become the norm of international dispute practice in a few decades, because of its ability to provide a simple but effective cultural and communication bridge. This will put demands on the mediation community to ensure that the quality of international mediators can match this need.

Whether setting up a mediation in a negotiating context or legal context, parties without a formal contract procedure still have to decide exactly *how* to approach the other side with a suggestion of moving into mediation as a next negotiation phase. This could be heavily influenced by whether the project has been completed, at which point the parties are more likely to be in a legal mode of communication through lawyers. Or whether there is an ongoing commercial relationship, in which case there may be more opportunity through direct contact via engineers, technical personnel or managers. In general parties should seek to find the best point of communication contact in existence and should use this as a vehicle.

In our experience, proposals to mediate need to be restrained and exploratory in tone, inviting dialogue rather than seeking a yes/no answer to an ultimatum. This is partly to compensate for inevitable concerns about the proposal being interpreted as a gesture of weakness, and also in recognition of the fact that entering a mediation is a form of *joint* project management. For this reason recommendations of appropriate mediators and recommendations on process detail are best discussed jointly rather than be unilaterally proposed at the outset. Mediation organisations can provide a safe space for this to happen.

How to get into mediation without losing face

'Tell me, I may listen, Teach me, I may remember. Involve me, I will do it'

Chinese Proverb

Among the options for addressing the issue of not being seen to suggest weakness by proposing a dialogue are:
- Use previous negotiating efforts, business relationships and other contacts as an informal platform for exploration of the proposal;
- Acknowledge that there is a genuine stalemate so that third party involvement in the form of advisers and arbitrators etc looks inevitable – given this is the situation suggest the parties involve an experienced mediator to work with the parties within a tight time frame, what is often termed a 'rapid track' or 'final-shot' approach before formal legal proceedings;
- Ask a neutral organisation or mediator to talk to both sides without obligation on anyone's part to enter mediation until they are satisfied that the process has benefits for them;
- Stress your interest in positive negotiation and willingness to listen in

the context of neutrally-managed negotiation, stressing also that nevertheless you currently believe your case is a valid one, which you are happy to test before a neutral mediator;

- Note (if appropriate) the possibility of forthcoming court-directed ADR;
- Refer to contract provisions which either require ADR or which imply it – for example, references to best or reasonable 'endeavour to find amicable settlement';
- Re-label the process in terms that are more likely to appeal to the other party, for example as an 'independent chair review' or 'Board-level appraisal' with independent assistance;
- Offer to hold all meetings in the other party's country, to accept a qualified mediator of their choice, to complete the process in 40 days, to pay the costs of the procedure – or any other tactical offer which overcomes specific objections raised by the other side. Of course, many of these detailed points only become issues for discussion once the parties are exploring mediation in principle;
- State (if appropriate) that it is your company/client's policy to use mediation to achieve fair and cost-effective settlements.
- Treat the deadlock negotiations as equivalent to an 'operational shutdown'. One would not leave a power plant or a software failure to simmer on a backburner for a number of years awaiting third party resolution. In the same manner, one should react to stalemate in negotiations in a timely manner and bring in a neutral expert hired to work for all parties to bring the failed negotiations back on track. Tell the other party that this is your corporate culture of getting things done.

Where there are multiple parties and strong sensitivities, cultural or otherwise, *the entry to mediation should be regarded as a mediation process in its own right.* The matter should be approached as a delicate negotiation using, where necessary, skilled third party brokers to open up a dialogue. In political conflicts, for example, this has led to the phenomenon of 'Track Two' diplomacy, where the negotiations are conducted away from the glare of publicity on any formal negotiation process – this was used in the early 1990s when a little-known Norwegian team produced a framework for negotiation between the key players in the Israeli and Palestinian conflict.

What can a mediator achieve?

You may be asked by your own team or the other party what a mediator can do that an experienced negotiator has been unable to achieve. Whilst acknowledging the experience and ability of the negotiating teams you can explain the reasons why (see Chapter 2) and how a mediator can add value to the negotiating process including:

- Intractable issues may become less intractable with a fresh mind, neutral management of discussions and detached creative thinking;
- The dispute is too complex and hard to manage in straight negotiations – for example because there are too many parties, in too many locations, delicate issues or relationships that need to be managed. An experienced mediator can work at all levels of the dispute and break down some of the complexities to get at the core issues;
- The risks are relatively low that an experienced mediator will make the problem more intractable. It is more likely that the mediator will, at the very least, untangle some of the issues and give the parties a clearer understanding of what is at stake, therefore fresh reason and opportunity to resolve the problem. One objective is to get opposing parties to see the legitimacy of each other's positions – this is quite distinct from the *legal* effect of these positions;
- If the mediator cannot help the parties resolve the issues, he can at least either narrow the gap between the parties, or convince everyone there is no alternative to proceedings, or help the parties design a better dispute resolution approach. For example, if the parties require an independent appraisal from an arbitration panel the mediator can seek agreement for a smoother, more cost-effective process than would generally happen if the parties get entrenched into an attacking, adversarial mode. One outcome could be an agreed fast-track arbitration procedure that was not possible to agree outside of mediation and was not provided for in the contract;
- The process usually gets results and has essential business, 'bottom-line' benefits – in terms of cost, time and relationship savings;
- Finally, provide examples of cases where a mediator or mediation has worked successfully with parties to bring about resolution. (*See* Part 2 and throughout this text.)

Mediation selection: skills, personality, status

'The purpose of a summit is to intensify the pressure on both sides, making it easier for leaders to justify difficult decisions. There was nothing routine about such an event. To bring the parties along required thousands of hours and hundreds of meetings and phone calls on the part of the President, me, and our team. It was hard, *painstaking work. But that is the only way progress toward peace in the Middle East had ever been achieved. As we made final preparations for a summit, we were well aware that our task had barely begun.'*

Madeleine Albright, *Madam Secretary*

The go-between wears a thousand sandals.

Japanese saying.

You may be asked how you can be confident of the skills of the mediator. Ensure you have a selection of candidates to offer and can speak of their track record or have an organisation which can supply such references. Most mediators are invited to assist parties only once the parties are deeply entrenched in an adversarial process and procedure. If mediators have demonstrated success in that environment they are likely to have the skills necessary to help. The selection of the appropriate mediator or co-mediation team is important. It is the belief of the authors that parties should look for trained and experienced mediators. It does happen from time to time that a well known individual from politics or international diplomacy is prepared to take on such a role or essentially required for that role by reason of their status impact. In our experience they are generally willing to work, and can work better, as a member of a team with an experienced and trained mediator.

A number of organisations publish lists of mediators but not all mediators are trained the same way, and only a few organisations insist mediators go through a formal evaluation process or continuous updating of skills. Some panels, for example, focus on background expertise, such as prominent legal qualifications or other professional expertise. Experience shows that good mediators can come from a range of backgrounds. Again it is the authors' view that non-mediation expertise is only a secondary quality in terms of mediation effectiveness. The parties will usually already have invested much time and resource in obtaining their own experts' views. There is only a real need for the mediator to be an expert where the technical issues in the case really are the overwhelming stumbling block to settlement. More importantly usually are the neutral negotiation project management skills learned in intense mediation practice. However, mediation's flexibility is again a strength if parties differ in their views of what is required in the mediator. Except in the low value cases, parties would usually be justified in agreeing a mediation team, one reflecting process skills, the other expertise in subject-matter or culture, or preferably having both these attributes. It is

51

our view that complex mediations justify appointment of two mediators. Mediation is a process which is more demanding on personal energy and fleet-footedness than adjudicative roles. It is therefore helpful to the mediator and the parties to have a colleague who can share the energy demands, act as a sounding-board for discussions of mediator tactical choices, and share some of the tasks of information-gathering, relationship-building and logistics of the mediation project. A lead mediator with an assistant mediator can also work well, or a mediator with a technical assessor for highly technical project disputes.

In an international setting the co-mediation model therefore presents additional opportunities. One is able to address the broader requirements of international mediation in terms of language, culture, expertise, and appointments can also provide for an experienced mediator to work with a less experienced mediator to meet the needs of the international community. In multi-party mediations another advantage of a co-mediation team is that the mediators can, if they deem it to be for the benefit of the process, work with the different teams and split roles. They need to have a high regard and trust of each other for this to work. The intensity and energy required for a complex multi-party dispute means that mediators are considerably advantaged by being teamed with another effective mediator.

There are a number of methods of selecting mediators which include:

– Dialogue with an organisation with a track record in international mediations;
– Pre-mediation meetings with a shortlist of potential mediators. These 'beauty parades' often take place with all parties forming part of the interview panel and themselves can help to create a bridge for communication between parties;
– Face-to-face meetings with potential mediators;
– Personal recommendations from other mediation users. Some organisations have feedback procedure following mediations and keep records on mediators, their characteristics and success or otherwise.

In terms of discussions with mediators one should examine their career experience and subject matter expertise, their availability, flexibility and willingness to work in a relatively short time frame. It is also important to check their willingness to work with the parties should a settlement not be achieved within the agreed time frame, as it is not uncommon in international mediation for some post-mediation work to be required to tie up all issues. Parties can be extremely disappointed if their chosen mediator is not available to them, and the negotiation can collapse without proactive third party effort. Career mediators understand the importance of availability and follow-up after the mediation.

There are a number of general qualities (some have been referred to) one would look for:

- background and status;
- track record;
- style of approach;
- credibility;
- humility;
- diplomatic approach;
- intellectual rigour;
- integrity;
- patience;
- persistence; and
- energy.

Mediators have to adapt to different parties and different situations, and have to remember that they are the agent to all the parties. There is a range of styles and backgrounds already available in this field. When talking to potential mediators ask them to provide referees and, when talking to their selected referees, ask for the names of other parties who were involved in the same prior mediations so that you have the opportunity to see how effective the mediator was from the point of view of all parties involved in the prior disputes.

Overall, one is seeking a certain elegance of approach that works across cultures, personalities and specialisms.

Building bridges

As this chapter has illustrated, the entry phase of getting into international mediations can be particularly sensitive. There are a number of reasons.

First, the suggestion of mediation may be difficult when immediately following on from stalemate in face-to-face negotiations. The threat of actual implementation of arbitration may seem more appropriate. It should always be remembered that one can instigate a mediation in a tight time frame against the backdrop of commencement of legal process if the mediation fails, or can set both processes on track together.

Second, the climate of conflict which is likely to be in place can make mediation procedural decisions themselves into very sensitive negotiation issues. This will be exacerbated if parties and advisers bring the habits and mindset of traditional arbitration and adversarial negotiation into the process, making each point a battle to be contested fiercely if it is perceived to give some ground to the other side. In our experience a neutral mediation body can be of major assistance to facilitate agreement on entry, process and mediator selection. In the last several years many very complex, high stakes disputes with multiple parties have been brought to the mediation table. This can involve several months of work by experienced mediators.

Third, there will be many situations where international commercial mediation is an unfamiliar option or where it may be unclear whether the parties are communicating about the same kind of process. It is very common for parties to confuse arbitration, which essentially requires a third party to decide on an outcome, and mediation which essentially facilitates a party re-evaluation of the issues in a commercial context, to lead to an agreed and binding party-controlled outcome.

In all these circumstances parties and mediation organisations have to learn to treat preliminary matters, particularly choice of mediator, as themselves issues for a mediation process requiring the same skills and sensitivity as a mediation of the substantive case.

We predict that international mediation will grow rapidly because its flexibility and project management potential is particularly suitable for the complexity of international disputes and cost-effective in comparison to existing alternatives. Case selection and entry to mediation should therefore become a less critical issue, and current lack of awareness of mediation will be overcome by court-annexed and contract developments. As the process becomes more established, it is equally important that the mediator community can sustain the quality needed for this regular practice tool and deliver the process framework and experience that the case and party circumstances require. We turn next to the process itself.

Chapter 4. 'Form and Flexibility' – The Mediation Framework

'There is in our work as mediators, when it is going well, a ... blend of learned structure and conventions, and improvisation strongly supported by talent and intuition. It is jazz: There are a few orthodoxies and a lot of ad hoc ensemble invention.'

Howard Bellman, US Environmental/Labour Mediator.

FORM	MEDIATION	FLEXIBILITY
Confidentiality Independent Mediation Agreement Law of the Mediation Legal Presentation Disciplined process structure Discipline of deadline Agreed binding outcome	Dynamic balance managed by neutral	Executive participation Commercial dialogue Infusion of common sense Imaginative solutions Financial analysis Balance of risk and reward Principal to principal contact Case and business overview combined Agreed workable outcome

There are a number of issues in terms of legal and procedural framework that need to be considered when advising on the use of mediation as a tool for resolution of an international dispute. These include the following:

– design of process;

– confidentiality;

– law of mediation agreement;

– termination of the mediation;

– impact on other legal processes;

– role of commercial managers/lawyers/other experts;

– how long to prepare – pre-mediation work;

- how much time to allow for the mediation sessions;
- where to conduct the process;
- documentation;
- estimate of costs of process;
- authority to settle – necessary steps; and
- enforceability and workability of any settlement (See Chapter 7).

We pick up some of these points in more depth in later chapters. This chapter outlines the skeleton framework of a typical mediation process and highlights some of its cost benefits compared to an arbitration.

Process design

If you are working with a mediation organisation it will have its own blueprint/guidelines for the mediation process. An example of the main elements of such frameworks can be seen in Part 2 of this book. This covers most of the issues outlined in this chapter. In more complex multi–party cases there may be a need for a carefully negotiated process design. This dialogue would be a first phase of a confidence-raising entry into further substantive negotiations.

Confidential and without prejudice

Mediation is often described as a 'safe haven' to explore opportunities for settlement. This requires the parties to have confidence that what they say in mediation to each other by way of compromise suggestions, and what they say to the mediator in private sessions, are treated as confidential. In many common law jurisdictions, negotiations in the spirit of compromise are protected from evidential disclosure, particularly if the parties contract with each other and the mediator to preserve confidentiality. In such jurisdictions there is likely to be case law to support the statement that the mediator cannot be required to divulge confidences made in the course of mediation. Precedent also supports the position that parties cannot present evidence of what was said in the mediation (though there are some exceptions to this general rule).

In a jurisdiction – some civil law countries – where compromise negotiations are not always so clearly protected, the parties should consider whether this lack of protection would preclude them from having negotiations as such. If not they should treat the mediation as an extension of the negotiation process – which is what it is – provided that a third party to the negotiations has the same legal protection afforded to the direct negotiators.

If there is a problem of a less favourable legal environment, the parties should consider whether they would prefer to opt for a mediation agreement that is governed by the law of a jurisdiction that protects confidentiality, thus ensuring that the mediation takes place in a more favourable jurisdiction. This consideration should also extend to selecting a mediator whose training and professional code of ethics supports adherence to mediation confidentiality (for an insight into variations even across Europe, see *The EU Mediation Atlas*, Part 2, Further Reading).

There is also the issue of the appropriate use of documents or other evidence produced at the mediation. Typically mediation agreements and general law would distinguish between documents created specifically for the mediation process, which can be protected from later disclosure in legal proceedings, and documents contemporaneous to the dispute which evidence factual and technical issues. The latter category of information will not be protected from disclosure in arbitration or the courts, if this information would in any event have been admissible and required to be disclosed. If in doubt parties may seek to use the protection of mediation confidentiality to disclose a document to the mediator only (if they can be sure that the mediator is not compellable as a witness in the jurisdiction).

Mediation is intended to be 'without prejudice' to any party's right to continue or pursue legal proceedings if the case does not settle. This is an essential feature of the process to assist the parties by providing a legal cloak of safety over the 'no risk' aspect of mediation discussions and settlement offers. If the case is a court-referred mediation, the court in some jurisdictions may, however, keep an overall view on progress, or the costs of the mediation may be subject to later judicial direction.

Also mediation may in some instances be an essential step under contract procedures before a court will permit proceedings to be initiated. A good illustration of this position was *Cable & Wireless Plc v IBM Ltd* [2002] 2 All ER 1041 (COMM) where an ADR clause that specifically referred disputes to mediation was upheld notwithstanding vague language due to the fact it provided for CEDR rules so had institutional back and clear rules. The judge said the rules and procedure of the institution provided all the necessary clarity to hold the parties to their bargain.

The Australian Courts have upheld the enforceability of mediation clauses since the early 1990s. In Europe, clauses have been upheld in

Austria, France, Italy and Sweden. There is also a trend developing of parties amending their international contracts at the time of the dispute to provide for mediation procedure.

Absolute answers are not available on many of these questions of the detailed implications of mediation internationally. As a new process, mediation case law or statutory protection is still evolving within and across jurisdictions. The United Nations Commission on International Trade Law (UNCITRAL) has attempted to develop a broad Model procedure (on Conciliation) to achieve consistency across jurisdictions globally (see Part 2), as has the US for cross-state purposes (Uniform Mediation Act) and the European Union for its member states (Draft Directive on civil and commercial mediation).

Law of the mediation agreement

The law of the substantive contract may be deemed to govern the mediation agreement, unless otherwise specified. It is often simpler to have the same governing law but it is important to consider if this will have any undesirable results in relation to confidentiality as previously discussed. Setting the mediation in another jurisdiction from that of the contract (or parties) may further complicate the legal position. A mediation agreement should also normally provide that any settlement will not be legally binding unless and until it is reduced to writing and signed, to avoid scope for misunderstanding over oral agreements apparently reached during the process. The authors encourage parties to use a mediation agreement governed by English Law. Our experience is that parties are happy to work with this framework even where the governing law provision of their contract is different and the mediation is outside of England.

Termination of the mediation

The essence of mediation is that the mediator cannot impose any settlement on the parties or compel them to stay in the process. The parties will want to define therefore when it is clear that the mediation is finished. A mediation agreement will provide for termination at any or all of the following points:

- a party withdrawing from a mediation with notice;
- a written settlement agreement is concluded; or
- the mediator decides that continuing the mediation is unlikely to result in a settlement; or

- the mediator decides that (s)he should retire due to ethical concerns which may be covered in a mediators' code of conduct.

It is common practice for mediators to make contact with parties after an unsuccessful mediation session. The mediator or parties should make clear that such communications are intended to be covered by the appropriate provisions of the mediation agreement, ie confidential and without prejudice.

Stay of arbitration or litigation proceedings

Where the parties are engaged in or contemplating a formal legal process, they can agree to stay further steps during the course of the mediation process, or they may wish to continue in parallel with a mediation. If legal proceedings or arbitration have not been commenced they can agree (subject to the general law of the jurisdiction allowing this) to withhold action subject to avoiding problems with legal rules on time periods within which legal proceedings can be started. It will depend on the jurisdiction, and on the tactical deployment of arbitration/litigation, as to whether there is any disadvantage to proceeding in one or other manner. In recent times parties have tended to defer the commencement of arbitration or litigation and to try mediation first, to save costs. But advisers should ensure they protect any rights to formal proceedings.

Record or transcript of mediation/mediation outcome

The nature of mediation as a facilitated negotiation makes it inappropriate to keep formal transcripts of the proceedings. If there is a settlement then the mediator and parties should ensure that the parties prepare a written agreement and take such other steps as appropriate to ensure a workable and enforceable settlement. This should be done as soon as possible, preferably at the termination of the mediation itself. The mediator may need to help the parties resolve disagreement over the drafting of the terms of settlement.

The responsibility for drafting the settlement is for the lawyers. A useful checklist of issues to cover could include:
(1) Time and method of any payments.
(2) Currency, any provision for fluctuation of currencies.
(3) Transfer of real property – how and what restrictions exist.
(4) Transfer of intellectual property, how will it be accomplished.
(5) Any cross-border tax implications.

(6) Continued relations or actions, how they will be managed, and by whom and by when.

(7) Any corporate, public or regulatory statements required, or other exceptions to confidentiality.

(8) Actions or dispute procedure if any default.

(9) Law governing the settlement agreement.

In many complex international cases the mediation session may end with a memorandum of understanding – to allow the detail to be worked out over the weeks ahead. This type of arrangement in our experience needs to be carefully managed to ensure that the deal does get implemented. In some instances it will be appropriate to keep the mediation process alive until a final binding workable settlement is signed.

Where there is no settlement, the parties may want to request that the mediator prepare a non-binding written recommendation on terms of settlement. This generally will not be an attempt to anticipate what a third party body would order but rather would recommend a settlement that the mediator believes the parties may be prepared to endorse once they have had time for reflection. Where one is dealing with a government body or state owned entity, the parties may want to agree that the mediator makes a clear recommendation. This can help a party 'sell' the agreement to senior managers or within the context of an audit trail. In some cases, the parties have wished the mediator to go further and state in writing, for example, that the agreement is a 'reasonable' settlement for that body to enter into. Most experienced mediators will delay giving any such recommendation until they are certain that they have exhausted all other routes for the parties to agree their own terms.

Arbitration route – mediator commentary
In one case mediated by the authors, an Asian public sector organisation asked the mediator to include a statement on the estimated costs of taking the case to arbitration had it not settled, to reinforce the case for settlement. If parties are aware in advance that a case may need this kind of outcome, there is a strong case for including an appropriate expert to work alongside the mediator.
Mediators will usually test a figure with the parties before proceeding to a written recommendation. Another way of handling a non-binding recommendation is to have each party put in a recommended figure for settlement and the mediator can take the proposal that seems most

*reasonable. This type of approach, the 'Baseball Settlement' recommen-
dation (taken from 'Baseball Arbitration') can drive each party to a
more reasonable conclusion based on the gap at the end of the mediator
negotiations.*

Venue for mediation

Location is particularly an issue for international cases. However, it is
important in international mediation not to be overly concerned on the
neutrality of the venue. There may be considerable benefit in locating the
mediation where the project is or has taken place. This will assist with site
visits, access to local managers, access to political and economic decision
makers, cost saving for one of the parties.

The atmosphere and psychology of the physical environs at mediation is
important. It is not uncommon for difficulties to arise from accommodation
being chosen that is not conducive to positive negotiation discussions.
Venues in overseas mediation will very often be hotels. Care needs to be
taken to choose venues with appropriate facilities for the basics of the
process – private meetings, joint meetings and preservation of confidentiality, as well as access to business centres. Mediators should be willing to
accommodate the parties and they will generally travel to countries of the
parties' choice.

Venue variations – adapting to local expectations
*A mediation team arrived in a small Asian country for a mediation. The
'home-team' showed us to the meeting room. They had booked a local
palace great hall and had set out tables and chairs as if for a formal
inquiry with two banks of tables linked by a large head table 20 feet
away, despite advance notice of the type of accommodation required. An
early start already arranged for the first day allowed the mediation
team time to set up new arrangements more productive for mediation
negotiations.*

In the last number of years London has frequently been chosen as a neutral
seat for international mediations in matters not involving English law.
However, it is important for the development of international mediation that
parties recognise the flexibility of the process and the ability to have the
mediation at whatever location is likely to provide the most and best
ingredients for resolution. In a longer-running mediation, for example,
meetings can be conducted in each party's country in turn with perhaps a

final meeting in a neutral country to emphasise the psychological difference from earlier stages in terms of finality.

Time and duration

The timescale and duration of mediation needs to be assessed carefully in international cases. The choice may be whether to have a single mediation event or to lead up to the mediation with a number of pre-mediation events and meetings. Most mediators prefer to engage with the parties before the main mediation event to develop a rapport and understanding of the issues and to help the parties design the best approach, particularly in multiparty and more complex problems. Equally however, this needs to be balanced with one of the benefits of mediation, that it is not protracted in the same manner as arbitration or international litigation.

Generally mediators will want to get the 'mediation process proper' on track within three months of engagement and to limit preliminary stages to a few meetings and/or telephone calls, and reading of mediation submissions. Mediators or parties may limit preliminary meetings if the parties are clear that they are seeking a 'last-shot' attempt at settlement negotiations following a number of earlier efforts. The typical international mediation event, even with multi-parties, lasts somewhere between two to five days. It is unusual for a mediation to last more than two days at a stretch but not unprecedented to have a first and second phase, totalling five days. The break in the process may be necessary to get government or corporate/ insurer approvals, or to bring in other third party elements which could not be incorporated in the first round. Sometimes it may be a necessary gap in time within which the mediator or parties can seek to 'rescue' the process and negotiation momentum.

> *Last Call – mediator emergency services*
> *In a $1bn pharmaceutical distribution dispute between a European and Asian company, the parties had finished two days of mediation with a negotiating gap remaining of $500m. At the end of the two days, the parties agreed with the mediator to reconvene for a third and final effort one month later prior to which time each would consult with its CEO. One week after this agreement the European company pulled out of the mediation saying that it was unrealistic to expect further progress. However, the mediator continued telephone discussions via the lawyers, testing various proposals. Four calls later, the parties had bridged the gap, and settled the case.*

The length of the mediation day is also flexible, closer to corporate negotiation than arbitration/litigation practice. In some mediations the mediators will work into the small hours of the morning if that is likely to benefit the process. This may not always be sensible or appropriate and one has to be cognisant of the cultural expectations and energy of all the parties involved. The important objective against which questions of timing are measured, is as to whether the mediation can create an energetic environment. A pace needs to be created so that the parties feel engaged and have a sense of momentum towards settlement, with appropriate breaks for review and reflection of negotiation issues and progress.

Participants – 'Decision makers are critical'

The right team at the table for each party will be important to the success of the process. The general unswerving principle of mediation is that commercial decision makers are critical to the success of the process. It can also help to bring a fresh mind to the problem, a commercial decision maker with no earlier direct involvement in the project and who does not have the need to justify past actions or who can take a more detached perspective. This can be an advantage if organisational politics allow. It can sometimes be the case that in-house counsel play a lead role as the commercial representative, but a commercial executive will normally be preferable. Technical experts, external lawyers, accountants, project managers and process experts may also have a role. Most mediations involve lawyers but principals should have a much more central role. It is the authors' experience that, where possible, smaller, more focused teams are most effective.

Involvement of advisers may depend on the type of case and on exactly where a party is in the dispute. Early in the negotiations and in the commercial stages, it may be more appropriate for managers to be closely involved, perhaps teaming with in-house lawyers, and only later in the project or post project would external lawyers be brought in. On the other hand, if there is a lot of value in the dispute or an important contract interpretation, or when commercial principals want additional advice on the likely result of going to court or arbitration, early external advice may be advisable in order to decide on a negotiating position. The authors have had experience of adjourning mediations, to allow one or other teams to get further advice from a leading law firm or barristers, and then sharing this advice on a confidential basis with the mediator to oil the wheels of the negotiations. Sometimes the clients have commissioned a joint non-binding expert view to help the next steps of the negotiations. If this additional input is managed well, it can be beneficial to assist in breaking the impasse. It is nevertheless our experience that, notwithstanding the comfort some may achieve from an expert view, the commercial imperative is nearly always the greatest driver. (The involvement of a state owned enterprise is probably the exception to this experience, such parties often being driven by legal advice or political agendas.)

In practice parties may also be influenced by whom the other side choose to bring along, and to some extent there may be a 'tit-for-tat' approach in this. Closer to legal proceedings parties may wish to use the trial team in order to demonstrate to the other side the strength of their case and demonstrate their level of preparation. They may also want to control the risks of disclosure in mediation, or to assess the strength of the other side's case if mediation were to fail.

One should bear in mind, however, that the process is fundamentally a commercial negotiation process rather than a legal one and that, however strong the back-up team, there will be need for a core commercial negotiating team at some stage of the mediation. For this reason in some cases there may even be an argument to separate the negotiating team very strongly from the team involved in any court or adversarial or arbitration process. In one international dispute involving long running litigation, the US in-house counsel told the mediator he had flown to London to participate in the mediation to assess the performance of his London lawyers. The mediator was nevertheless able to assist all the clients to reach a workable settlement.

Outside experts may also be important. They could be appointed by party agreement to give joint non-binding neutral advice to the parties and/or mediator. Otherwise the mediator has to facilitate dialogue between party experts and assess common ground and differences. It is important that experts are there for reasons of reassurance and confidence within the management team, or to engage in dialogue with the other side. However, there is a danger that they can take the parties into fixed positions that do not reflect the full commercial risks. Managers have to retain their ability to make a commercial judgement as to how far to go along with the expert assessment.

In international cases there may be a need for local advisers on the situation, or local agents who can explore the wider implications and attitudes blocking or facilitating the negotiation. For example, local commercial or political circumstances or potential future opportunities for contracts or tenders can influence the negotiation position taken.

The management team directly connected with a project – or a key witness of fact – may equally be an important element. In a particularly technical case, it would clearly be important to have technical managers with the appropriate know-how and confidence to influence and persuade the other side, if not to educate their own senior management and advisers.

The effective team

Overall in choosing a management negotiation team or legal negotiation team, one would also bear in mind their personal abilities, attitudes and experience. The overriding need is to find co-operative, effective negotiators with a good track record of building relationships and doing deals. In practice, a team focused on the end game, which is about resolution rather than gamesmanship or winning outright, is going to be the most effective.

In an international mediation, where parties sometimes have to travel considerable distances, it is important that each team is satisfied that they have the right team and that the other parties bring key decision-makers to the mediation table. The mediator can have a key role in facilitating an agreement to have the right personnel and decision-makers at the mediation table. They should explore with parties or their advisors before the mediation, just what are the likely negotiating dynamics between the teams in terms of who could be there, or should be present.

As we have mentioned, some of the most effective mediations have involved small teams – highly focused and efficient. It is certainly true that if the clients come to mediation early there is a much greater chance of a small team being used. A good example of this was a case mediated in Europe where one team had the Finance Director and corporate lawyer and the other a Commercial Director and corporate lawyer. There were many elements to the dispute including highly technical, financial and environmental data. The mediator had been well briefed by both teams, and felt the process was so successful due to the authority and commerciality of each team. Two days were needed to unlock the deadlock but including more personnel would not have made this a more successful process.

Authority to settle

Authority to settle is a key ingredient of most mediation agreements, and vital to effectiveness of mediation. However, in practice, the situation can often be more complex. Insurers or company boards or government ministers may need to give approval to any negotiated settlement. Even senior commercial managers may enter negotiations with limits on what they can offer. Where the dispute is with a state-owned entity or government department, it is often unlikely that anything more than a recommendation may be achieved from the mediation unless within clearly delegated authority.

In-so-far as possible parties, and particularly the mediator, should be clear as to the power and constraints of the decision-makers. Ideally this would be established in advance of the mediation. However in practice in international cases, it is only by working closely with the teams and building up confidence and awareness, that the mediator gets a clearer picture of what can be achieved and the limits on parties' authority. This should be factored into the negotiation and mediation efforts, and may require adjournments either for proposals to be relayed home for consideration, or for new authority to be brought to the table.

In some cases, the mediator or other parties may need to arrange to meet government officials, or make informal contact with local trade consulates or funding agencies in order to assist in the influence process, or to confirm what systems are in place (including telephone contacts during the process) to 'deliver' a workable deal. Clearly such contacts have to be handled with considerable sensitivity, for confidentiality and political reasons, as well as their effect on the negotiation process. The key objective is for the mediator and mediation process to sustain momentum even if there appear to be roadblocks on authority. This can again call for effective follow-up to mediation meetings.

Mediation structure

There are generally three core phases to a mediation. Given the flexibility of mediation, a mediator's own personal preferences and the range of types of case, there can be considerable variation in the details of how this structure is acted out by mediators and parties (more detail will be given in Chapter 5).

Phase one – preliminary matters

In this phase parties will work through most of the issues highlighted in this chapter, with the mediator and/or ADR organization. It should not be forgotten that this phase itself may be important in re-opening dialogue and contacts, although often it reflects a background of distrust in terms of skirmishes over a number of issues such as confidentiality, participants, venue, etc. A preliminary meeting with the mediator may also take place, jointly or separately and on one or more occasions.

Phase two – exchange of information

The information exchange will usually involve a prior exchange of documents with a subsequent review of positions in the presence of each party's full team in the first joint session of the mediation. In addition to the mediator's formal introduction at the joint meeting, the opening meeting offers the opportunity for each party to set out their view of the issues that confront the parties – legal, factual, financial, emotional and procedural. This serves both as a summary of case to remind each side and the mediator of starting positions, but may also signal new information, arguments or settlement proposals depending on prior activity and case strategy.

Phase three – the negotiating process

The heart of mediation practice takes place in this phase, where the mediator, in a series of joint and private meetings, encourages the parties to explore and reassess each other's case, and assists in the search for options that will lead to serious bargaining over the terms of a deal. To be truly effective in this phase, the mediator will want to work with a smaller core team with the commercial decision-makers at its heart. In most of the large international mediations the Phase Two team can often be six–ten strong whereas the Phase Three team is more often two–three participants from each side.

The economics of mediation

Costs can be classified under two basic headings:

1   Mediation costs

These can vary according to the mediator and/or mediation organisation used, and will cover any referral costs, preparation including reading time, and fees for the mediation meetings. Practices vary but reflect the range of models found in professional work generally, namely:
–   hourly rates;
–   daily basis;
–   fixed fee; and
–   success fees (though this is unusual and often barred by professional codes).

These may be linked to the value of the amount in dispute. Parties normally agree to share the costs of the mediation equally although this may vary, for example if one party or an external project funding agency has agreed to pick up the costs in order to facilitate entry to the process. Also, with the increase in court-referred cases, parties may leave open the question of seeking a costs order from the court or arbitrator to recover their costs (mediation and/or party costs) if a mediation 'fails' and they go on to succeed in the action.

2 Party costs

– management time;
– legal team preparation, experts etc; and
– expense of travel, accommodation and venue.

In Part 2 of the book we provide more detailed examples of international mediations based on real cases. This draws on a range of the kinds of value at issue ($200,000–$1bn), time taken to mediate and at what cost, and the result. The cases handled demonstrate that mediation can work with different sizes of cases from small to large in financial scale, and two–party or multi–party. Our experience also confirms that even high-value, complex cases can be mediated in two-three days with one-two days preparation, at a mediation cost to the parties of around $10,000–$60,000 (and excluding travel costs and other expenses of the mediator).

The economics of mediation have to be measured by a number of criteria:
– the amount in dispute;
– the likelihood of achieving a satisfactory solution;
– the future transaction costs of an alternative arbitrated or court solution;
– the management investment in time which should be compared with the time that will be involved in achieving an arbitrated or court-based outcome;
– any reputation costs; and
– the opportunity costs of achieving a result in mediation, ie freed-up management time.

Hidden cost of conflict – iceberg effect

The core accounting approaches to disputes (if used at all) often take no account of the 'iceberg effect'. The greatest impact is hidden below the surface – and will include:
– damage to company reputation;
– exposure in the public domain;

- effect on personal reputation or health;
- damage to business relationships;
- loss of customers;
- damage to company or executive/staff morale;
- increase in staff turnover or absenteeism;
- failure to meet targets;
- missed opportunities and diversion of management time.

Research into the real cost to business has confirmed that one of the severest consequences of disputes on business is the effect on management time, with (according to a recent survey) 87 per cent of businesses affected. High-value or complex disputes in particular can call on years of management time. CEDR in 2006 estimated the cost of conflict to UK business to be exceeding £30bn a year. Against this backdrop it is clear that the future of mediation as a tool for business is very great indeed.

'Two key pressures on business in the twenty first century are to be socially responsible and, as always, maintain low operating costs ...So the question is – how much money, not to mention business goodwill, is being lost by lack of practical know-how in accessing skilful independent intervention? It goes without saying that every business in a dispute today must ask itself – "can I afford not to mediate?" '

Sir Peter Middleton, Chairman, CEDR

Here is a comparative example of clients in one case who made the choice to mediate before arbitration (with estimated total arbitration costs):

The Choice between international mediation and arbitration

	Mediation Costs	**Arbitration Tribunal Costs**
Amount at issue	€ 20 million	€20 millon
Time to reach result	2–6 months	24–36 months
Management time	100 Hours	700 Hours
Cost of mediator/ arbitrator panel	$17,000	$350,000–$750,000
Legal costs	$90,000	$400–600,000
Result	Agreed Commercial Solution	Binding Award, still to be enforced

We have assumed the same hourly rates apply for mediators/arbitrators and have made some averaging assumptions about the model of arbitration used, and of lawyer time and costs. Both arbitration and legal costs can have significant variations internationally and, in some cases, a significant percentage of legal and arbitrator costs may be recoverable depending on the award outcome and enforcement likelihood in the case.

On the basis set out in the example above one could see that the following was achieved through the effective use of mediation at the appropriate time (and the earlier in the dispute the more benefit that will be derived). The potential benefits include:

– **Certainty of Result.** The clients kept control of the decision-making but were guided by the mediators to understand the issues at stake and the real difficulties with handling the dispute from a purely legal perspective.

– **Effort appropriate to result.** Of course there is a small chance that a mediation would not achieve settlement either at the mediation or soon after. In the small number of disputes where this is an outcome, the clients will definitely have a much better understanding of the risks of not finding a solution and the groundwork will have been done to make a better strategic decision for what to do next.

– **Timeliness.** In the above example money was paid within a few working days and bank guarantees were surrendered immediately. A fully workable settlement was achieved. An arbitration award may have to be enforced and takes time to implement.

– **Management time.** In this example one can see that in addition to the settlement amount there is potential minimal management savings of at least 600 hours. There is also the avoidance of the 'Dispute Distraction' phenomenon, leaving management to get on with future acquisitions, building their business and achieving targets. Many mediations may involve an opportunity to achieve some commercial objectives, for example return of bank guarantees or variation of contracts.

– **Transaction savings.** The earlier a decision is made to mediate the greater the level of efficiency and savings. In the above example we estimate the savings were in excess of $1m. If one factors in the travel and fees for experts, fees for the arbitration panel and management time, the cost savings could be double that.

The decision to mediate can therefore be dramatic for business

International business will face conflict on a daily basis – it is how managers decide to manage the conflict that will separate success from failure.

'We relied on CEDR's mediation services to successfully resolve a difficult international dispute. The CEDR team were so diligent and professionally focused on the objective that we placed our full confidence in the mediation process. I highly recommend to any international company facing the problem of dispute resolution to [use mediation]'

Director, Japanese pharmaceutical company

Finally, it is not an uncommon occurrence in mediations that parties resolve more than the dispute that brought them to mediation, or for them to identify other commercial deals as part of resolution. This is a common feature in disputes involving financial institutions or corporations that have more than one piece of business together. It is, however, a myth that mediation solutions require continued business relationships. Probably at least 60 percent of international mediations do not have the feature of a potential future business relationship. Clearly, however, in major joint ventures and project finance initiatives involving major construction and engineering projects going on over a number of years, there ought to be a commitment to develop a solution that allows the parties to work together or to terminate in a manner that is least disruptive.

Mediation therefore has significant 'Form and Flexibility' to make it a tool that suits the needs of lawyers for structure and business people for commercial opportunity, 'fairness' and adaptability. Both business people and their lawyers stay more in control of costs, process and outcome, and hence reduce the risks of alternative adversarial combat.

Chapter 5. Preparing for Success in Mediated Negotiations

'*A basic fact about negotiation easy to forget in corporate and international transactions is that you are dealing not with abstract representation of the "other side", but with human beings. They have emotions, deeply-held values, and different backgrounds and view points and they are unpredictable – so are you.*'

Roger Fisher & William Ury, *Getting to Yes.*

'*Let us never negotiate out of fear. But let us never fear to negotiate*'.

John F Kennedy

When we have talked to international hostage negotiators and asked them how you break deadlock in very difficult and life-threatening situations, there emerges a powerful set of golden rules:

- ACTIVE LISTENING

- ACTIVE LISTENING

- ACTIVE LISTENING.

This is an easy thing to say, but much more difficult to achieve, which is why it is worth emphasising at the outset. Active listening is harder to achieve than most negotiators appreciate. A key question to ask when preparing to mediate is – how will we help their team listen actively to us? And how do we show we are actively listening to them? As people and their business culture are at the heart of any deadlock, you need to understand their motivations and concerns. This requires great patience and perseverance. It is not at all surprising that most of us run out of steam when faced with our own intractable conflicts. The mediation process, because of its structure and approach, brings greater discipline and framework into business negotiation. For one thing you have to allow a full day or two for the dialogue. It is a tough but potentially rewarding process *and it is definitely worth preparing well for.*

Good preparation for mediation calls into play a need to cover some key elements, or *agendas*, to reflect the multilayered character of the process, alongside *levers* to create mediated negotiation effectiveness. These fundamental ingredients of a mediation recipe will be mixed in different ways to reflect the particular circumstances and people in a specific case. However, they will all be present in some form in any case.

Many of these factors of course will be present in direct settlement negotiations. What mediation does is to add greater ability to explore and develop them by the nature of the process, as well as adding the direct impact of the personality and approach of a third party. In addition to providing an overview of the elements for preparation therefore, we will focus most of our attention on what third party engagement distinctively brings to the preparation process.

Key agendas in preparation

In-depth review of case/project issues – legal/technical/financial

Mediation provides an opportunity for advisors and managers to get to grips with the range and proportionality of failure and success of the project in dispute and how the other party sees this. What are the failures really attributable to? For example in a reinsurance coverage case, could it be poor risk analysis/bad underwriting in addition to possible non-disclosure? How can documents or 'witnesses' or experts best be used to convey this? There are often a number of reasons for failure shared between the respective parties to a project. In a formal legal process the unravelling of causation and liability can become protracted, and unhelpfully 'forced'. Any remedy is likely to be therefore a blunt instrument of resolution. However, in a mediation context there is greater fluidity in the process to enable the parties to *design* an outcome taking account of the technical and commercial failures, successes and proportional contributions of all the parties, rather than being purely focused on the legal effect of failure, which is entirely blame orientated and usually black-and-white in judgement and restrictive principle. The mediation process and remedy is capable of creating a more equitable, commercially 'fair' outcome. Preparation for the process should therefore factor in how best to address 'proportionality' of contributions and set them in a broader context if appropriate. This also allows for a greater sense of 'give and take' and therefore positive spirit in the negotiation. It should of course also address normal negotiation and risk analysis perspectives – best, worst and satisfactory outcomes likely from the negotiation, or from an alternative process.

Taking a commercial perspective

As mediation can convert a legal or technical dispute into a commercial negotiation, it is of course essential to review key financial and business drivers for all parties. How might these be raised or developed in the process? Related to this, while mediation may begin with a review of past problems and history, it can then powerfully switch the negotiating dynamic and content to include present and future commercial interests, eg future business opportunities, cash flow or political imperatives etc. What are the opportunities and potential for this? How is this potential best released? What role can the mediator play?

Understanding the human dynamics

This requires an examination of the nature and route of dialogue between the parties in the past as well as alertness to the present potential for better dialogue. In international disputes, distance, cultural mismatch, political interference and more pressing domestic agendas can further damage difficult dialogue. Before one can establish the route to effective dialogue in mediation one has to have examined how and why previous dialogue failed to address the issues. Mediators will want to understand the human dynamics as much as, and sometimes more than, the legal interpretation. The mediator will usually have the trust of both parties and can therefore more easily convey messages, filter communications to make them more powerful or less provocative, test resistance to new offers, and assist in identifying how to encourage better communications.

All of these elements will play some role in a successful mediation outcome. Even with preparation, parties have to be as flexible in the mediation as they should be in any negotiation. New information may emerge, or new understanding of the resistance of the other side. Relationships may need to be built between senior managers in the mediation in order to make compromise acceptable. Time may need to be devoted to a genuine review of how to deal with a technical problem – for example a power plant or IT system not operating to original expected performance – not for the question of legal blame, but instead how to remedy the situation so that the other party can go back with a face-saving or commercially viable deal. In one dispute involving a failure of electricity generators in Central America, one allegation involved the failure of a linchpin. Notwithstanding the presence of 40 individuals from Central and North America, and Europe – the missing piece to resolve the dispute were the manufacturers from Europe. After two days of mediation a memorandum of understanding was signed and parallel negotiations were put in place with the missing manufacturers.

As one party stated 'the mediation was a success in that the parties are all on the same page and there is a way forward'.

'Getting on the same page' is again and again repeated as an observation in mediations as to why and when deadlocked negotiation turns into mediated progress. Previous project failures, breakdowns in communication, piecemeal and fragmented efforts to negotiate directly or via legal correspondence – time and time again there remains a fundamental misperception by each party of where the other is coming from. The mediator's neutrality and objectivity, together with a structured joint process, help build the bridge.

Negotiation levers

In addition to the substantive agendas that will play out at the mediation, parties should also factor into their preparation the question of how best to use the *negotiating levers* at their disposal. Not least the role of the third party mediator and how to make optimal use of the role and the fact of a third party process. There are at least four elements in this part of the matrix of factors and choices of how to progress negotiation diplomacy.

Measuring the practical and financial context and effect of the problem

Good preparation and presentation of financial profit or loss calculations or other technical data is always valuable in an effective negotiation. In our experience if the detail is prepared with the same persuasive tone and marketing pitch of negotiating documents, and not legal documents, it can be more effective. Often not enough attention is paid to financial data and its presentation. Or the data is drawn up by a technical manager with little thought on how to make it really meaningful to the principals/lawyers. Or lawyers who are driving the case have limited numeracy or presentation design skills. The data should be considered in terms of all parties' positions. This element of course also suggests that a good mediator should have good numeracy skills.

Potential sources of influence and persuasion

As in all effective negotiation, planning should factor in what is the best way to present a case, how it should be presented, who should present it, to whom is it best addressed. In mediation there are opportunities for more formal presentations, but information can also be channelled via the mediator. In one IT dispute the German commercial director was very influenced by listening to both technical teams talk through what had gone wrong with the specification, but some of this was reinforced in further private discussion afterwards with the mediator. In all mediations one of the key benefits is the fact that senior managers can hear – sometimes for the first time – an in-depth analysis of what is being said by not only their own team, but also by the other side's experts, project managers or lawyers.

Imaginative methodologies for finding solutions

In one dispute involving multiple contracts over diesel engines, one team produced a simple text financial analysis acknowledging some of the financial loss. This enabled the mediator to convene a private session with the commercial directors – and help them jointly negotiate a final figure. In another case an insolvency practitioner in a property development case gave in confidence a spreadsheet showing agreed settlements to date with other creditors. This helped the claimant adjust psychologically to a discount on his claim against company assets. In all difficult negotiations it is helpful if parties have worked in advance on alternative ways of persuading the other side to their way of thinking. Mediators can also bring some lateral thinking into 'stuck' discussions, either by way of background qualifications or merely because they bring a fresh mind to an intractable problem. Mediation is about being prepared and being creative in presentation and with ideas. In one Anglo-American intellectual property dispute, the US trial lawyer used all her trial and mediation experience to pull off an effective PowerPoint presentation. In another international case there was a very much less effective video with a CNN voice-over that had a very unhelpful effect on the other team. It presented the case in a partial and arrogant way and caused the negotiations to begin in a highly negative and adversarial atmosphere. The art of negotiation is not a science – you want to engage your audience and keep them listening to you. If they at least listen, you can be on the way to possible breakthrough – *Active Listening* is the goal.

Optimising third party impact

All of the above elements that parties bring to negotiation are of course 'mediated' through the fact of an international mediation process. This is a vital factor to consider in preparation, of how best to 'exploit' the process to deliver the best value one can extract. Otherwise the parties would have tried direct negotiation. One should not underestimate the contribution that may be made by a third party 'neutral' in assisting parties to develop fresh perspectives – to face up to realities; to open up better communications; to consider new routes to resolution. Good preparation for mediation will factor in decisions on how best to tap into a mediator's potentially powerful contribution. What documents, preliminary conversations and tactics in the mediation itself will help? How can we help the mediator persuade the other party? Equally, one or more parties may have been unrealistic or ineffective in past negotiations. In these circumstances, the value of the mediation may lie in the mediator's ability to 'reality test' about futures, and in the power of the process itself to bring parties to an environment that resembles 'imminent adjudication' – the ultimate moment where they have a choice of a commercial outcome before negotiations close.

Mediation will often produce unexpected directions for discussion, because of its fresh and catalytic impact. In preparing for mediation parties should therefore be ready to engage in some fresh thinking and challenge their own views and assumptions. This can best be accomplished by infusing fresh blood into the team, perhaps also running through a rehearsal of negotiations to help think themselves into the other party's (and mediator's) shoes.

When one is dealing with multiple parties there may be a need for a third party facilitator/mediator to assist in the preparation and ensure a coherent approach to procedure, negotiation preparation, mediator selection and lead up to the mediation event. Multi-party problems present the greatest challenge for negotiators and is an area where mediation – either of process or substantive issues – can provide the most effective mechanism to enable effective communication.

Mediation preparation as a structured project

In the last chapter, we covered the formalities of the mediation legal framework. The first part of this chapter has dealt with the substantive preparation rather than procedural. A starting point in preparing formally for mediation procedure in any large international case will involve the following 'project management' approach and building blocks to mediation. These represent the structural development of a mediation, or 'mechanics' of the process.

Project management approach

All Party Building Blocks

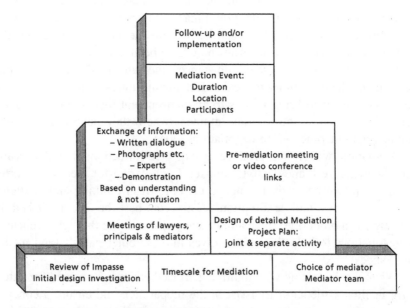

Measure of Success of Project Management

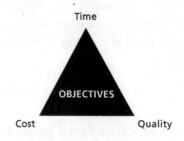

In most large international cases the preparation for mediation starts with the decision to mediate. Once the parties have decided to travel that course they have to agree on:
- facilitation or ADR Organisation Support;
- the mediator/s;
- the team for mediation;
- formulate a project plan that gives discipline and cohesion to the process;
- the timetable – generally working backwards from the date of the mediation event (or anticipated date of implementation of mediation follow-up);
- exchange of information that will assist the mediation process;
- decide on the negotiation teams;
- detailed preparation for mediation event;
- language;
- place and venue;
- mediation agreement/confidentiality;
- dates and times; and
- authority to settle.

In practice once parties have agreed to mediate, the most important issue is selection of the mediator and for the selected individual to make contact and help the parties agree on date and venue. Once a time is agreed it creates a psychological pressure to get everything else resolved. At CEDR we will convene pre-mediation discussions to have 'talks about talks' to cover all the sensitivities and help parties build trust and explain their concerns. Our experience is that if you can get such talks convened by a neutral body you can normally get the process underway successfully.

The mediators – selection

We touched on this important element in the last chapter, but it is worth developing some of the issues.

In international cases there is a tendency for parties unaccustomed to mediation to view mediators in the same role as international arbitrators and adopt the approach that they will strike out the other party's selection or each seek to nominate their own favoured candidate. This approach fails to understand that the parties maintain control of the outcome and that the mediator should be appointed who can effectively help all the parties not only re-evaluate legal, factual, commercial and financial issues but also address the human dynamics in communications. The mediator/s do not adopt party positions and are less likely to be effective the more they are seen to do so. Indeed some parties see a distinct advantage in selecting a mediator whom another party has proposed in the belief that the mediator will be more effective in facilitating change or broadening views of the proposing party and, therefore, increase the chances of a favourable settlement.

In many large, complex international mediations the parties tend to appoint a co-mediation team rather than a solo mediator. This provides for a broader range of skills and abilities and energy. The co-mediation team do themselves need to have a clear strategy on how they will work together and their roles, and this needs to be clear to the participants. (In one case we were asked to act as umpire between co-mediators in case they disagreed over procedure).

Where there is significant disagreement as to the choice of mediator, it is worth revisiting the criteria which each party is looking for, to see if these can be embodied in a particular mediation team or if there can be priority given by agreement to selected criteria only, or some rank order/weighting system to apply to a panel of mediators from whom to choose.

It is important that one considers the likely influence of the mediator/s on all parties and the negotiators in each team. A number of key factors will be important:
− experience and track record of the mediator;
− style/chemistry;
− authority, balanced with humility;
− patience and persistence;
− ability to work with a range of people;
− creativity and persuasiveness;
− language and cross-cultural skills.

In preparing your team, consider what skills are most important in terms of your own team and the other party. List the priorities and ensure that your core negotiating team is involved in the mediator selection procedure, if possible.

We referred to the practice of taking references and soundings on mediators in Chapter 3. It is, however, important not to destroy the neutrality of the mediator; so these soundings may be best undertaken through a neutral body and/or as part of a co-operative approach with the other parties. The authors have experience of international parties teaming together to work on mediator selection. In some very large cases the approach has required a very difficult facilitation exercise because parties could not agree. The goal of facilitation on appropriate mediator selection is that all parties ultimately should have confidence and trust in the mediators. However, in the event of complete deadlock over mediator appointment, parties should always remind themselves that in mediation, unlike arbitration, they have the ability to walk away at any time, or to insist on direct discussions during mediation, thus lessening the risk of an appointment.

One question often asked is 'should the mediators have expertise in the subject matter of the dispute?' The reaction from clients is often yes, but there are dangers as well as perceived benefits to this belief. A mediator with knowledge of the subject matter may well be able to get to the central issues more quickly, but the hidden danger is that the mediator will become an evaluator or an adjudicator or may not be as well trained in mediation skills as a more generalist commercial mediator. A well-trained mediator will understand the problem of premature evaluation. Therefore a good approach is to appoint either:

- a well-qualified mediator with a good mediation track record and with some expert knowledge of the sector through mediation or professional qualifications; or
- a well-qualified and experienced mediator, working if necessary with the assistance of a subject expert.

In very significant international cases there can be some benefit to including an individual with high profile and public respectability who nevertheless has a mediator's qualities of patience, perseverance and humility. Their involvement can add weight, status and an edge of additional importance to the mediation effort. In appropriate cases this will ease influence and persuasion or make it easier to sell any final agreement to each party's constituents. However, it can be a challenge to find the right person who can and is willing to work with the content and timescales of commercial cases. A neutral ADR organisation is best placed to find a co-mediation team that can match this and all other requirements.

The demand for high-status ('big-hitter' or 'big-shot') mediators has led, at national level, to more frequent recourse to retired senior judges. A 'health warning' should accompany such practices. Judges bring with them a distinguished track record of 'judging' but only a small percentage in our experience can adapt well to facilitation in a negotiating environment. A second group of high-status neutrals emerging in global business diplomacy are retired senior politicians and businessmen already used in political diplomacy in the traditional 'good offices' sense. More at home with diplomacy skills in direct negotiation, these groups often still need effective learning or effective briefing in professional and commercial mediation approaches to give of their best and to deliver an optimal mediation process.

The psychological impact of status in mediation is that it encourages humility in the parties as well as that which should be shown by the mediator! Overall remember that status is no substitute for skill and substance, ie always look for natural mediation skills even if 'big-hitter' status is felt to be a necessary ingredient in the process.

> *Missing the point: mediator insight*
> *An Italian lawyer advised his clients to issue proceedings in Boston, Massachusetts for alleged breach of supply contract. The local Court ordered a mediation by a Court appointed retired Judge. Both parties welcomed the opportunity to resolve the dispute. The mediation was derailed when the mediator Judge told the US party their defence was hopeless. They felt obliged to resist this as they had wanted to settle on better terms. Equally, the Italians had wanted early resolution and had been prepared to make concessions. Fortunately both parties after the mediation made direct contact and eventually agreed on a deal.*

The mediation process is extremely robust and difficult conversations will take place. However, the skills are more aligned to those of coaching parties to negotiate and giving them some room to manoeuvre. Mediators come from a range of backgrounds, the key is that they are effective, experienced and skilled as mediators whatever their earlier career experiences. A background and career experience of working with international clients will of course be helpful.

The authors have worked with all combinations of mediators including former judges and senior politicians. As mentioned, confidence in the mediator is very important so that in large international cases we would recommend that the selection and appointment of mediators be approached with care and diplomacy. Good mediators come from a variety of professions: legal, financial, diplomatic, psychological practice and academic backgrounds predominate.

Team members and roles

Parties have to decide who will be present, and what roles they will play. The first part of mediation will involve a larger Phase 1 and 2 team. In most mediations there will be one person given the role of the key opening presentation supported by experts who can present factual and technical information in summary form. Even if not given this role in the first joint

session, the lead commercial negotiator should also make some opening remarks to help begin the process and establish a climate of dialogue. The presentation should therefore:
– be persuasive;
– address concerns of each team;
– recognise blocks to resolution;
– provide a platform for further dialogue; and
– affirm good faith intention to negotiate a settlement.

If the external lawyer takes the lead in making the presentation, the task is still to facilitate a well thought out and thorough approach to mediation. The lawyer should stress that the presentation and approach to mediation is non-adversarial, inviting a helpful and thorough examination of the legal, financial, commercial, emotional and political issues that underpin the case.

The approach to preparation of the case should reflect the potential for mediation to embrace a broader agenda, even if a party wishes to concentrate initially, for tactical reasons, on a more limited agenda. A useful framework is to consider working with the agenda headings and negotiation levers outlined at the start of this chapter – the three sources of agendas, and the four levers in mediated negotiation.

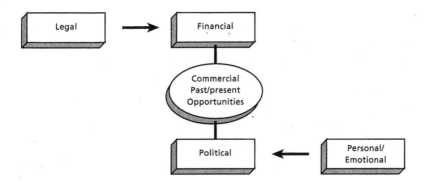

The managers and technical experts, including lawyers, should plan their presentations and roles in advance of the mediation. The appointed mediator can meet with the teams to discuss what would most help them to get appropriate understanding of the issues that they feel need to be addressed. In practice in our experience, this is not happening enough. There is a real role for the mediators as a coach to each team to ensure they make the best of the process and prepare adequately. Parties should consider how best to factor this into the process.

Presentation clash
In one intellectual property dispute the US party through their lawyers
wanted to concentrate on the alleged theft of trade secrets and breach of
fiduciary duties, while the European business party wanted to do a very
technical presentation to demonstrate that the technology was entirely
distinct. The mediator had to work privately with each team before and
during the mediation to manage their very different expectations. The
result – both teams were able to do effective presentations dealing with
their perceptions, felt listened to, and ultimately reached an agreement.

A carefully managed approach to preparation for mediation can in itself help
the team ascend to a new level of negotiating understanding. If this is
combined with cross-team contacts or investigations, these can lay a helpful
foundation for a powerful mediation process or even lead in some cases to a
settlement before mediation.

Preparing to get a negotiated result – role of the team

In preparing the team for mediation, consider three things:
- how the team will work together;
- how to influence the other team effectively;
- how to work with the mediator.

Generally it is better to have smaller teams. There is a danger of redundancy
if the group is too large. Additionally a team member there to play one role,
for example technical expert, may continue to do so inappropriately once the
negotiating process is underway. Absence of a real role can lead to team
members inserting themselves in a way that does not help the fluency of the
negotiation process. In some mediations a team may not possess adequate
knowledge or skill to help unravel complex points on financial or technical
data.

When considering who might be necessary team members, think
through the importance of technical/financial/legal/commercial know-how,
and how their expertise and understanding will assist a practical presentation
of:
- the issues;
- possible solutions;
- negotiating options;
- face-to-face contacts.

But most importantly will it achieve 'ACTIVE LISTENING?'

84

In one reinsurance mediation involving parties from the US and London – one team provided a very detailed probability and decision tree analysis as part of their presentation – the problem was that it assumed all participants were mathematical and informed on this type of thinking – this was incorrect. It therefore failed to have the desired impact and in fact soured the atmosphere.

It is worth having a conversation with representatives of the other teams attending the mediation. Discussions with them about their constraints and concerns may be a very positive building block in the process. You should also identify individual decision–makers within your own and the other party's team. Discuss any limitation on authority. When you are dealing with government bodies or state-owned entities understand their decision-making process and how it will intersect with the mediation process. Also remember that managers with local knowledge, cultural fluency and on the ground negotiating experience of local conditions may be critical. In a technical case, it will be important to have technical managers with appropriate knowledge and confidence to influence the other side.

In an IT dispute the mediator convened a technical session where both teams' middle management involved in the specification and implementation talked through the project. At the end of the mediation the Senior Commercial Director of a global automobile manufacturer said the session had been influential in his decision to settle.

Personnel and Action Plan

Ensure you and your team have:
– Authority to settle and flexibility to respond – Commercial decision makers.
– Know How – Technical managers.
– Language and cultural fluency.
– Commitment to the time lines.
– Energy and commitment to focus on the problem.

Consider the Negotiation Dynamics
– Brainstorm with your own team to consider options.
– Brainstorm with your own team to consider the other party's perceptions of the issues and possible solutions.

- Engage a negotiation coach who can facilitate your thinking and approaches.
- Test your assumptions with your team and the other parties' team. Consider BATNA (your Best Alternative To a Negotiated Agreement) and WATNA (Worst Alternative that could happen to you if agreement fails, you lose the case, etc). WATNA is the challenge to the BATNA in reminding parties of the tangible, real risks they run in not settling. Also consider your desired settlement range, and the other party's likely position on all these perspectives of the case.

Remember, the aim of mediation is to get all parties *focused*:
> **F**orward thinking
> **O**pen dialogue
> **C**ommercial dialogue
> **U**nderstanding the reason for deadlock in respect of all parties
> **S**trategic approach to solutions

Even though the mediator will have a major role to play in achieving *focus*, parties can assist in this by being well-prepared.

Remember, the negotiating team needs to blend 'Form' *and* 'Flexibility' eg legal case with commercial necessities or interests. Parties should bear this in mind when preparing written documentation for the mediation process. The emphasis will depend on how mature the dispute is. If the parties mediate early in the dispute there will be less spotlight on legal issues and costs.

Best information to be effective

Mediation requires the parties to inform, but not deluge, the mediators and the other party. The guiding principles for written materials are:
- Present in a business form – executive summaries – avoid technical legal submissions that fail to inform;
- The content should be accurate, concise and restrained – seek to influence and not harangue;
- Address issues or understanding that may be blocking settlement;
- Cover the factual background of prior negotiations, those involved and proposals made;
- A chronology of key events, a list of individuals involved and a glossary can sometimes be of assistance and speed up the learning curve;
- A summary of common ground, differences and reasons for differences between the parties is an excellent document for mediation.

In short, the documentation should aim to educate efficiently but emphatically the mediator and the other teams' decision-makers. *Effective education assists persuasion.*

Length of written materials varies but generally in international mediations the mediator will invite the parties to confine the written submission to 15–20 pages and provide an indexed bundle of other documents (3–4 files, 100 pages). The authors recognise that this is a challenge but some very complex matters have been effectively summarised in this way. The preparation of the written documentation in this way will get each party *FOCUS-ed.*

Checklist of key information

(1)   Key participants;
(2)   Summary of facts and context;
(3)   The client position on legal and technical issues;
(4)   Negotiating history – present position;
(5)   Common ground and differences;
(6)   Chronology of events;
(7)   Glossary of technical terms;
(8)   Financial spreadsheets and calculations – alternative calculations;
(9)   Schedules of key documents, experts' reports etc;
(10) Draft settlement/negotiation proposals.

Where fully covered by confidentiality provisions, the legal framework of mediation also allows parties to agree that some documents on sensitive issues (such as legal opinions they have obtained) may be restricted to the mediator's eyes only. Limited use should be made of this possibility because the main intent of the process is dialogue between the parties. However inevitably the parties will try to influence the case they want the mediator to communicate and may wish to disclose in confidence why certain claims have credibility or are structured in a particular fashion. The privileged nature of the process may, however, allow them to exchange some opinions in draft form with the other party.

Involving decision-makers in mediation preparation

Decision-makers should have been involved at an early stage of preparation. They should be actively involved in:
–   mediator selection or be aware of selection procedure;
–   review and approval of the written materials;

- team preparation;
- formulating and testing negotiating options, and planning how best to present them;
- education on how best to work with a mediator; and
- decision-makers should also be thinking strategically about how to assess the key agendas of each party, which negotiation levers can be brought to bear, how the team should be organised for optimal impact.

Where parties are reluctant to mediate: trouble shooters and mediators

The authors have been called into a number of complex, usually multiparty, disputes where no one really feels that mediation will work, or one party is deeply resistant so that the process of preparation cannot even begin. In such cases our role as 'troubleshooters' still utilises mediation objectives and techniques, but it is a less structured role. This process focuses more on informal facilitation, either to convince parties of the value of the process, or to help them design a process that will work for them. But it can also be a process that mediates key blockages to allow for a further stage of formal mediation. Often after we broker a mediation agreement and preparation to mediate, we then 'hand the baton' to a different team to handle the final phase and the mediation event. (Usually because we have become too familiar with the parties – although sometimes this also leads to a preference that we stay with the project.)

This type of division is most common in large multi-party cases where there are a number of parties to persuade to negotiate through mediation. The facilitation phase will involve many meetings covering:
- visits to all affected parties;
- persuading them to consider mediation;
- dealing with their concerns;
- assisting with the selection of a mediation team;
- helping to design a project management plan and agreed time lines;
- assisting in overcoming obstacles to mediation – for example, concerns over information;
- facilitating exchange of information;
- design of agreement to mediate including confidentiality, costs alloca-tion, etc;
- briefing the mediators; and
- continuing support of the process logistics and intent, and any after-math.

In this type of case, the mediators for the final event have probably confined themselves to a few pre-mediation meetings thus putting their emphasis and energy on the 'Final Mediation Event', a defining climatic event to a long-running saga.

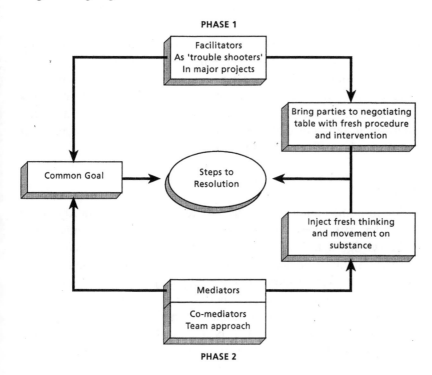

For the most part there is a benefit to parties if mediators do not become extensively engaged over a long period of time in preliminary and procedural matters. There is an advantage to early involvement for the mediator has a better acquaintance with the case, and with the parties. However, this has to be balanced against a tendency to staleness, reduced impact, and the danger of mediators being drawn into procedural adjudication. If this occurs, there might be perceived to be bias against particular parties before substantive issues are really addressed. Or the troubleshooter may be seen to know too much about the 'skeletons in the cupboard' or financial difficulties of one party. One of the advantages mediation brings to entrenched parties is to inject 'fresh air' into the dispute, 'fresh thinking' and 'new leverage'.

Both phases are therefore critical for the success of the process in major situations of impasse. The authors have learned from experience that avoiding staleness and keeping free from some of the undercurrents that are

89

inevitable when bringing parties to mediation is a real advantage to the final mediation process. However, this is not to deny that for a certain type of case mediator involvement is best at an early stage, particularly where all parties are reasonably agreed to mediation in principle. Developing the consensus on procedure often creates the necessary dynamic path for a successful outcome.

The authors recommend that parties limit the number of pre-mediation events with the mediator and, if this is not possible or the circumstances and parties are very complex, then consider separating the facilitation from the mediation team. Where case complexity does not justify the two-phase model, parties can achieve a similar effect by working with case managers in an ADR organisation or with mediators working only with advisers, then with clients at a later focused negotiation stage.

Conclusion

Preparation for a mediation event is usually regarded more seriously than is the case for less structured negotiations. The fact of third party intervention and the knowledge that there is a real possibility of 'the event' controlling and delivering an outcome, lead to a sense of greater structure and status of the process, and therefore more effective preparation. This in itself can at times lead to a negotiated outcome before the mediation event. Parties should therefore enter mediation as a major opportunity for a 'best shot' at settling difficult issues, and bring their best active listening and commercial skills to the process. Decision-makers in particular have to be won over both to the process, and to the key role they play in making it a success.

Chapter 6. Steps to Settlement: the Negotiating Dance

'Convert your opponent into your partner – every negotiator needs help and the person who is in the best position to give this help is the opponent.'

Janos Nyerges, former Director General, Hungarian Ministry of Foreign Trade, *Ten Commandments for a Negotiator.*

'When one is willing to see all conflicts ... as dances of energy, and to accept them and to blend with them, options and opportunities for successful resolution emerge, powerfully and elegantly. The ability to remove the unfortunate contest-mentality takes courage, tact, a sense of well-being, and a strong commitment to developing fulfilling relationships.'

Thomas Crum, *The Magic of Conflict.*

Six steps to mediation settlement

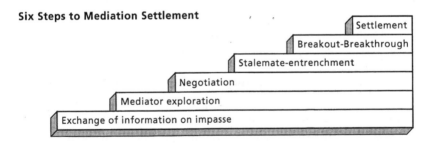

Six Steps to Mediation Settlement

- Settlement
- Breakout-Breakthrough
- Stalemate-entrenchment
- Negotiation
- Mediator exploration
- Exchange of information on impasse

The six steps outline the typical key stages in working through a mediation process. We describe some aspects of them in more depth in this chapter, and the settlement stage in the next chapter. Another way of capturing a typical long day of mediation in terms of energy and effort demands, is set out later in this chapter in a diagram of the Mediation Cycle.

Preliminaries: preparation and opening

A significant amount of preliminary work is needed even in the simpler international cases in order to enter the formal mediation process with the ability to concentrate on the essential negotiation issues between the parties. The mediator will usually have had prior contact with the lead players, or more often their advisers, in order to set the scene. This contact will begin to establish relationships; help agree on the goals and format of the process; check that all administrative arrangements are in place. In a more complex case, contacts within and between parties will also have been needed on logistics and negotiation agendas. In many international cases the preparatory mediation work undertaken by an ADR case manager and mediators could be in the order of 15–20 hours and sometimes more.

The mediator should also have taken the opportunity to 'gently coach' each team on the most productive approach to mediation, particularly the question of the opening presentations and role of principals/advisers. The mediator's coaching on the opening presentations is likely to stress the need for parties:

- to listen actively to the presentations;
- to address the other team's commercial clients;
- to focus on issues that may influence the other team's negotiating positions;
- to look for clues as to possible negotiation objectives and preferences; and
- to recognise that the mediator is there to assist the parties to negotiate.

In international cases, the mediator often needs to acknowledge the special concerns of overseas parties, particularly if they are experiencing mediation for the first time. The intervention of a third party negotiator may be met with some scepticism – particularly if the parties have been persuaded to mediate by a local court.

In one intellectual property dispute between American and British parties – the mediator learned from talking to the lawyers in San Francisco, that although they had a great deal of mediation experience, they were not familiar with the British practice of talking to clients without Counsel present. These early conversations paved the way for a successful mediation where the mediator did meet privately with principals.

Where pre-mediation meetings have not been possible, telephone or video conference discussions are the next best option. Even if there have been effective pre-mediation contacts, the mediator will also want to ensure on the first morning of the formal mediation meeting (or a day earlier) that everything is in place in each team, particularly in relation to principals' attendance and to time availability. It is good practice for the mediator to meet with each party immediately before the opening plenary session and to begin to establish or build relationships. The mediator will want to ensure that all members of each team (including interpreters if present) understand the process and to check whether individuals have any language or time concerns. These initial introductions may also provide further helpful information to the mediator on team structure, dynamics or agendas.

Joint Meetings – exchange of views

The mediator will be responsible for identifying the room and seating logistics which are most likely to assist early positive reactions and progress. This could include the mediator inviting parties to take certain seating arrangements with a view to having some of the commercial team near the mediators and able to make appropriate eye contact with each other.

The mediator will, following introductions, open the session and remind the parties of some of the following:

- the opportunity that the mediation presents to resolve the issues or previous difficulties between the parties; that it will be a tough process, a 'pressure chamber' for negotiations; that there will be low points but the mediator will encourage the parties to continue through these difficult phases;
- that patience and persistence are necessary qualities for the mediator but also the parties;
- that any party should be willing to make recommendations to the mediator to help move the discussions forward;
- that the mediator will facilitate dialogue between selected members of each team, particularly the commercial members, as seems useful, and not just engage in formal dialogue across whole groups;
- that it may be a long day. The mediator will check again on any potential time constraints to avoid surprises of early tactical departures;
- that the process is voluntary but all parties are encouraged to stay and persist with the negotiating effort;
- that the parties have signed a mediation agreement which protects the privileged and confidential nature of the discussions;
- that the process will be a structured series of open and private meetings, and other logistical details.

The mediator will want to take control over the process and stamp her authority and chemistry on the process to give the parties confidence that they are in safe, experienced hands.

Party presentations: aim – active listening

Opening presentations by the parties vary in length but in a mediation the parties are encouraged to be brief, say between 20–30 minutes. However, they may last up to an hour if one party feels it is important to set the scene. Presentations by one party that are longer than an hour should be actively discouraged as they are likely to have limited additional impact, and may even be counterproductive. It is better to revisit information exchange, if necessary, later in the process. The mediator will generally ask the 'claimant' team to start the round of presentations followed by the other party, but there is no formal rule, unlike litigation practice. Indeed there may be reasons to reverse the order in a particular case.

The most effective presentations cover the range of issues facing the parties:
- commercial;
- legal;
- financial;
- political;
- personal/emotional – acknowledgement;
- other factors.

The presentation should be in business style, and concise, in order to engage everyone's attention. Good mediation practitioners always acknowledge the other team's concerns, whilst at the same time protecting the integrity of their own constituents. They will generally remind everyone that their objective is to resolve the issues and be quite confident and upbeat in style. Often the presentations are done by the lawyer, with some brief views and comments from the principal client. Presentations predominantly by the client are more appropriate if there is a strong business relationship and dimension to the disputes, or if the presentation will help the other side take a measure of the personality of the presenter (for example, if the senior managers have not met previously).

IP Technology – different waves
In this case Party A did a presentation based on legal analysis, whereas Party B did a presentation based on the technology. This did not block

progress but actually facilitated it as it gave an early indication to each party of where the other party felt their strengths lay and opened an early dialogue on both dimensions.

There is definitely scope for parties to be more creative and imaginative in how they capture the other team's attention and make an appropriate impact. The presentations that tend to be less effective are those that are lengthy, or focus on the pleaded claims and reiterate the issues in a legal framework. If presentations are losing their impact and going on too long, the mediator may well interrupt and suggest a shortening of the process.

When the presentations are completed, the mediator may do a variety of things, depending on the mood and tone of the process:
- open up the dialogue; encourage a broader discussion and exchange of views;
- chair a question and answer session recognising that a party can reject requests for further information;
- allow parties to respond more formally to other presentations;
- adjourn for parties to reflect on what they have heard, and reconvene for one of the above;
- break up into caucus (private) sessions immediately.

The next step depends on the mediator's judgment as to what is most likely to help the parties understand the major aspects of their differences, and as to what will help create a platform for moving on to exploration of positions and, beyond them, to an acceptable solution.

Less experienced mediators may have a tendency to want to separate hostile parties. In international cases with more experienced mediators, parties can expect a greater willingness from mediators to let parties air their views together. If mediators close down a plenary too early they deprive themselves and the parties of the opportunity to learn more about the real issues and concerns, and/or to observe the character of relationships between the parties.

Airtime – getting to in-depth understanding
In a dispute over an IT system, involving German, English and American parties, the mediator decided to continue into a phase two of the plenary after an adjournment, at which point many more of the commercial players contributed commentary on why things had gone wrong in the project. This led to all parties accepting, for the purpose of negotiation, that no party was blame free – but the parties did not alter their legal arguments. The plenary therefore gave the commercial

negotiators and the mediator more information to work with.

The role of the mediator in the plenary session is to give the parties confidence that the procedure is controlled and to inject some trust, energy and sense of structure into search for a solution. These sessions lay the foundation for the rest of the mediation. As mediators we will often point out to parties that our task is to facilitate a dialogue where the parties can re-evaluate all issues (once they are identified). To do this well all the core issues have to be identified as part of the mediation 'due diligence'.

The role of advisers is to ensure a measured and sound presentation that will get the other party's attention and to ascertain any new information that will assist the process. Advisers also usually welcome the opportunity to address the principals on the other side who previously may only have been exposed to their own team's partial viewpoint.

The role of the principals is to set down the marker that ownership of the solution rests with the corporations which they represent.

Once the mediator forms the view that the plenary sessions have exhausted their value at least for the time (she may reconvene the parties at a later stage and certainly if there is a settlement), she will ask each team to retire to their own rooms and will start the round of private meetings with each team.

One can expect the mediator, before the private sessions, to give some indication of how long she will be with each group and to set some kind of timetable for the day. She may well ask those teams she is not meeting with to review certain issues or find out additional information if, in the mediator's judgment, issues have come to light in the plenaries that could be usefully explored.

'Tasking' parties

In a franchise dispute the franchisee made certain allegations concerning damage and loss of profits. The mediator requested that this Middle Eastern party work with his lawyers to fully identify the measure of damage – this recommendation was made privately. Mediators will generally task parties on a confidential basis unless a party has explicitly requested information and another party is willing to facilitate the request. Mediators are always aware of their neutrality and want to avoid requests being interpreted as an evaluative appraisal on the merits.

Exploration phase

The mediator will visit each team to develop with them an interactive process of review of the case and discuss options for the progress of negotiations. Her initial objective will be to gauge the parties' reactions, positive and negative, to what they have heard in the plenary and, as importantly, to hear what the parties did not want to talk about or have not yet revealed in the open sessions. It is very important for the parties to 'open up' in the private meetings as this gives the mediator clues as to how best to facilitate productive discussions. Generally parties, and particularly commercial parties, will be quite forthcoming in expressing views and comments on the issues, although even in private sessions the degree of openness will depend on party strategy and how far the mediator establishes rapport and party trust in the process

At this stage the mediator will probably not want to spend too extensive a period with any one party, particularly if there are multiple parties to visit. She may well explore breaking down the negotiating teams into information exchange sub-groups, and want to find out who could be the appropriate spokesperson in such meetings with other parties. She will also want to check status and power balances in the group, and language facility issues that may influence the choice of negotiating sub-groups.

One problem for commercial managers at this stage is that they can be impatient and want things to move at a faster pace. Experienced mediators have to make judgments as to whether an accelerated approach from the exploration phase to the bargaining phase is likely to cause a breakdown and premature fixation on positions. Very often, if a mediator tries to accelerate the pace too far, the parties can retrench and go backwards.

Restlessness and impatience amongst parties because of a lack of progress is, however, often an issue for the mediator. (Cultural differences in patience may come to the fore here!) Some cultural/corporate groups are more accustomed to steadier paced managed meetings and negotiations. The authors can remember one mediation where a critical commercial manager announced that he had to take a flight to Rome at the mid-afternoon stage of the mediation. The fallout when he left nearly caused a walkout. It certainly caused bad feeling and gave the mediators a major task in restoring confidence and a sense of bona fides.

The role for advisers during these middle exploratory phases of mediation is to keep their team engaged, and to help the mediator to help them. Advisers often send messages to the mediator when the mediator is with the other party, if they sense an unhelpful dynamic developing in their team.

Mediators are always very grateful to experienced advisers for their input. Mediators will have asked advisers to work with clients on their best and worst case scenarios, helping principals reassess their understanding and priorities in negotiation.

Mediators always have to strike a balance between the investigation phase of mediation and the need to move on to looking at solutions, actively engaging parties in solid and forward negotiations. Inexperienced or over-evaluative mediators often put too much weight on the former.

> *Experts on tap – but not on top*
> *In one large multinational reinsurance case the legal teams were keen, in the middle phase of mediation, that mediators should hear Lloyds' market experts to test the parties' contrary claims on industry standards. As both parties were keen to have their involvement, the mediators agreed to interview the experts and to allow each team to ask questions. In fact, the process did not appear to accelerate the negotiating phase and it seemed that neither party was much influenced. However, for the mediators it was important to meet the joint wishes of the parties. They had judged that, while the experts' intervention would probably not advance the process, nor would it put the process in jeopardy if handled appropriately. In fact it probably did help the parties at least recognise that their assertions were not clear-cut in terms of the merits of the case.*

Sometimes parties will give an indication to the mediator that they are willing to acknowledge problems in their case. More often all parties will view it as the responsibility of the other team to take the first step forward and the mediator will have to find ways to get the parties' actively engaged. In other words, challenge the parties in a helpful way, or begin to make active proposals for resolution. If all parties are willing to acknowledge some contribution to the problems (very different from admission of legal fault), this will often help.

Mediators have to be sensitive to the parties' cultural customs and concern over issues of acknowledgement and apology. One tactic is to stress that discussions and proposals in caucus will not be communicated to the other team unless and until the climate is right for disclosure. Another tactic of mediators is to brainstorm with the parties and advisers – seeking their views and solutions to impasse. Sometimes these sessions work very well as cross-team sessions, in other mediations this will inhibit creativity.

Mediators also have to balance how much to intervene. For example, principals may ask the mediator to leave them to talk privately one to one.

Generally a mediator will not get in the way of such dialogue. A disadvantage, however, is that if the dialogue runs into further impasse, which it often does, the mediator will not have witnessed how and why it collapsed, and is therefore less able to recover negotiation momentum. However patience and re-engagement with the principals will normally get them 'back on track'. Another problem in international mediations occurs if the party decides to negotiate in their native tongue. As a result, the mediator may need an interpreter. However this is never as satisfactory as witnessing the subtleties of the dialogue first hand. A mediator or co-mediator with appropriate language skills will help considerably if such a dynamic is likely to develop in the mediation.

Finally, mediators have to balance their facilitation role with the need to unblock deadlock by 'robust intervention'. Mediators in international cases can deploy a range of intervention tactics to shift parties into better dialogue and away from intransigence. The *least* helpful technique in many cases is for the mediator to give a view of the merits of the case. Mediators are there primarily to find techniques and tactics which facilitate *party* re-evaluation of the merits and negotiation positions based on them. However there is no absolute rule in mediation, and there are certainly cases where mediators with acknowledged expertise have tactfully deployed this at an appropriate time, to assist in the re-evaluation by a party of its substantive case.

'A potent mix' – helpful rework
In an acquisitions dispute involving allegations that there had been an intentional reduction of inventory in a production plant, closure of part of a plant and lost capacity, the mediator worked through the calculations with the Spanish General Manager of the plant and suggested reframing some of the numbers to produce a more balanced appraisal. Her suggestion led to a reappraisal which helped move the negotiations forward. The mediator also helped the clients simplify their claims. The mediator was able to effectively coach each team to reappraise the detail and numbers, leading to a workable settlement.

'A new view' – The mediator flipchart
In a dispute over ownership of intellectual property in Europe and the USA there were proceedings in North America and a mediation in London. The bitter dispute was resolved when the mediator explained the different perspectives by means of a diagrammatic illustration. One of the inventors claimed that it was the first time he had really understood the dispute – the parties entered into a settlement agreement

four hours later.

The negotiating dance and the despair phase of mediation

'Trust is a fragile commodity.'

Stephen Davey, International Federation of Red Cross and Red Crescent Societies, CEDR-accredited Mediator.

In most mediations, parties move at least a degree closer and a settlement starts to look like a distinct possibility. Parties move from reviewing and attacking/justifying historical events and begin to explore options for present or future settlement terms. It is at this point that mediators should gear up their energy, creativity and patience because the normal pattern is for parties then to get stuck on their 'bottom line' positions which often involve a considerable gap! At this point, negotiation progress seems to have been permanently halted. Without a third party to keep them together, this would often signal breakdown and the end of the negotiation. However an experienced mediator still has a lot to offer.

Once parties start the 'Negotiating Dance' the mediator can play a number of roles:
- shuttle diplomacy to ease communication of positions and options;
- testing the basis for settlement *vis-à-vis* merits or BATNA/WATNA (Best and Worst Alternatives to Negotiating Agreement) or against commercial interests;
- absorbing and thereby defusing negative reaction;
- reframing offers to make them more acceptable, given the mediator's deeper knowledge of the other party's interests;
- giving reassurance of *bona fides;*
- chairing and managing commercial dialogue;
- keeping the dialogue moving;
- preventing impasse by finding new lines of inquiry or communication;
- brainstorming ways out of impasse;
- challenging impasse or providing reassurance/confidence that ways forward can be found;
- re-interpreting how each position can be perceived;
- giving parties a fair assessment of each other's positions;
- reminding parties of their progress in the negotiations to date;
- challenging their bottom line and commitment to settlement; and
- managing relationships within and across teams.

Some practical examples from real situations:
- a mediator joined a client riding on the hotel escalator to cool off this annoyed senior manager;
- a break in the mediation to make a call to the chairman overseas so he could join the mediation;
- a new settlement proposal made actively by the mediator to railway executives, to close the gap between the parties;
- getting the chairman to do a site visit on an African road construction project and 'walk the walk' to understand better the common-sense basis for client concerns.

With skill, judgment, patience and perseverance, mediators can help parties break down deadlock to reach agreements which they had felt were not possible. It is important to remember that mediators cannot impose settlements and should never bully parties. However, firm, strong handling of difficult situations is very much the order of the day as one moves into the low point of negotiation deadlock, before the parties can start to climb out again. Good mediators will maintain optimism even if a satisfactory end point seems impossible. The mediator will ensure that the parties keep focused. As creativity scholars have pointed out time and time again, focus on the underlying problem with sufficient intensity, and the solutions will suddenly emerge. Parties are often too focused on a premature outcome and on set positions, and so lose their way in their pursuit of 'winning the war at all costs' or because of indignation at the lack of realism of the other side.

Negotiations working through the mediator

Parties will use the mediator to test positions in the relative safety of the caucus. Generally the mediator will make an assessment as to whether an offer is likely to have an effect different to that anticipated. If a mediator takes the view that parties are taking very unrealistic positions, or are bordering on using the mediator in a manner that seems inappropriate, the mediator might caution against it or decide that a party should make their offer direct to the other party.

The mediator cannot and should not take all responsibility for a settlement. The most important goal for a mediator is to ensure that the parties have been given every opportunity to confront their differences, understand them and make every attempt to resolve them. This is the reason why they are at the mediation in the first place. The mediator's role is not to own the problem or the solution but to design and manage a process where all parties feel that they have been given every opportunity to find a solution, if one exists.

Breaking deadlock – direct talks
In one IT dispute between a German manager of a multinational and British/American company, the two directors were moving closer to an accord but a gap still remained. They lapsed into German and the mediator allowed them to conduct their own discussions. However, the German party subsequently approached the mediator affronted because he felt he was negotiating in good faith and that the other director, in his perception, was not negotiating in good faith. They were in deadlock and obviously both felt genuinely aggrieved and bemused – they wanted help. The mediator offered to take their best numbers confidentially and see if the bargaining zone overlapped. However, this was used, not to make a recommendation, but to open up a dialogue on how to narrow a smaller final gap which now existed between them.

Roadblock – rigid negotiations
In a multiparty dispute with claimant parties from eight countries, the mediators were faced with the problem of not being able to identify commercial decision-makers who could talk for the group or help the mediators identify important commercial interests. Their advisers were keen to keep everyone working as a group without breaking into sub-groups or discussion of individual interests. This gave the mediators much less scope for manoeuvre – they were essentially blocked by the advisers' over-control of the process. In this case, more preparation work on the participation and role of the parties in the mediation would have helped the mediators and the process. In preparation for international mediation, problems such as this can arise in making sufficient contact with commercial parties before the mediation. This then impedes the rhythm of subsequent negotiations within the mediation and narrows opportunities for free-flowing dialogue. In this case, however, the defendant party made enough progress to allow them to open up dialogue with sub-groups after the mediation until all but two parties had achieved settlement.

Video conference
In a large reinsurance mediation the mediators discussed the process
with the American parties in Boston from a London video conference
link. This had the advantage of giving the overseas parties confidence in
the mediators and the process before committing to travel to London.

The Mediation Cycle

The Mediation Cycle

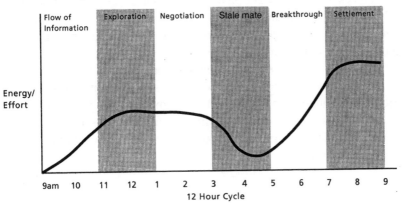

Pacing of Negotiations

One also needs to be mindful that in international mediations parties from
different parts of the world – for example West v East – will have very
different perceptions of pace and momentum and there is often considerable
mismatching. This presents the mediators with the task of handling this
different expectation sensitively.

One diplomat who has been involved in years of international negotiations said that one trick was to keep putting the clock back to midnight!
Inevitably, the mediators must be very committed and willing to work with
the parties, giving them every opportunity to use every second of available
time well. The mediator should have her finger on the pulse of a time
budget, and it is important that she and the parties use it well and wisely.

In most international mediations at the end of the allotted time, there
will be pressure for closure. This is because parties will be leaving the
neutral venue and travelling often long distances in different directions. The
opportunity to continue the dialogue face to face will diminish if not
completely close at the end of the mediation. This tends to concentrate the

minds of the parties but can also make the timing of offers and of deadlock a critical issue for the parties and the mediator. Parties should avoid over-reliance on the deadline as a bargaining lever, as this can inhibit effective time for exploration of the critical final bargaining zone between the parties.

However, if parties cannot resolve all issues, they should be encouraged to continue after a short break – a gap of some weeks may be all that is needed. This is not uncommon in international cases where the typical problems in most negotiations are exacerbated by the logistics of time, travel, distances and often additional needs in some cultures and organisations for extensive review and consultation over decisions. The authors have experienced some mediation processes where intermittent meetings have continued up to a year or more. If the mediator or parties suspect that the process will have an approval and consultation phase before final agreement, it is often wise to plan for this. A provisional follow-up date to the mediation can be agreed in mediation preliminaries, thus ensuring a managed timescale and a real, final deadline. This tactic has to be balanced against the risk that the negotiating stage may merely be extended into the time available for meetings.

Stop-start
In a dispute involving an African government and a construction contractor, problems of divergent views were compounded not only by the differing organisational cultures of the parties, but by the added requirements in that case of government consultation with a UK government project finance arrangement, requiring approval of the settlement within an aid budget. After the main event mediators continued with a process of separate meetings with each party for a year before settlement terms were finally agreed.

Building trust: Norwegian woods
In the build-up to the final Middle East Oslo Peace Accord, the Norwegian facilitators focused most attention on a slow and steady process of allowing the opposing parties to get to know each other. Regular dinners together in a country estate outside Oslo finally allowed a human face to be put on the relationship, and allow barriers to thaw. An ultimate agreement (of further steps), formalised in triumph on the White House lawn, was later shattered with the entry of new players and concerns. Trust is a fragile commodity ...

In the next chapter we turn to the final phase of mediation, 'doing the deal'. It may be useful at this point however to set out a diagrammatic reminder of the entire mediation process and milestones.

Pre-mediation

PARTIES	MEDIATION BODY FACILITATOR	MEDIATOR
ENTRY One party initiation or agreement Third-party brokered Contract clause Court-referred	Discusses and advises whether mediation is appropriate Contracts other party/parties to confirm parties willing to mediate and advises on next stage	
PROVISIONAL FRAMEWORK Agreement or mediated faciliation towards provisional agreement on: Mediator selection process Objectives, procedure, legal framework Cost allocation Preparatory steps - documentation, meetings, representation, authority	Identifies and shortlists potential mediators and assistant mediators Case management form and biographies of potential mediators sent to all parties together with details of: ● Mediator & pupil appointment ● Dates of availability of mediator ● Venue ● Mediation agreement ● Fees ● Supporting papers to be with mediator at least 2 weeks before date of mediation	
Preparation for mediation	Contacts all parties to confirm timetable	
	Sends appointment letter to mediator & assistant	
	Exchanges papers between parties with copies to mediator and assistant	Reads through papers
	Prepares and sends mediation agreement to mediator for signature in readiness for mediation	Meeting or telephone contract with parties for introduction; clarification of documents or procedure; sound out on expectations

Mediation

Mediation

Opening & Information Exchange	Mediator introduction Opening presentations Response & discussion Private reflection & review of issues
Exploratory phase	Further review of issues Mediator probing of context, case studies & strategy for solution Further exchanges to test other side's viewpoint Brainstorming & problem-solving
Negotiation phase	Framework for resolution offered/devised Detailed terms offered/discussed Proposals/counter-proposals Further brainstorming Mediator options Dealing with deadlock
Concluding the deal/mediation	Final terms agreed Provisional draft agreement drafted & tested Negotiation over omissions or uncertainties Signing memorandum of understanding or contract Adjourn for further consultation and commitment Regroup & review final sticking points
Follow-up	Implementation Monitoring implementation Dealing with outstanding disputes or initiating further actions Follow up by mediator

Chapter 7. Achieving and Implementing Mediation Settlements

'That eighty-five per cent of disputes referred to mediation result in settlement is surprisingly high in my opinion – it would indicate that mediation has a significant role to play in international disputes.'

Hans von der Linde, Senior Legal Counsel, Shell International.

'There are two problems with the deal orientation. The first is the practical difficulty of crafting, interpreting, and enforcing a legal agreement across multiple legal and governmental jurisdictions. The other more significant problem is the dynamic nature of the world. A deal orientation is essentially static in nature, while a relationship orientation is dynamic in nature. For both these reasons, working on developing a solid, mutually beneficial relationship is a better approach to a dynamic global environment than trying to craft a series of 'air-tight' agreements reflecting interests at a single static point in time.'

Griffin & Daggatt, *The Global Negotiator.*

The settlement phase of the mediation process

Mediated negotiations can be intense and will involve very concentrated work. Complex cases may run for several long days or sometimes over several months. By the time the deal is reached everyone will be very tired, nerves will be frayed and feelings may be bruised. At this point the temptation is to do some or all of the following:
- leave the legal advisers to resolve the written agreement;
- leave the agreement to be dealt with at a different time and place;
- rush out a memorandum of understanding leaving fine detail to be worked out later;
- spend hours late at night after a long negotiating session trying to get the details right.

All of the above approaches have some flaws. The best approach depends on the type of agreement, simple or complex, and whether the relationship is terminated or will continue albeit in some different form.

If the agreement has been negotiated by the commercial principals, then they should participate in the structuring of the agreement. The mediators should be available to assist as and when issues arise.

When the agreement is realistically going to take many hours to design, then ideally this should be factored into the mediation planning and timetable, so the parties will have the time and energy to get the agreement right.

Often the mediators and parties make an 'oral agreement in principle' their goal – whereas the goal should be a fully designed and workable agreement. One technique is to ask representatives of each team to work on possible design outcomes during the negotiating phase of the mediation. The mediator should help orchestrate this process by asking each team to test possible outcomes in draft form for workability and durability; also for legal and commercial obstacles and benefits.

If agreements are complex, might raise new issues and/or will benefit from a time break, then the mediators may well suspend the proceedings and bring the parties back for the final phase, asking each team to liaise on drafts or send them to the mediator for comment and review. In this follow-up it may be important to build on personal and professional relationships established during the negotiation process, to smooth the way to a final crafted deal.

If the parties have truly reached an accord then broking the right framework should not be a struggle. In mediation the preference is to have a written accord as soon as possible. However, if the proceedings are to be suspended then we recommend drawing up a memorandum of understanding which should identify a clear timetable and direction for the next steps, in order to reach a conclusion. Even during intensely difficult discussion on the details of agreements, parties should take comfort from the fact that the success rate of parties achieving agreement in international mediations is high. The mediator should expect to assist the parties in finding creative solutions to designing workable settlements.

In the absence of agreed terms at the conclusion of the designated time, parties will have to use their best judgement as to whether or how to continue. Options to be considered would include:

- agreed cooling-off period and stay of proceedings to allow time for reflection and further discussion if appropriate;
- further meeting of teams or sub-groups with/without mediator;

- non-binding report from mediator with recommendations on reasonable/ appropriate terms of settlement;
- adjudication by mediator/other expert on outstanding gap or unresolved issues;
- appeal to higher political/business level for more 'realistic' response;
- initiation or continuation of formal proceedings leaving open option to reopen negotiations.

Enforceability of settlements – the paradox of process outcomes

Concern is sometimes expressed at the voluntary nature of mediation compared to an international judgement or arbitration award which can be directly enforced under the New York Convention. It is important, however, to avoid confusion between two separate aspects of the mediation process. Parties may be required to mediate by a contract clause or court order, but they always maintain control over the outcome. Where the parties do reach a settlement, they will want to ensure that their lawyers draw up a legally binding settlement agreement. However, the 'non-binding' character of the process is paradoxically part of the strength of mediation. This encourages commercial parties to enter dialogue with some control and with considerably less risk of either the escalating costs of a binding procedure or of an errant judgement by a third party. Any outcome, however, will be 'owned' by the party controlling their negotiations, and so they are *more* likely to implement the binding agreement compared to an externally imposed outcome.

> '*Mediation is a flexible process conducted confidentially in which a neutral person actively assists parties in working towards a negotiated agreement of a dispute or difference, with the parties in ultimate control of the decision to settle and the terms of resolution.*'

(CEDR, 2005)

An agreement through mediation has at a minimum the equivalent binding character of a commercial contract. The terms of the mediation process, however, typically require agreed terms to be written down and signed before they become legally binding. A mediation settlement agreement can take two forms:

(i) *Binding commercial contract*

In international mediations this is the most common outcome. The agreement can be enforced in all the ways typically associated with commercial agreements – resort to litigation, arbitration or to in-built contractual sanctions such as performance bonds. While usually regarded as less 'safe' than enforceable arbitration awards, contractually-binding mediation settlements do have, as we say, the advantage that they are the product of intense negotiations under the supervision of the neutral. As a result, the 'buy-in' commitment by the parties will normally be greater than the outcome of an imposed arbitration award (which still has to be enforced for effectiveness). Sometimes it may even lead to greater commitment than the original contract terms, because the parties will have reached agreement in the knowledge of all the difficulties associated with an earlier relationship. Finally, mediation agreements typically are less complex or cover a narrower scope, than the original agreements in dispute. They are therefore more easily litigated or arbitrated, and enforced, if that is necessary.

(ii) *Consent award/court order*

If the dispute is already in arbitration or court proceedings, the parties may be able (or in some cases may be required) to return to that tribunal to seek a consent judgement/award on the terms of the mediation settlement. This method produces a result equivalent to an enforceable arbitration award. It is also the considered view of some leading figures in the field of international arbitration that parties can institute 'new' arbitration proceedings at the end of a mediation and before written agreement, with the purpose of converting a mediated settlement agreement into the form of an award, provided that there is a 'dispute' which is not compromised unless and until the parties have entered the consent award. Some of the delegates who have helped negotiate international model laws for mediation such as the UNCITRAL Model Conciliation Rules, have also aired the possibility of an international convention confirming the enforceability of mediated agreements, in order to put them on a par with arbitration awards.

In addition to these two forms, it is of course open for parties to agree to terms which are not legally binding. This might apply, for example, to apologies or acknowledgement, statements of good faith in future dealings, offers to consider for future business, or commitments to reform working relationships or organisational practice for the future.

'Workable settlements'

In general commercial parties are less concerned with the technical question of legal enforceability, than whether the agreement is at its core, 'workable'

– ie the parties have confidence that the actions and commitments agreed *can* be performed and *will* be performed.

Given a likely background of hostility or scepticism about party behaviour or promises, mediated settlements will often require that a party gives confidence to the other party of its commitment, either substantively or symbolically. This can start early in the process with demonstrated participation of more senior managers, readiness to travel or to go to neutral territory, or readiness to invest in the costs of the mediation process. In terms of outcomes it may involve personal commitments by senior managers, performance bonds, escrow accounts, dispute resolution procedures and other methods to assure implementation. Reforming the relationship may in some cases be as, or more, important than the details of the deal.

This background suggests that the phase of concluding settlement terms should not be short-circuited or underestimated. Parties and mediators should be prepared for last-minute hitches as details get worked out, and uncover new complications of understanding or implementation. Time-zone differences may also interfere to prolong problems of necessary consultation with directors back home. However, if the parties truly have reached an accord then outstanding details should be capable of being overcome.

The nature of the settlement will depend on whether the parties are:

– Terminating the relationship (or have already terminated, or are not in any relationship other than via a legal claim, for example over breach of warranties after a corporate acquisition).
– Continuing the relationship on similar terms.
– Transforming the relationship.

(a) *Terminating the relationship/non-relationship legal claims*

In settlements where termination or resolution of a pure legal claim is the mediated outcome, the parties will be concerned to ensure:

– All financial issues are tied up – generally a clean break from the relationship or legal claim with one or the other paying a sum of money in an agreed space of time. Parties will often discount for early payment and certainty. The longer the payment terms, the greater the concern of risk factors interfering with payment, such as currency fluctuations, political risk, government approvals.
– Transfer or structuring of any property rights, real or intellectual property or equivalent transfers.
– Confidentiality provisions.

- That all third party relationships or legal claims are resolved or a process mechanism is in place to handle them.
- Agreement on responsibility for outstanding costs of prior legal actions.
- Agreement on any public or third party statements.
- Agreement on dispute procedures/access to court, if there is failure to implement the terms.

(*b*) *Continuing the relationship*

In settlements where the parties have agreed to continue their relationship:
- They may defer monetary payment to allow for further project development or specified commercial review, or to explore another joint venture opportunity, or they may require monetary payments as a basis for going forward.
- They will want to clarify existing and ongoing obligations together with new arrangements.
- They will want to review whether legal, commercial and other structures which caused the prior dispute are modified and how they link to elements of the new agreement.
- They will need to consider whether any approvals are necessary for payments.
- They will want to consider effective procedures for resolution of issues and setting up appropriate project management structures.
- They will need to consider legal, economic and other incentives to make the relationship more durable.
- There may be other relevant elements as set out under (a) above.

(*c*) *Transforming the relationship*

This will have elements of termination, ie closing down the past framework, while continuing and maintaining what worked:
- Parties will need to decide if all obligations and rights are to be transferred or which are no longer relevant to the new agreement; if the prior legal and economic relations are to be maintained, how they dovetail with new legal and economic arrangements.
- Whether to structure the new agreement in the same legal manner – which law will apply.
- What will the parties do to avoid past pitfalls, how will the parties share risk and measure performance.
- What arrangements are in place for dispute resolution and termination.

- What negotiating structures are in place to deal with change – future use of mediation.
- Consider what third parties or external risks can or could affect the agreement.
- How will parties communicate in their ongoing relationship.
- Other relevant elements as in (a) and (b) above.

The emphasis in reaching an effective settlement agreement, whether it involves termination, continuation or transformation, is that the agreement should be workable. In the context of a mediated agreement, it is the mediator's role not only to bring parties to an accord but also to examine with each party the best way to structure the agreement so that the parties have got an agreement that stands a real chance of working. Mediators and parties should be concerned to diagnose the causes of past problems and have a real grasp of what has changed to make the future realisable and sustainable – in terms of legal or financial structures, dispute provisions, management or political relationships. The indications to date are that mediations do achieve settlement in over 80 per cent of international cases. Mediated agreements are generally simpler than the original dispute subject matter, force parties to work very hard together to reach settlement terms and involve senior executives and often lawyers in negotiations. The mediator will take shared responsibility (moral rather than legal) to ensure that the agreement terms actually are likely to deliver what the commercial parties believe they have achieved. These factors all assist in the durability of agreements achieved in mediation.

Chapter 8. The Challenges and Alternatives
to Mediation

'It's still a cultural challenge outside the US to go to mediation, though this will change in time. A significant number of the disputes we get involved with are very large. There is a psychological inhibition about going to a third party rather than court – it's the problem of the "If I can't resolve it, no one can" philosophy.'

Peter Bevan, Group Legal Counsel, BP.

Like any management or legal method mediation has its inherent limitations and also potential weaknesses where not managed well. A strategic view of mediation also requires that a business or lawyer have a sense of what alternatives to mediation are available in a conflict, and how these alternatives and mediation may interact. The principal structured alternatives available in international commercial transactions, apart from direct business negotiation or political influence, are arbitration or litigation. A good understanding of these options will ensure that when mediation is adopted, it is used wisely and appropriately. Our experience, however, convinces us that the power and flexibility of mediation, particularly in complex international cases, merits the process being positioned in management systems as a *primary or mainstream management tool,* no matter what other routes may be run in parallel. First, let us paint the canvas of what can complicate access to mediation or what factors can lead to it being inappropriate in some situations. We will then need to touch briefly on the options available outside the mediation process – when are they valuable, when should they be avoided, and how they interface with mediation.

Cultural and psychological barriers to mediation

Perhaps the greatest constraint on mediation usage is self-imposed, the fact that managers and lawyers often resist entering the process. This attitude may spring from one or more of a number of sources.
– *Distrust of new approaches.* Without the experience of a successful

114

mediation, parties are sceptical of the added value it can bring to a negotiation. This will be reinforced in jurisdictions where mediation is not commonly used in domestic legal disputes. However, where a company indicates it wants a genuine dialogue about a business problem, such distrust is easily overcome. Our survey of senior in-house counsel from multinational companies reveals that, whilst experience of commercial mediation is relatively limited, the overwhelming view is that mediation has a significant role to play in international disputes and is likely to grow in the future.

- *Desire for autonomy.* Managers instinctively prefer to manage their own business problems and tend to call in third parties only in crises, particularly if such assistance is associated with failure – organisational psychotherapists after all are less in vogue than 'consultants' or 'coaches'! In some settings, junior managers have this mindset even in terms of concealing problems from their own senior managers. Recognition of this psychological tendency reinforces the value of top management strategically embracing mediation as an explicit core practice. Thus linking it to a culture of positive and intelligent relationship management approaches, rather than to a perceived system of legal risk protection.

- *'Macho' management/advisers.* Adversarial position-taking is both a common outcome, and also a source, of conflicts. Lawyers or managers raised in a culture of adversarialism and point-scoring, can see offers of mediation as a sign of weakness. Lawyers will also tend to discourage dialogue before 'enough' information to bolster their case is available or until they have confidence that clients will not concede too much in personal discussions. (Insurance coverage requirements often formalise this to protect against claims.) This creates enough difficulty for triggering a mediation process if only one party takes this view. Where all parties hold this view, there can easily be a dance of delay, isolation, escalation of conflict and mutual damage to the point where the costs become disproportionate to the business value claims. This dance of mutual damage is most often witnessed on the international plane in terms of ethnic conflicts, but it is also regularly echoed in business arbitration and litigation practice. Often, the complexity of litigating international cases and absence of effective accounting of transaction costs against outcomes, conceals the 'irrationality' of the legal process being undertaken.

- *Political constraints/decision avoidance.* Arbitration and litigation have political advantages for some parties and in some business/cultural situations, insofar that the outcome is outside of the parties' control. This may make it easier to justify a final negative outcome (loss of action or sum of damages) to senior managers, political or audit authorities, or other constituency members, than would be the case for a negotiated outcome of a similar kind. It is easier to cast blame on an externally imposed adjudicator for a decision and to avoid personal or internal accountability. Related to this phenomenon is the fact that it can be challenging to use mediation in cultures where 'deal-making' is not undertaken lightly or where broader social or organisational consensus is a cultural norm. (In one case we mediated in Asia, civil servants had just been sent to jail the week we arrived. They had negotiated a settlement in a similar case and accepted a bribe to do so. This created quite a blockage on a deal mentality for our mediation!)

–   *Cultural definitions of mediation.* Just as different cultures approach negotiations differently, so one must expect differences of approach in mediation. Americans might value its commercial flexibility and 'deal-making' character, whereas the Japanese might favour its amicable settlement emphasis and face-saving avoidance of imposed decision. The novelty of professional mediation as a process may also lead to uncertainty as to whether parties have a common understanding of the objectives of the process. For example, in some cultures and contexts mediation may be regarded as less formal than 'conciliation' where a third party opinion is issued, in others the definition of the two terms is reversed. Increasingly however, 'mediation' is being recognised globally as a flexible process of professionally assisted, structured negotiations. Clarity, consensus of understanding and mediator robustness are nevertheless an important part of preparation for effective mediation. Particular problem areas which typically arise are:

(1)   *Lack of urgency* – some parties will be seen to 'drag their feet' at each stage without other pressures to sustain momentum. In this respect mediation is no worse than negotiation. In arbitration or litigation, delay and prevarication are common experiences although usually there are ultimate sanctions to impose. Parties should stay patient and focused for results;

(2)   *Lack of authority* – promises of 'full settlement authority' may appear to vanish within the heat of negotiations. Progress may appear to stall because of delays for parties to make telephone contacts with their home executives, or adjournments required for

consultation or to engage appropriate managers. Firm commitments and understanding before the mediation event will avoid many problems.

(3) ***Lack of preparation*** – fragmented international contacts and problems of distance mean that principals and advisers often may only convene the day before, or even on the morning of, the mediation. Time needs to be factored into the process to allow for this, as well as for work within and across teams on negotiation material and documentation.

The importance of these psychological barriers is that they are, of course, 'real' obstacles in many cases. They need to be recognised and dealt with as part of overcoming potential limitations to mediation in particular conflicts. That is not to assume that they make mediation impossible, only that a party seeking to use the power of mediation, must design the mediation process in a way that overcomes some of the resistance or likely cultural and psychological barriers, or that factors in an appropriate expectation of the patience and project management required.

Tactical avoidance of mediation

This is one of the most difficult areas when deciding whether to mediate. On the one hand the decision rests primarily on judgment as to when direct negotiations do not require third party assistance. On the other hand, you may feel it is time to show to show that you are serious enough about a claim to go down the route of imposing sanctions (commercial or political), or to involve more 'extreme' third party interventions such as arbitration or the courts. In other words, between these two extremes, when is a case really 'ready' for assisted negotiation? Cases may *not* be ready if:

– Parties are capable of effective and efficient direct negotiations and/or sufficient time needs to be given to direct negotiations before the case will be 'ripe' for mediation. (Question: when and how will you judge inefficiency/ineffectiveness?).

– The other party is unwilling to negotiate realistically unless further legal/economic/political sanctions are applied. (Question: will you know this for sure unless you offer or really test an initial dialogue?).

– One or more parties lack sufficient information to negotiate effectively (or may need the weight of legal process to acquire it). (Question: could its production be facilitated by mediation?).

– No effective decision-maker exists on the other side (eg due to economic or political upheaval). (Question: how will this impact on alternative routes to resolution?).
– Other routes will be more effective than negotiation, eg economic pressure or political lobbying. (Question: but will a mediation damage this route?).

Recovery – what process?
An international bank had been the subject of a trading 'scam' on a developing country's stock exchange, losing hundreds of millions. It began legal proceedings and also lobbied for an ADR approach. Its most successful tactic some years after the incident, however, was successful lobbying of government officials for the establishment of a special tribunal to hear the case. (Estimates of ordinary legal proceedings in the country had predicted a period of 25 years, with appeals, before it would otherwise have recovered any funds.)

Unsuitable disputes

In some cases it is clear, in terms of the issues at stake, mediation will not be the most appropriate first choice for an effective outcome. These fall into a limited range of categories:
– Urgent or unilateral rights protection. Where rapid protective action is required to protect assets, evidence or reputation, eg abuse of intellectual property rights.
– Legal or industry precedent or signal required from a decision, eg a public judgment on an important clause of an international franchise contract.
– Formal legal proceedings need to be initiated before limitation periods expire (although parties could consider an agreement to extend the period or an agreement to mediate in parallel with formal proceedings).
The vast majority of commercial cases fall outside these categories. And even within the categories, mediation may have a complementary role if seen as a robust negotiation tool – for example, many intellectual property cases begin as 'rights' disputes but end up with negotiated licensing deals. The overriding test for deciding suitability is to ask oneself of a case – could this in theory be resolved by direct negotiation even if this currently seems unlikely? If the answer if yes, mediation will be worth considering and testing.

118

Unsuitable disputes

International cross-border litigation

Litigation is, in theory, often the 'final' option for international business parties where mediation may not work, or be unsuitable for a case. (In practice parties often start proceedings and then choose to mediate.) However, litigation as an approach is often avoided in international commercial contracts unless the parties have clearly specified an appropriate forum in their contract. Without an effective court jurisdiction clause, or alternative arbitration remedy, the parties will have to litigate regardless if they seek a legal remedy for a claimed wrong. One of the preliminary problems to be addressed will be to determine which state court will have jurisdiction. There are various technical rules for determining in a particular case which courts have authority to intervene, but they are not always accepted by the other side once a dispute evolves, nor always clear. Once the forum is determined, the litigation procedure will be set by the local courts and the timetable is not in the control of the parties. Every issue may have to be pleaded in a highly formalised procedure, and the case may have to be argued through locally qualified professional practitioners who are registered to practise in the jurisdiction.

In litigation the decision-maker, the judge appointed, often does not have subject matter expertise. Litigation is, of course public, and in most jurisdictions use of the courts is free with the exception of the court fees for issuing the process.

One of the major concerns with international litigation is whether the national courts will have a bias against an overseas party. Even if more perceived than real, it is nevertheless a concern. There are also issues of serving of process and taking evidence with fundamental differences of approach between civil law and common law jurisdictions. In a civil law jurisdiction, the judge plays a much more active role in conducting the proceedings and the findings of fact. The hearings are shorter, more paper-based and would normally concentrate on procedural matters and legal argument. Under common law systems the judge traditionally has a more hands-off approach and the lawyers were much more in control. The English system has more in common with the American than the continental civil law jurisdictions, although the discovery process under the English jurisdiction is more contained than that of the US system. Recent developments internationally have in common, however, a search to develop a stronger judicial case management approach. This is pressing closer, if slowly, to a global standard of active case management through the courts.

The other important issue in considering the litigation option is the question of how to enforce the judgments of foreign courts. In Europe, the Brussels and Lugano Conventions oblige signatory states to enforce judgments from other signatory jurisdictions. The United States is not party to these Conventions. As between England and the US, judgments will be enforced under the Reciprocal Enforcement of Judgements Act 1933 and enforcement would require at least the issuing of a summary process in the other jurisdiction, but can be complex.

It can be seen from the general outline above that litigating international business disputes is not without risks, and is usually a costly process requiring several professionals or expert advisers. If one is going to adopt litigation as the preferred ultimate resolution technique, one should ensure that parties have clearly contracted for the forum (with exclusive jurisdiction to avoid multiplicity of proceedings), and in most cases it would be appropriate to have the same law governing the substantive contract, rather than have a foreign court applying different law. Clients should ensure at the outset of any litigation that their advisers present them with a clear strategic brief, setting out objectives, predicted stages, time and costs, possible outcomes and probabilities.

International arbitration

Arbitration is the traditionally popular 'alternative' to international litigation. In arbitration, the parties have the right at the outset of the relationship to make their own rules for adjudicating privately any conflicts, or to decide whether they wish to submit to one of the international arbitral institutions. Most international arbitration rules leave open the possibility of a court order for interim remedies, such as preservation of assets, although in some jurisdictions it is necessary to make these applications prior to the designation of the arbitrary tribunal. For complete clarity one can provide in the contract as follows:

> *'Jurisdiction to issue pre-arbitral injunction, pre-arbitral attachment or other order in aid of the arbitration proceedings and the enforcement of any award.'*

In most international commercial transactions, parties prefer arbitration to domestic courts. Parties can predetermine the methodology at the contract stage, and can avoid local courts and possible prejudice toward one or other party that may be perceived in a foreign jurisdiction. Jurisdiction for arbitration arises from the agreement to arbitrate; by and large domestic courts will uphold the parties' agreement provided the clause is properly drafted.

Arbitration clause

When selecting arbitration as the ultimate method of dispute resolution, the contract drafter should consider:

– The areas of dispute that are to be resolved by arbitration and the rules of procedure to be adopted. Generally the law of the venue for arbitration will govern the procedure of the arbitration. So if London is the seat of the arbitration, the 1996 English Arbitration Act will apply. Under the 1996 Arbitration Act the court will have very limited jurisdiction over matters such as discovery. Parties can go further in specifying rules or procedure if they wish at the outset to ensure, say, a fast-track arbitration approach.

– The parties can choose to have the involvement of an administrative body, such as CEDR, the International Chamber of Commerce, the London Court of International Arbitration, JAMS or similar centres in North America, Scandinavia or Australasia which have clear and developed guidelines for the control of arbitration and for the selection and appointment of arbitrators. The parties will have to pay a fee for the assistance of this outside body, but the use of their established rules, procedures and contract clauses which have been well tested, are in most cases to be recommended. Administration bodies have experience and knowledge of moving the process along and of typical problems that arise. They may give much comfort and remove suspicion of each side's counsel, a third party effect in itself.

– The number and background of arbitrators should be decided and provided for in the contract. In complex disputes it is not uncommon to have three arbitrators although this is more expensive and does raise severe logistic challenges with regard to timetabling of meetings. Generally, one will be selected by each party and the third nominated by the administrative organisation (or other arbitrators) as a means of broadening expertise while preserving neutral balance. The nationality, background and experience of the arbitrators are extremely important. Choice in arbitration brings with it the responsibility to ensure that the parties will be well and fairly served. One cannot, however, overlook the additional costs involved and, for certain types of contracts, the parties may prefer to choose one arbitrator which will be considerably more economic and administratively far easier.

– The place of arbitration is relevant. One needs to consider the convenience to the parties as well as the local court's power to govern procedure and to provide interim remedies or to overturn the arbitral award – in some parts of the world this is a distinct possibility.

– The language of the arbitration should be considered: what language will the witnesses give evidence in, and what will be the language of the transcripts.

– Applicable law of the contract should be determined as should the procedural law, although they will often be the same. Failure to address these issues at the time of drafting the arbitration clause can result in challenges to jurisdiction by a party, requiring preliminary litigation to determine the challenge.

Importantly, enforcement of arbitration awards is possible in most jurisdictions providing all the procedural steps have been properly followed, most countries being signatories to the 1985 New York Convention. However, many commercial clients have stories to tell of the problems they have faced in enforcing arbitration awards.

Weaving mediation into other approaches

Either of the adjudication routes, arbitration or litigation, will typically create problems for commercial parties. They usually raise the stakes in the conflict; they can be a diversion of time and energy; they will add to their cost of the dispute; they lead to a loss of control over process and outcome (in theory arbitration gives parties more ability to determine the process). However, because mediation does not guarantee an outcome to the assisted negotiation, parties will always have to face the choice at the beginning of the contract, or once a problem arises, as to what they want as the 'backstop' to a dispute. This gives a degree of discipline and deadline, to close off the uncertainties inherent in commercial arguments and disagreements over actions required.

However mediation also has the strength of flexibility in timing of its use. It is not therefore excluded as a possibility just because parties resort to adjudication. In an increasing number of international contracts, a mediation phase is built into the contract's dispute procedure *before* access to one of the binding process options. Similarly, mediation's power to 'rescue' parties from deadlock and drift towards litigation, means that an increasing number of national court systems either encourage or direct parties into mediation as part of regular court procedures.

Chemical reaction: amiable agreements
In a dispute following the acquisition of an Italian company – the Portuguese and Italian lawyers amended the Sale and Purchase Agreement to allow for mediation before arbitration. The multiple claims were mediated in two days and all matters resolved – avoiding arbitration entirely.

Down under express
An Italian firm was supplying an Australian restaurant chain with coffee maker machines. The Australians complained about defects in many of the machines and refused to pay the Italian company. The Italians took the Australians to court in New South Wales. There the judge at an early point in proceedings required that both parties try mediation and referred them to a court master. The master arranged a telephone conference between the parties and talked them through the issues in a joint session, then by separate private calls. The issues were not resolved during the calls, but the parties made progress and were able to negotiate a compromise agreement within two weeks of the conference call.

'... mediation is making a very positive contribution towards dispute resolution. This is especially so in areas where specialist concerns are involved, where the accusatorial process is sometimes unsuited to give the tribunal a grasp of the issues involved, and where necessary expertise, particularly if a full panel is to be constituted, can be hard to find. Specialist mediators therefore have a real part to play as does the process of mediation itself in an ever more specialising world.'

(Robert S Webbs, QC, General Counsel, British Airways)

While court systems increasingly recognise a parallel mediation track, this is much less true of private arbitrations. International arbitration centres increasingly, following CEDR's lead, have added mediation or ADR rules to their standard arbitration rules. However, once an arbitration tribunal is formed, it is usually only required to follow arbitration procedures and has little financial or procedural incentive to encourage parties into a mediation that might settle the arbitration matter before the tribunal hears it. Having said that, there are exceptions in terms of the traditions of some Asian and continental European arbitrations where the arbitrators will also seek to encourage the parties to settle the case. However, these are usually fairly informal or low-key efforts compared to the intensive and disciplined professional forum of a separate commercial mediation. We touch below on a more formal approach to reconciling mediation and arbitration in 'med-arb'.

Experience demonstrates that getting parties into structured settlement talks creates its own momentum with a very realistic prospect that a settlement will be achieved because of, or following on from, the mediation efforts. It is important therefore for contract clauses to include a mediation stage, rather than relying on chance that a litigation or arbitration tribunal might encourage mediation. Once litigation or arbitration has begun, parties often lose control or allow the process to generate negotiation 'inertia' where lawyers continue 'the action' until ready to settle on the steps of the final hearing. Sometimes parties are reluctant to include mediation clauses in a contract as they feel it might tie their hands in the event of a dispute, or generate delay when it is important to begin legal proceedings. However, most of the objections to mediation clauses can be met by appropriate refinement of procedures. For example: time limits on the mediation phase to avoid undue delay (as agreed *ad hoc* or set out in contract); providing for an appointing authority or broker in absence of agreement to a mediator, to ensure a mediator is actually appointed and other process decisions taken; exemption for parties from mediation provisions of a contract where a party is justified to protect legal rights (ie to deal with urgent or unilateral rights cases).

The law governing the effectiveness of mediation contractual provisions is still undergoing evolution internationally. In some cases parties may seek to argue that the mediation clause was a mere statement of intent and not contractually binding, if they are concerned about using mediation at the time of a dispute. Much depends on the jurisdiction and the particular wording of a clause as to whether parties will be held bound by a court to follow a contractual mediation procedure before moving to litigation or arbitration. In general it is important to ensure such clauses are clearly worded, and refer to an independent centre's rules of mediation procedure. (For a clear example of this see *Cable and Wireless v IBM Ltd*, 2002 where a leading judge of the Commercial Court in London held that a reference to the use of CEDR with its Model Mediation Procedure, gave sufficient clarity to allow the court to enforce this stage of contractual procedure).

Drafting the appropriate multi-track dispute-resolution approach

Model Mediation and Arbitration Contract Clauses are included in Part Two. In all cases, those drafting contracts are reminded of the points raised above concerning the necessity of providing for the governing law of the contract and any dispute resolution provisions – not assuming them to be the same – together with the place and language of the dispute resolution procedures.

Provision of a mediation stage in contracts ensures that the parties have a flexible procedure in place for a neutral to assist with the project management of conflict. Further, the fact of providing for various 'steps' before ultimate adjudication ensures that the parties give themselves every opportunity to resolve a problem at the most appropriate level.

One of the biggest international infrastructure projects to utilise the multi-step philosophy of conflict resolution was for the construction of the new Hong Kong Airport in the early 1990s. Core contracts for the project made mediation a mandatory procedure for contractors and client (Hong Kong government). If mediation was unsuccessful, the contract provided for adjudication by a single adjudicator. Adjudication was defined in its new technical sense in construction contracts as only an interim decision which binds the parties unless and until one appeals within a set time period to the final phase of arbitration.

Construction projects internationally are frequently the source of innovation in dispute resolution because of the character of the industry and variability of conditions and client requirements. The information technology sector is likely to follow this pattern. In addition to interim binding adjudication decisions, other major infrastructure projects have used project monitoring by 'Dispute Review Boards', 'Dispute Resolution Advisers', or 'Project Mediators/Neutrals'. These processes ensure that conflicts are tackled early by a neutral but knowledgeable project third party manager who can assist parties to avoid project breakdown on an ongoing basis. Some of the aspects of this are discussed in chapter 10.

Med-arb – a hybrid versus tiered approach

Typically, contracts provide as seen above for a sequence of dispute resolution efforts moving from formal negotiation, through mediated negotiation, to final determination by arbitration or a court. There have also been attempts to blend the elements in a single process, usually called 'med-arb'. A med-arb process can also be constituted by an *ad hoc* agreement at the time of dispute.

The distinguishing feature of med-arb is that under the agreement the appointed mediator seeks to resolve all issues by negotiation; if this is not achieved within a defined time period, the mediator converts to the role of arbitrator and hands down a binding award on any outstanding issues.

The advantage of this technique is assumed to be its cost-effectiveness and finality. Parties enter a process which combines mediation flexibility with arbitration conclusiveness. And the parties avoid the time, expense and duplication of educating a separate arbitrator if mediation does not succeed on all or some issues. It can, therefore, seem to be a powerful pragmatic business approach in the right kinds of case.

However, while attractive in concept, care has to be taken in applying the approach to cases of any significance or high value. A number of arbitration bodies expressly prohibit the process, and some experienced mediators or arbitrators will not engage in this approach. It has the disadvantage that parties may feel inhibited in their negotiation – the prospect of an arbitration award by the mediator, if mediation fails, may inhibit flexibility and frankness. It also raises issues of fairness and principles of natural justice, in that neither party has had an opportunity to respond to possibly inaccurate or misleading statements made to the mediator in the other party's private sessions. However, the procedure has had its successes and supporters, and there are examples of statutory provisions which seek to prevent challenge to med-arb decisions by parties arguing subsequently the natural justice claim (for example in Singaporean law).

A number of variations in the med-arb procedure have been suggested in an attempt to overcome some of these dangers. These include:
–   Two neutrals are present for a longer opening presentation, one then dropping out of the procedure unless recalled for an arbitration phase;
–   The procedure offers a formal summary arbitration phase at the end of the mediation and the mediator is required to dismiss from his mind any statements made in private sessions;
–   The mediator writes an arbitration award after the opening sessions but does not reveal it to the parties unless the subsequent mediation session is unsuccessful (this process is sometimes called arb-med to distinguish it from med-arb);
–   Either party has the right to veto the mediator's switch of role at the end of the mediation phase (ie they will only proceed if they continue to respect the mediator's objectivity);
–   The arbitration phase is restricted to 'last-offer' arbitration, ie the neutral has to choose between each party's 'final offer' rather than attempt a

more sophisticated case review. The theory is that this streamlines arbitration evidence and argument, and encourages parties to converge towards a more reasonable position that an arbitrator might select.

Given the difficulties in determining whether med-arb, or which kind of med-arb, will be exactly appropriate for a future dispute under the contract, it would not normally be recommended as a formal contract provision as opposed to a timetabled, tiered approach. The parties are free to agree to med-arb if appropriate when they first initiate ADR, or to agree that the mediator should provide a binding or non-binding opinion, at the conclusion of the mediation process.

The whole approach to the dispute resolution part of the contract has to be in harmony with the manner in which the parties have designed and anticipated their day-to-day operations. This shall ensure that the parties, even when requiring external help, are less able to walk away from the problem. They will have to work with the lawyers and other appropriate participants as part of a team, and to both control the outcome and optimise the opportunity of an outcome. Joint project management of negotiations is an essential feature of sustainable business relationships and of efficient resolution of the terms of withdrawal from a relationship.

A sophisticated corporate policy on the management of conflicts (and lawyers) is the best answer as to how to overcome tactical and psychological barriers to mediation, and how to avoid the worst features of international arbitration and litigation. The benefits of mediation, set against the costs and risks of the alternatives, justify that mediation should become a fundamental part of any international business manager's know-how and practice.

Chapter 9. Forging Leadership in International Mediation

'What people often mean by getting rid of conflict is getting rid of diversity – and it is of the utmost importance that these should not be considered the same.'

Mary Parker Follett, 1900, *The Creative Experience.*

'How can the rapid acceleration of contact among diverse cultures be turned into cooperation rather that conflict? How can demand for cultural integrity be reconciled with the dazzling rise of the global village?'

His Highness Prince Aga Khan, 1996

Mediation in International Business Conflicts

A transformation is already under way in the interconnection of global commercial, legal and political structures, systems and traffic. Begun at the end of the 18th Century and the early 19th Century, it will prove to be one of the great management and social challenges of the 21st Century. Within this reconstruction of the human race's development, conflict systems are only a small part. Yet they are a vital ingredient. Unfortunately, like dispute clauses in a contract, they are often neglected until the final wrap-up sessions of negotiations, or left to the lawyers.

Yet effective structures and systems for handling conflict are an essential ingredient for the new global social marketplace. Conflicts can be handled to optimise their constructive elements or to exaggerate their destructive capacity. Conflicts can be managed efficiently or inefficiently. If severe enough and handled badly enough, they may only leave destruction in their wake, 'Lose-Lose' not 'Win-Win' in the jargon of negotiation scholars.

The upsurge of mediation practice globally is witness to a subtle shift in the recognition of what is required for effective conflict management. The 19th and 20th centuries saw substantial progress in the professionalisation of

128

rules and structures concerned with methods and principles of legal judgment. Litigation and arbitration remain still essential backstops to conflict resolution, as sources of authoritative public rule making, and boundary setting, within commercial and social conflicts. However the complexity of global business is also calling for a new approach to the management of conflict. International commercial mediation, like international diplomacy, promises to offer a vital tool for extending the potential for effective justice systems in the global community.

International commercial mediation offers the global business community, at a minimum, a vital tool for commercial relations that are in crisis. Mediation gives the business world more positive and effective control of the 'problem review and decision' process in serious conflicts. It offers a neutral third party to assist proactively with facilitation and project management of difficult dialogue and problem-solving. It provides a rigorous vehicle for ensuring focus in conflict discussions, considering them against current and future circumstances, and testing the realistic prospects of best and worst case outcomes from litigation or arbitration. It offers a process more in harmony with the essential character of free market commercial transactions – of negotiated, rather than imposed, commercial order. It loosens the constraints and the paralysing effect on negotiations of over-rigid rules of legal process, or of jurisdiction and forum sensitivities, and instead moves in favour of a more fluid balance between formal independent intervention, and a flexible review of a case that takes into account the specific circumstances and needs of the parties.

So how do we realise the optimal benefits of mediation in future international business conflicts? The answer to this turns on the evolution of developments and leadership at five levels of current activity: in justice systems including regulatory authorities; in the practice of lawyers, both private practice and corporate counsel; in the international arbitration community; within the emerging mediation profession; and of course finally within the business community itself.

Justice and regulatory systems

Encouragement of dialogue once parties have reached a crisis point is often best fostered by the institutions of the justice system. As we have described earlier in this book, the players in a conflict often feel reluctant to 'concede' that they are willing to compromise to resolve a claim or defence once positions have been asserted. Avoidance of the 'who blinks first' problem crosses cultural and geographical boundaries. Leverage from a third party who can exercise power over the parties is often therefore an important or essential ingredient in making mediation happen. Courts and regulators, once seized of a dispute, have clear authority to encourage or direct parties into 'settlement conferences' or mediation. Parties will often welcome this, not only because they are not seen to initiate the discussion, but also in international cases because often they will escape the uncertainties and possibly perceived biases of the domestic court system.

There have indeed been remarkable developments in the last 20 years, and continuing, in the way justice systems have been adapting to this new approach. Begun in the harsh litigation context of the US and spreading around the common law world, the approach is increasingly being adopted more formally in civil and Asian law practices. For example, at the time of writing, it is anticipated that the European Union will pass a Directive on civil and commercial mediation. This will not only give official parallel recognition and encouragement of mediation as a process alongside national court systems, but will also bring a degree of harmonisation to differing national legal practices within the EU to support mediation's impact. The Directive is likely to cover areas such as: the consistent treatment of the 'without prejudice' nature of mediated negotiations; a common standard in relation to the effect of mediation on time periods within which legal claims must be registered; immunity of mediators from being required to give evidence of mediated negotiations. Similar considerations are under way in many other national legal systems outside the EU. (Even in the EU, the importance of mediation has already found its way into legal reforms in the countries of Central and Eastern Europe which have sought accession to the EU in the recent period.)

The significant adjustments in juristic attitudes to legal processes and conflict resolution options have also fuelled rethinking of conflicts affecting public sector bodies or the community at large. Thus many countries have extended the role of mediation in neighbourhood or family disputes, or applied mediation options to government commercial contracts (the UK government for example, pledged in 2001 to agree to alternative dispute resolution in its disputes). Such developments can spill over into inter-national work, such as in family inheritance cases, or cross-border personal injury, insurance or consumer claims. Public and administrative law also has begun to be more receptive to the possibilities of mediation. (See, for example, the 2005 Report on reform of procedures before the European Court of Human Rights by Lord Woolf, former Lord Chief Justice of England and Wales.) Consumer disputes are also increasingly being diverted

130

from traditional courts into other more cost-effective or consumer-friendly alternatives such as tribunals or ombudsman, though these tend to be more adjudicative in approach.

At the same time, mediation practices are increasingly being written into the rules of regulators or international trade blocs. Treaty provisions or regulations of bodies such as the World Trade Organisation, the International Centre for the Settlement of Investment Disputes, and the North American Free Trade Agreement, include the potential for disputes to be resolved by conciliation or mediation as well as arbitration. The OECD Guidelines on Multinational Enterprises governing the corporate social responsibility of multinationals include a 'Specific Instances' system for dealing with employment or stakeholder disputes by mediation and facilitation of dialogue (adopting the definition of mediation developed by CEDR in 2005). Mediation is also used for 'domain name' and other IP disputes in a successful programme initiated by WIPO, the World Intellectual Property Organisation of the UN. In the UK the Financial Services Authority became the first major regulator to pursue an active mediation scheme for its enforcement proceedings, followed by Office of Fair Trading requirements for mediation in relations between major supermarkets and their suppliers. In 2005 the UK Patent Office became the first international patent office to promote a mediation service as part of its procedures for hearing and settling cases of disputed patents. Others are likely to follow.

Improvements in justice systems in a more global world, also more easily become capable of imitation. An appreciation of the benefits of ADR in civil justice have led international funding organisations, such as the World Bank or Asia Development Bank, to encourage countries to adopt ADR practices and training in the interests of good governance. These leadership developments have to be tempered, however, with the realisation that each country has to learn to adapt mediation and ADR systems to its own unique social, cultural and commercial context.

Legal professionals

It goes without saying that for mediation's potential to be fully realised, legal professionals inside and outside companies must be made aware of the process, and should be skilful in adapting it to the needs of a case or sector. In the case of external lawyers, there can be initial resistance not merely because of unfamiliarity or scepticism about the process, but also because it may appear to be economically threatening – a settled case does not continue to generate fees. The answer to this is threefold. Lawyers in companies and their managers have to insist on what business expects by way of support for more cost-effective dispute methods; good education and awareness-raising is required; and finally there needs to be a recognition amongst external lawyers that they have everything to gain from, and ultimately no alternative to, delivering the services that clients really need and expect. Most national legal professions have swung around in support of mediation, eventually, though there is still much work to be done. Increasingly major international bar associations have incorporated recognition of the process into their activities – for example the American Bar Association has a Dispute Resolution Section; the International Bar Association has a Mediation Section; the Union Internationale des Avocats has a Forum of Mediation Centres and mediation interest section. The International Bar Association's Mediation publications have profiled mediation developments in over 20 countries from Finland to Argentina. See also CEDR's '*EU Mediation Atlas*' for detailed coverage of developments within the European Union.

International arbitration community

The traditional 'alternative' to national courts has been the international arbitration system, mainly dominated by specialist private practice lawyers though also served by key international institutions such as the International Chamber of Commerce in Paris, London Court of Arbitration in London, China International Economic and Trade Arbitration Commission in China and similar centres in most continents and many countries. The growth of international business has also fuelled growth of the international arbitration system and the role of arbitration contract clauses, as companies have sought to free themselves from national court oversight (though certain jurisdictions such as London and New York retain a historic popularity, partly driven by national interests, partly for their reputations of objectivity). Most of the major arbitration centres have come to terms with the growth of mediation as an alternative to both arbitration and litigation, by devising their own mediation rules and contract clauses. However for many this has not been an easy or effective transition. There are two key reasons for this. First the traditions and business model of such centres do not easily adapt to the faster-moving, short-term flexibility required for business mediation (and frequent upfront costs and skilled effort required to engage parties in the process). Second, most of the centres rely heavily on outsourced case referral to sole practitioner arbitrators (lawyers) appointed by the parties if not the centres. Their practices, and the traditional rules of arbitration, do not easily allow for referral to mediators in the same way as the public courts can do. Publicly funded judges are often seeking to reduce their workload or are driven more by juridical principles of trying to improve access to justice and the quality of justice processes.

However, arbitration is not immune from such national developments given that its practitioners come from the same cultural and professional groups as public justice; also some arbitration jurisdictions (like some national courts) have a tradition of seeking where possible settlement within the process, for example amongst Chinese or Swiss arbitrators. However, such settlement practices are usually fairly 'light touch' approaches compared to the more focused process of mediation, so there remains a gap in the arbitration world's processing of cases. As an adjudication process driven by lawyers, arbitration remains prone to many of the weaknesses similar to the litigation system. Reform is, therefore, most likely to come from either statutory reform of arbitration practice, from pressure from the business community for arbitrators to simplify and streamline their practices, or from innovations and greater acceptance of a med-arb approach in international business conflicts.

Mediation profession

The rapid growth of mediation has fuelled, and has been fuelled by, a remarkably fast growth of a community of individuals interested in the practice of mediation around the world. Taking CEDR's training alone, we can point to engagement with trainees from over 30 countries, and every continent. Add in the work of other trainers, and national systems of training, and there are undoubtedly now tens of thousands of individuals who have received basic training in mediation skills and techniques. Of course, basic training and experienced professional practice are different matters. There is still a wide gap between the two groups, particularly where it comes to regular international mediation work. However, each new wave of national mediation impact fuels further experience, and creates connections inevitably into the international business community and its conflicts. Alongside voluntary developments, international institutions such as the World Bank, European Union, Asia Development Bank, USAID, British Council and Department for International Development have helped fund further in-country training as part of their support for developments in justice systems or corporate governance programmes. (Recent examples at the time of writing are CEDR projects in Kazakhstan, Azerbaijan, Pakistan, Croatia, Nigeria, Slovakia and Russia. Some of our partners in CEDR's international mediation alliance, MEDAL, are also extensively involved in such programmes internationally, eg across the Mediterranean countries).

Mediation training has appealed to individuals from a wide variety of backgrounds including lawyers, construction professionals, IP and IT specialists, management consultants, healthcare and arts professionals. Mediation training is popular for two reasons. First it is more of an add-on to existing professional or managerial skill bases, rather than a major vocational programme in its own right. (Though, within the European Union, some countries such as Germany and Austria are requiring courses of 200 hours, rather than the more typical 40-hour and apprenticeship system in other jurisdictions.) And second, there appears to be an inherent fascination and satisfaction for many professionals in working as an independent with clients and advisers with the goal of helping resolve difficult conflicts over a short time frame.

This background has, however, also had its drawbacks. The supply of mediators outstrips the demand for mediation services in every jurisdiction. At the same time, the 'vacuum' in terms of mediation's obvious openness as a process to a variety of professional backgrounds, has led to some competition for ownership between lawyers and others (including regulators), or between attorneys and organisational providers, or attorneys and judge-mediators. Ultimately, the mediation profession will be shaped of course not only by its leaders, but by client choice in terms of best and most cost-effective service, but like any market there are 'imperfections' which legislators and the emerging profession will have to wrestle with. This is likely to be begun at a national level, then echoed in international developments.

Mediation services, as with other professional and justice services, need to sell to, and meet the needs of, the international marketplace. Promotion of the mediation 'brand' by publications, education and training, is therefore essential but not sufficient for implementing global business diplomacy. The field also needs effective practice and effective systems of training, both of mediators, and of representatives in mediation. Word of mouth recommendations of the effectiveness of mediation are a helpful but relatively slow method of promotion in a global market. Proving the case for using mediation clauses in international contractual arrangements will speed up required access of businesses to mediation experience. Similarly the growth internationally of programmes where courts direct or encourage litigants into mediation is also providing leverage to multiply the experience of mediation.

The business community

The obvious source for leadership to promote and develop international mediation is often missing from the table. Business conflicts are bad news, and regarded as one-offs in many industry sectors. However, quite apart from cost control considerations, the development of global business, and particularly business activities built on relationships and reputation, make it essential that executives find ways of regaining control of their conflicts. Mediation offers managers the opportunity to manage and control costs and outcomes in conflicts. For the more farsighted, it allows them to become better in the first place at preventing conflicts and their resulting costs – a reason that has led some companies to encourage legal reporting to their Chief Finance Officer. Chief Legal Officers of companies have a particular opportunity to take a leadership role that not only applies to questions of the adoption of mediation in a case. It can also apply to management policies and decisions concerned with the management of external lawyers, to business plans, corporate statements and contract clauses. Senior in-house counsel, executives and international advisers need to demonstrate courage and leadership in the deployment of mediation and policies which support mediation. This not only extends to management education programmes but also suggests they get to know well the mediation profession, and find ways to encourage its emergence and development. Effective use of mediation procedure in political and supra-national trade disputes will also help serve as a leadership model for business-to-business conflicts.

Of course there are many business settings and disputes where it is 'rational' to engage in, or to sustain, conflict or hold strongly to positions as a manager or business leader. However, in considering arguments for the rationality of other approaches to conflict than mediation, managers need to weigh costs and benefits of process alternatives properly in the balance. And the reality of much corporate life is that instinctive reactions of 'fight' or 'flight', are often mis-judged in their value and effect.

Resolving major conflicts by recognising the power of assisted dialogue, often requires senior executives to act with more courage and imagination than they realise is needed. However the 'bridging deadlock dividend', for businesses managing conflicts well, is potentially immense. This is particularly the case if mediation can be brought fully 'into the business bloodstream'. We consider how this can be done in the final chapter.

Chapter 10.   Diplomacy at the Heart of Business

'... all the good-to-great companies had a penchant for intense dialogue. Phrases like "loud debate", "heated discussions" and "healthy conflict" peppered the articles and interview transcripts from all the companies.'

'... Iverson dreamed of building a great company, but refused to begin with "the answer" for how to get there ... "my role was more as a mediator." '

Jim Collins, *Good to Great*

Some years ago we were running a negotiation seminar for senior international contracts executives for a major multinational telecoms company, and asked the question, 'How many of you have had a serious dispute in the last 12 months?' Two hands out of 16 went up. 'And how many have had serious difficulties in negotiating a contract or contract performance in the same period?' Twelve hands went up. The truth is that 'disputes', particularly those reaching a stage of arbitration or litigation, are only the tip of the iceberg of business relationship challenges. Breakdowns in communication, mismatched expectations, aggravation and 'hassle' are a major part of the fabric of daily organisational life, far exceeding formalised disputes. Getting things done in a complex business and human environment typical of international business, is like setting sail in challenging seas, full of potential hazards and changeable weather conditions requiring regular course adjustments just to stay on track – never mind the possibility of running into a submerged iceberg or being blown over by a sudden squall.

International mediation has in the last 20 years begun to register its effectiveness as a professional approach in the context of international dispute resolution. However, just as disputes are only the tip of the iceberg of organisational conflicts, so is current mediation usage only the tip of the iceberg of the potential transformative resource available to business for rethinking approaches to 'regular' conflict or mainstream management difficulties. Preventive approaches are always harder to initiate and sustain than are rescue efforts, but have enormous power when they become integrated into standard operating procedures. The 'next generation' challenge in international mediation is therefore to find ways to build it into

136

accepted management practices, to free it from its association with 'break-downs' and crisis, and convert it into a 'maintenance and prevention' management tool.

Why do we believe in the power of mediation as a transformative management technique? At a theoretical level, the answer to this lies in revisiting the simple rationale for mediation's effectiveness that we have outlined throughout this text. Mediation brings into play a combination of an effective outside project consultant, a sense of focus and discipline, a catalyst for ensuring *real* management engagement with a problem. These can so often be absent when disputes are allowed to drift in the swamp of legal systems, ad hoc management and distaste for tough conflict dialogue that characterise the typical business dispute and manager. The remarkable power of mediation to overcome apparently intractable deadlock, or to initiate a step-change in previously stuck positions, is well proven. Because of this proven value, imaginative managers should at least consider how they can harness the same proactive methodology with all of its strengths to a wider management arena.

But it is not only at a theoretical level where this discussion can begin. There are already practical insights into how to engage mediation and introduce it into the business bloodstream. The following is based on our experience of areas where insights on this already exist. Also, as mediators working on many cases of business deadlock, we regularly see cases (perhaps as much as 80 per cent) where, with better systems or skills in place at an earlier stage in the business dispute, we believe that it would have been possible for such problems to have been averted. It is, therefore, valuable for managers to consider where and how mediation or related techniques would assist in *pre-dispute* management practice, and we set out below some key areas for reflection and example.

A key issue in considering the application of mediation experience to management is to differentiate between the scope for *skills integration*, from that of *technique adoption*. Managers' practices may benefit by merely being trained in mediation skills and techniques, which they can then incorporate into their own management of dialogue at work. Most of the managers who have attended our intensive mediation training programmes say that they think differently about their own negotiations afterwards. In other words, they are better able to empathise, to think into other people's situation, to recognise and work with differing perspectives, to work with patience and optimism through decision impasse. This kind of empowerment can run alongside the adoption of further formal mediation applications into the business bloodstream, in other words adapting regular work practices to ensure that there is a genuine third party element brought into play. Both approaches should be adopted for the areas we discuss below, but we concentrate for current purposes on stressing how the more radical approach of adoption of mediation practice can be undertaken. *However, managers who are trained in mediation as a core management competence will be better able to recognise when to access formal external mediation* (whether that be to call in a further level of manager, or an external mediation resource).

Corporate governance/employment in the global market

International businesses sometimes exploit the fact of differing labour or tax markets to generate greater profit potential. However, in an increasingly 'connected' world, this approach is frequently subject to challenge and risk. Companies can also be accused of applying differing ethical standards to different parts of the world. There is, therefore, a trend towards finding processes for resolving employment relationship issues which can reflect the flexibility inherent in different labour markets, while providing independent judgement and assistance that can encourage coherence and perceived fairness. In response to this trend, many international organisations, particularly those linked to public sector norms of fairness, equity and transparency, have increasingly been adopting policies which give employees or departments with a grievance access to independent third parties. Sometimes these programmes have been described or run as internal 'mediation' systems, sometimes they have been crystallised in the concept of an organisational 'Ombudsman or Ombuds-person', sometimes they work with tribunals or existing established third-party intervention systems in a society.

Mediation is also in harmony with the growing recognition by global business of its social and environmental responsibilities. But more challenging is the ability of businesses to respond to other relationships such as shareholders or 'stakeholders' represented by local communities or environmental NGOs. This requires that businesses find means to engage in dialogue that is managed and responsive. 'Partnering', 'relationship marketing', 'strategic ecology', 'business alliances', 'stakeholder dialogue' and other stock phrases of commercial development and corporate governance, resonate with the need to find ways of making the benefits of global competition be implemented through constructive and socially responsive business methodologies. The frequent failures of business interconnectedness also are a testament to the need to find a simple mechanism to manage difficult dialogue. Sometimes public agencies and courts can act as intermediaries but the sensitivity of the issues often raised, and of the politics of such engagement, should encourage business and public agencies to find channels which reflect not a specific interest at the table, but which can focus attention purely on the project of managing dialogue and making negotiation effective. An effective liaison with relevant public agencies can be part of the brief of the mediator or mediation team.

In its Guidelines for Multinational Enterprises, the OECD (Organisation for Economic Co-operation and Development) has developed a voluntary code of conduct for companies, with a linked national government monitoring mechanism of 'National Contact Points'. The Guidelines focus on corporate social responsibility, in areas such as human rights, supply chain management, labour relations, environment, taxation and bribery. They encourage use of facilitation of dialogue through processes such as mediation. They particularly recognise the potential for practical application in a 'specific instances' procedure for dealing with conflicts between multinationals and local stakeholders. By 2005 the OECD was able to report over 100 instances of intervention through the procedure, covering such matters as Trade Union recognition, corporate impact on local community land use, child labour practices, management of prisons. Discussions within the OECD also have recognised the need to take such approaches to a new level, to optimise the potential gains from effective mediation practice.

An even more elementary aspect of corporate governance is how boards or executive committees perform. While the concept of the auditor is well established for external verification of financial probity and health, the only equivalent approach to effective governance of corporate decision-making, is the non-executive director concept. Although this could be characterised as an informal mediator role in potential, the reality is often that non-executives find it hard to sustain such a role because of their shareholder interest, or because of their close engagement personally with executives. Recognising the value of calling in a 'true' mediator, can assist non-executives perform their role well when they find themselves caught up in boardroom conflicts or personality clashes. We have ourselves been called into a number of such situations, particularly where venture capitalists have been involved and were reluctant to see their investment drain away under pressure of unproductive conflicts in a fledgling company. Sometimes these interventions do result in an executive coming to terms with the impossibility of the team continuing and the need to depart, but such a 'divorce' will come less painfully, and with less expense, when there is assistance by a mediator to help parties face up to necessary decisions and to get real issues on the table. Similar considerations apply to the frequent interdepartmental/ unit squabbles within major organisations; or indeed to the 'family business' character of many major private international companies.

Goods and services in the global market

Supply of goods and services: IT systems, transportation and distribution, wholesale goods supply – these are such core areas of effective business practice in most businesses, that adoption of early mediation access by contract or procurement managers should be an elementary management principle. The same can be said of distributor and agency relationships, or licensing agreements. There have been traditionally many management practices and philosophies which have treated supply contracts as adversarial contests, where the aim is to squeeze the supplier to the limit. Such approaches, of course, would not find mediation intrinsically attractive since mediation use implies a readiness to make adjustments or to 'give-and-take' as an outcome. However, the areas of business life where such exploitative attitudes hold sway are on the decline, in recognition of the interrelationship between supplier commitment and quality, and purchaser needs for customer performance and satisfaction. Nor does mediation prevent managers from doing rigorous deals. Sometimes the process can actually achieve a higher value outcome, by stretching out the negotiation in a more professional, considered and articulate way. And even in cases of hard bargaining philosophies, the onset of legal claims from suppliers can quickly undermine the apparent gains made from driving supplier prices down. (The parallel with employment practices is obvious.)

The easiest way to incorporate mediation into management practice in the supply of goods and services, is to ensure that appropriate contract clauses are drafted, thus triggering a notice of dispute and resort to mediation if one party attests that performance or payment has not been satisfactory and that the case is about more than simple non-payment or non-performance. However, our experience of mediated disputes is that even in cases where contract clauses contain reference to mediation, managers often do not trigger such intervention when they should. This is due partly to managers often being unaware of the detail of contractual terms, and perhaps never realising that lawyers have inserted a boilerplate dispute resolution clause. It can also derive, however, from the inertia of managers used to working on their own account, or where calling in outsiders is seen to require effort or to signal a sense of 'failure' before senior managers. Therefore good business practice suggests that it is important to train managers early in the principles and practice of mediation, and to focus on its power-enhancing capacity rather than worry about its diversionary or oversight capacity. It is not enough to leave it to a written contract as a basis for professional management.

Consumer disputes are also increasingly open to fast-track mediation or adjudication approaches, with the emergence of Online Dispute Resolution (ODR), although at a business-to-business level ODR has been largely restricted to areas where disputants are happy to use a computerised system for trading financial offers.

Intellectual property in the global market

IP assets are increasingly both a subject of enormous value in global trade and also (not unrelated to this), a source of major contention and debate both at the level of cases and at the level of concept and regulation. Traditionally associated with claims for 'rights' and 'infringement', the IP world mindset is often initially bemused by the idea of mediation as a process. However, the reality of the IP world is that it is awash with 'deals' on licensing and other ways of managing IP risk and reward. Mediation, therefore, can often be applied to add value to such negotiations or conflicts. We have mediated many such cases ourselves. Experience of the role of mediation in IP has led to regular professional support and conferences on the topic, and to industry associations or particular companies (such as British American Tobacco) developing active ADR policies for regular problem areas. In 2005 the UK Patent Office became the first patent agency internationally to build mediation into its portfolio of intervention approaches. Others are likely to follow.

Contract clauses

While the typical 'amicable negotiation' clauses (ie escalating any formal dispute to senior executives for direct resolution) have a vital place in international business dealings, mediation – third party assisted negotiation – multiplies the inherent advantages and effects of the basic negotiation clause. It increases the formality and seriousness of impact of the procedural stage, yet retains and enriches the core business focus. It avoids the delay and inherent 'political' problems which are often found in applying purely amicable negotiation approaches. As we have seen in Chapter 2, mediation has a range of benefits for business suppliers, partners, or in complex project management, because:

- It deals with the root of problems by bringing in a detached third party for an overview;
- It improves the parties' communication skills and capability;
- It gives the parties a forum that enhances their ability to find a 'zone of agreement';
- Mediators act as joint advisers rather than partial advisers;
- Mediation is non-coercive – the parties can abandon it, if appropriate, and avoid the risk of imposed third party findings;
- Mediation can still lead to a binding settlement and does in most cases;
- The parties have greater control over the result and more scope to make it commercially acceptable or beneficial;
- The success rate is very high, over 80 per cent of mediations result in binding settlements, with satisfied parties on both sides also common. The case summaries in Part Two reflect the breadth of scope for mediation.

The importance of ADR techniques for contract draftsmen is the flexibility the process offers, thus being more adaptable to the context when differences arise. Without this flexibility it is easy for draftsmen to misjudge the person/procedure needed at a later date – for example, requiring appointment of a technical expert adjudicator when the dispute which arises is actually based on deep commercial, or political, rather than technical, difficulties. Also the process offers better opportunity to reduce the transaction costs of third party intervention.

Practical experience of this flexibility and cost saving potential is leading more and more businesses and advisers to insert mediation provisions into commercial contracts. For example, a direct outcome of the mediation over the wood-pulp processing plant described in Chapter 2, was that the Scandinavian lawyer redrew all the contracts of his client to insert a mediation provision. As previously mentioned, mediation was also included as a stage in one of the world's largest recent infrastructure projects, construction of the new Hong Kong airport. Further tiers (eg fast-track adjudication between mediation and arbitration), can be added to reinforce the safety-net impact of the dispute clauses (non-binding as was practised in the Hong Kong project). Recently international shipping companies have provided for mediation in charter party disputes.

International joint ventures/business alliances/mergers and acquisitions

Experience and research indicate that the overwhelming majority of strategic alliances, or mergers and acquisitions, fail to achieve the objectives they set out to achieve. This is particularly the case with international alliances or acquisitions. Failure to manage conflicts effectively is part of the source of this bleak picture.

Reasons for failure are typically inequality of competence in business and technical matters, failures of initial commitment, and failing to sustain commitment to making an alliance work.

> *'Among the hard lessons that experience has taught is that without ongoing attention and focus on common goals, partnerships wither and die ... partnerships have to sort out how to link their decision-making process, how they are going to resolve conflict, and how to build in the flexibility to make incremental improvements.'*

Gene Slowinski, Alliance Management Group.

Lack of identification of, or regular communication between, point people from both companies is also a common factor in the breakdown of continuing relationships. It is interesting that a number of major companies such as Disney and Hewlett Packard have appointed formal 'Alliance Executives'. Some companies such as Lotus and Xerox have set up separate Alliance Groups. Other ventures are supported by partnering philosophy and statements of principle. The essential features of effective alliance working focus on mutual outcomes, continuous improvement and problem/conflict resolution philosophy. When any one of these three dynamics is missing the relationship is at risk.

Continuous Improvement

RELATIONSHIP
OBJECTIVES

Conflict Resolution   Mutual Outcomes

The assisted negotiation model provided by mediation offers an opportunity for failing or failed joint ventures to be put back on track; and where this is not going to be the desired result, the parties have an opportunity to find the least destructive exit routes. (Planning for effective exit mechanisms should of course also be part of the conflict prevention thinking of the original contract draftsman.) The strategic objectives that seem an essential part of joint ventures or business alliances are increasingly recognised in global business conditions, and are also important in supply and other contracts. Competitive pressures mean that effective businesses need to partner with their suppliers and customers. Requirements for mediation in the contract provide a structured way of crystallising this culture into business/legal practice. Effective alliance thinking must really begin before a deal is signed. How to handle disputes as and when they arise should be considered in a positive rather than negative light, with acknowledgement that even in the very best of strategic alliances there will necessarily be differences. It is how they are handled that will distinguish the good from the mediocre or disastrous alliance. Methods have to be in place to handle these differences in a timely and appropriate manner. In this context, mediation provides a unique tool for crystallising the most constructive business approaches to alliance differences.

The contract drafter should therefore understand how the 'partners' intend to make their relationship work on a day-to-day basis at the operational and business level as well as for the strategic objectives. This will provide valuable clues as to how to handle more serious disputes if and when they arise, and where best to locate mediation.

The challenges are greater in an international strategic alliance because of different cultures and business practices. Therefore, there is an even greater need for positive dialogue, investigation and commitment to make the contract terms work, both on a day-to-day basis and over the longer term. Even businesses which do not anticipate breakdown of relationships will still benefit from a tiered structure of formal dispute resolution provisions which will respond to the seriousness, duration and potential risk of differences.

Clients do not want to feel that the lawyers have hijacked their business venture but there should be a recognition that, in order to create a viable legal structure that works for the client, it is important that the lawyers and the clients first work with each other to develop the goals of the alliance, and then do the same with the other side's team. In other words, the ideal relationship between lawyers and their clients should model that of an effective partnering contract.

Major project management and mediation

Most organisations engage in complex projects, either on their own account or more often engaged with other organisations. Some kind of relationship or communication breakdown is a real possibility over the lifetime of such projects, it is *a known risk*. Building in access to mediation is common sense, making clear what and who can trigger resort to it, and when. Even more powerful however, on any project of major complexity or size, is again not to work with mediation only as a crisis measure, but as an integral part of the project framework and process. It is relatively little cost against the typical cost of such projects, to enlist a 'Project Mediator' (or Project Adviser/Neutral) who can be appointed at the outset of the project and run with it as an integral part of the accepted management. Typically such an individual would run an early communications workshop to educate the team on negotiation and conflict management issues, get to know the programme, personalities and the project objectives, and would then stay in touch and be available to intervene when there are early signs of the project 'going off the rails'. This approach also leaves the neutral free to suggest a more formal mediation process if he or she has grown too close to the players over the course of the project. A similar appointment can be used in formal business alliances.

The nature of some businesses (or public sector bodies) is that they will already be involved in major projects – construction, energy, or major IT businesses, for example. Many of them have developed some of the best practices brought to conflicts by external mediators and absorbed this into in-house culture. However, our experience suggests that even those companies still have a missing element in failing to recognise the added value of the appointment of a project mediator. For example many of them run 'partnering workshops' at the outset of their projects, then fail to build infrastructure for dealing with potential breakdowns other than relying on internal management teams busy with their own operational and budget priorities. Others have implemented concepts close to the Project Mediator – for example the 'Dispute Review Board' is widely recognised as a third party tool for major international construction projects, although more formal and detached.

Other companies can still learn much from studying how major construction or energy companies have structured best practice in complex projects, in order to develop a systematic project management approach for their more occasional engagement with major projects. Areas to consider in design of a better-structured project management approach would be:

- An agreed project team – including technical, financial, legal, personnel to monitor ongoing results of the venture/project.
- If possible ask the other party/parties to the venture to have a similar project team.
- Ensure that all major developments, successful or otherwise, are notified to the members of the project team of all parties on a timely basis.
- Design incentives for managers based on joint problem-solving activity with their own team and the other party's team.
- Identify individual decision-makers within your own team and the other party's team.
- Where you have to deal with government bodies, understand their decision-making process.
- Ensure that your team has lingual fluency and cultural competency.
- If your project plan and contract do not respond to the way the project is actually developing, re-design them, keeping the protection of the original document and framework until the new plan emerges.
- Brainstorm with your own team and the other side's team to find solutions to problems, including improvements.
- Transfer personnel between contracting organisations to build a relationship and to create some bridges for future issues.
- Engage in negotiating and problem-solving training as a team and ideally involve the other party. Build these training costs into the original budget.
- Track success and failure. Use different measures – financial, technical, legal, commercial, future opportunity, use of time and management.
- Test all assumptions in your own team and the other party's team.
- Consider 'principled bargaining techniques' in your own team and with the other party's team.
- Track the success of the project where you use this systematic approach against others where the approach is less systematic.

Contracts and relationships worth potentially millions in earned revenue and reputation deserve an ongoing commitment to make them work. The challenges are greater in an international venture because of the differences of culture and business practices, and require an even greater need for positive dialogue, investigation and commitment. Each party in a negotiation has to be clear as to their mission, able to identify their own and other parties' decision-makers and able to understand the resource each party has in terms of time, costs and other influencing factors. In order to get the necessary information, negotiation needs to take place in a calm and reflective manner, able to address one's own trouble spots as well as those of other parties. They should also be prepared to engage in constructive yet firm negotiations, and to keep the momentum of communication moving. All of this is more easily achieved if the organisations involved have already 'bought' in to a Project Mediation approach to relationship issues as well as to the operational project issues. With adoption of a Project Mediation approach, risk management and relationship management are brought into a common arena, a shared space. Ultimately the question in complex international project management should not be 'Can we afford to invest in the extra cost of a Project Mediator?', but instead *'Can we afford to take the risk of the additional conflict costs by not having a Project Mediator?'*

> *Facilitating corporate strategy*
> *An oil company found itself in an adversarial relationship with its myriad of retail sub-contractors across several countries. It recognised the competitive disadvantage this created against other companies where mutual gain had become a business norm. The company set in motion a cultural revolution, bringing in a mediation team to facilitate substantive dialogue on management systems and commercial relations. The mediation team worked with the company and its retailers not only to establish new terms and conditions of the relationship, but also to build up a long-term internal mediation facility which could intervene to prevent future 'slippage' on the new cultural values and impact. The new facility enabled both internal and external mediators to be deployed quickly according to the seriousness and sensitivity of conflicts arising.*

Regulators and public sector organisations in the global market

While the public sector has its own culture and constraints that typically infect it as much as national cultural considerations, it is equally prone like business (sometimes more so) to partial perspectives, groupthink, positional stances, conflict avoidance – all the problem-solving and negotiation failings that can beset private sector players. Public sector bodies are now just as often part of an international fabric of stakeholders and connections as most major businesses, and sometimes major international institutions in their own right (UN, WTO, World Bank, NATO, European Commission, OECD etc). National states are also regularly engaged, not only with other states, but also with public, private and NGO communities. All of the advantages and areas listed above for bringing mediation into the bloodstream of active business organisations apply equally to public sector bodies. Governments and public agencies act as contractors of services,

147

deliver major infrastructure projects, develop and work with political and economic alliances, are national and international employers and have critical stakeholder and governance challenges. In all these areas there is scope to enlist deeper thinking about creative design of relationship and risk management, and to attract support for this by pulling in the best of mediation understanding and players.

Key constraints in public bodies of course have to be recognised – especially their need for consistency, transparency and for verification through audit trails, as well as their sensitivity to public mood and attitudes, and to the legal frameworks in which they must operate. All of these have echoes in business practice, but generally loom larger for the public body. These constraints do not bar mediation as a concept, but do call for parties and negotiators to learn how to adapt it to the public context. For example, to be more open about the process and its outcomes, to structure mediations to give more time for consultation over recommended outcomes, to develop precedent agreements for regulatory application, and so on. It is likely to be an especially challenging arena of international mediation practice, but again one where mediation can deliver a socially striking contribution to 21st century governance and rule-making.

Infrastructure for global business Diplomacy

Promotion of international mediation practice and theory is only one half of the overall equation of how global business diplomacy can develop. Equal attention must be paid to the suppliers of mediation services. Questions inevitably need to be addressed regarding the quality and effectiveness of the industry, of the systems in place to provide not only effective dispute resolution services, but also the kind of products and ideas that can ensure mediation will be adapted and absorbed into the business bloodstream. And new systems and leadership need to be ensured in order to sustain and grow the field.

In this respect there is still considerable work to be done. Effective training of mediators and mediation teams able to operate globally is still in an early stage of evolution. Credibility of providers is also still at an early stage, although rapidly developing. Investment in the infrastructure of mediation organisations, by governments or business, remains modest compared to legal system support. Companies operating from economies where mediation is still in its infancy, also have more of a learning gap to help them regularly access mediation as a global management tool.

Infrastructure for global business Diplomacy

Strong domestic mediation developments, however, are hastening the creation of a global infrastructure. The first truly global alliance of mediation providers was set up by CEDR in connection with the potential conflicts anticipated following the 'Y2K' problem, ie, computers failing to recognise dates after 1999. The worst-case predictions for the 'millennium bug' anticipated an explosion of subsequent litigation and business disputes. CEDR, at the request of Cable and Wireless plc, an international telecommunications company, put together a global initiative, 'The Millennium Accord', to ensure an effective mediation approach was available to potential disputes. The initiative also drew in other ADR organisations worldwide in recognition of the important international connectedness of Y2K issues.

While the Y2K 'doomsday' phenomenon was thankfully never realised, the concept of identifying a need for accelerating development of a global mediation capability remains. It cannot be realised by loose associations of individual mediators if it is going to achieve the kind of impact on our society that we have identified as possible and necessary in the last two chapters.

Since our first book, we have worked on developing another international alliance of mediation providers, now described as MEDAL (the international mediation alliance). See Part Two of this text for its rules of case referral. This runs alongside other initiatives by mediation and arbitration bodies, including efforts by the international professional legal bodies to create a community of mediation specialists. Finding a brand and a business structure that can support substantial growth of global business diplomacy, remains a key challenge.

All of these efforts foretell a significant revolution in both dispute practice internationally, and in best business practices in conflict management. If successful as a professional project, international mediation practice will help create a bridge between eastern and western, ancient and modern, legal cultures. Also, between the formal traditions of national legal cultures and the fluid forms of negotiated rule-making that will be necessary to support the global marketplace of the 21st Century. The art of international commercial mediation 'ambassadors' will be to help make global business diplomacy through mediation, the 'common sense' option for business executives and justice systems in this new, volatile and competitive global marketplace. The 'flattening' of the world through global business/ political developments needs also a 'rounded' or holistic system and methodology to address the richness of culture and conflicts in our global community. International mediation is a key pillar in building that structure.

Diplomacy at the Heart of Business

'While there can be a competitive element to negotiation, particularly in determining the division of gains, it is usually counterproductive to think of negotiation as adversarial. Negotiating models built on gamesmanship, in particular, lend themselves to military and sports analogies. Such adversarial models break down on one important point: you can't have a loser in a successful negotiation. If you approach a negotiation with the objective of 'defeating' an 'opponent', your chances of winning from the process are poor.'

Griffin & Daggatt, The Global Negotiator.

PART TWO

Cases and Materials in International Mediation

1   Cases

Introduction

In Part 2 we have drawn together a number of international cases mediated through CEDR, many by the authors, to provide the reader with a flavour of the type of disputes where parties have made real progress in resolving their disputes by working with a mediator and the disciplines of the process. The nationality and some facts have been changed where necessary to protect identity of the parties. The international elements or the essence of what occurred has not been diminished by these amendments.

The instructive part of the case studies is often the feedback from the clients. A summary of their observations includes the following key elements:
(1)   The benefits of early mediation.
(2)   The value of face-to-face dialogue managed by an experienced mediator.
(3)   Understanding the case and the psychology behind it can be critical to unlocking the negotiations.
(4)   The positive benefits – the certainty and control over the result coupled with huge savings in fees and time.
(5)   The experience of mediating drove the impetus to incorporate mediation into future contracts and to use mediation before arbitration.
(6)   The legal team have emerged with satisfied clients.
(7)   The benefits of mediation for complex disputes where there may be key question marks regarding conflicts of laws.
(8)   Mediation is very suited to dealing with cultural differences of doing business.
(9)   The small organisation can feel there is a level playing field because of the independent intervention in the negotiation.
(10) The ability to ask for and receive a non-binding recommendation is very helpful in some international infrastructure projects.

Construction and Engineering

(a) Nationality of Parties: Italian and Saudi Arabian

Facts: The parties involved in this dispute undertook a project in consortium in Saudi Arabia. The project description was for a water transmission system. During the execution of the Project a dispute arose between the Consortium Partners related to the Scope of Work between the parties for the design and supply of electrical items.

Amount in Dispute: US $240,000

Route to Mediation: With respect to the Consortium Agreement, the second party to the dispute decided to take the issue to Third Party Arbitration and informed the Consortium Partner. After considering this proposal, both parties agreed to utilise the services of CEDR.

Time Between Decision to Mediate and Final Outcome: Two months

Mediators' Pre-mediation Work: Eight hours of preparation

Length of Mediation: One day

Cost per party (includes preparation): US $2,500

Conclusion/Post-mediation Work: The parties settled their dispute through the mediation process. The settlement agreement was that the Consortium Leader would pay a substantial percentage of the cost of the supply of the items in question and the second party to the dispute would pay the remaining percentage. The engineering of surge vessel lighting would be done jointly by both parties. Apart from lighting design, engineering works for cathodic protection, cable sizing and routing would be carried out by the Consortium Leader.

(b) Nationality of Parties: Malawian and British

Facts: This dispute arose between party A, a Malawian employer, and party B, a UK Contractor, in connection with the construction of a road in Malawi funded by a public body. The Contractor presented a number of claims for extra time and payment. The Engineer gave his decision on the claim, as required under the relevant clause of the Conditions of Contract, and the Contractor registered his disagreement with this decision.

Amount in Dispute: US $19.2 million

Route to Mediation: The Contractor declared a dispute, requested an Engineers' decision under the relevant clause of the Conditions of Contract, declared his dissatisfaction and gave requisite notice under that same clause of referral to arbitration. Subsequently, both parties agreed to attempt an amicable settlement to the claims as envisaged under the Contract by entering into a CEDR mediation. CEDR had previous contacts with the public body financing the Project.

Date Arbitration Commenced: The possibility of arbitration had been discussed but had not commenced.

Time Between Decision to Mediate and Final Outcome: Ten months

Mediators' Pre-mediation Work: Preliminary meetings were held between CEDR, the public body funding the construction project and the Contractor. Prior to the start of the mediation process, the Mediators and Expert Adviser conducted two days of preparation.

Length of Mediation: Six and a half days

Cost per party (includes preparation): US $52,000

Conclusion/Post-mediation Work: The parties settled their dispute through the mediation process within the range recommended by the Mediation Report.

Comments from those involved:

The Contractor stated '... *I believe mediation to have some merit in that the costs associated and the timescale experienced in this complex case have been significantly lower and shorter than had we been required to proceed to arbitration,' and estimated cost savings of 'probably not less than $240,000.'*

(c) Nationality of Parties: Spanish and Norwegian

Facts: This dispute concerned a contract for the installation and laying of offshore piping for the construction of a sea outlet sewage pipe in Southern Europe. The sub-contractor (A) claimed from the head contractor (B), and alternatively the pipe manufacturer (C) who engaged them to install the pipes, payment for work it carried out under the Contract. A claimed from B, and alternatively, C, repayment of sums expended under the Contract. B also claimed unspecified damages, liquidated damages against C, an account between the parties, an indemnity from C for any liability B had to A, interest and costs. Along with costs, C claimed against B, for the amount it was found to be liable to A; similarly, against A, for the amount it was found to be liable to B.

Amount in Dispute: US $1,549,702

Route to Mediation: Due to the costs of arbitration proceedings, the parties agreed between themselves to refer the matter to mediation.

Time Between Decision to Mediate and Final Outcome: Eight months

Mediators' Pre-mediation work: Ten hours of preparation

Length of Mediation: Two days

Cost per party (includes preparation): US $4,332

Conclusion/Post-mediation Work: The mediation itself was unsuccessful in settling the dispute but it helped to create an appropriate environment for subsequent settlement. The end of the mediation saw the conclusion of all

155

matters except interest. The ultimate settlement was not far from the position reached at the end of the mediation and avoided a 12-week arbitration.

Comments from those involved:

One of the parties stated, '*The advantage of mediation was bringing the parties face to face and enabling them to carry out reasoned without prejudice discussions with each other with the help of an experienced mediator.***'**

(d) Nationality of Parties: Far Eastern and Canadian

Facts: A contract was made between Party C, a Canadian company, of the one part and Parties A and B, Far Eastern Companies, of the other part in which was set out the terms and conditions for the completion of a construction project. Following completion and delivery of the Project, Party C alleged certain deficiencies and uncompleted work and made a number of claims against Party A for costs allegedly incurred by Party C in rectifying the alleged deficiencies and uncompleted work. Party A denied liability to Party C for the alleged incurred costs and this formed the basis of the dispute.

Route to Mediation: A partner in a London law firm recommended mediation. It was decided to hold the mediation in London since London was regarded as a neutral venue.

Amount in Dispute: Approximately US $50 million

Time Between Decision to Mediate and Final Outcome: One month

Mediators' Pre-mediation Work: Ten hours

Length of Mediation: Three days

Cost per party (includes preparation): US $7,700

Conclusion/Post-mediation Work: The parties settled their dispute shortly after three days of mediation.

Comments from those involved:

One of the parties stated, '*There is no doubt in my mind and I am sure the principals agree, that without the mediation process which you [the Mediator] and [the Assistant Mediator] conducted there would have been little hope of settling this matter prior to trial ... Once again, I wish to extend my thanks and appreciation ... for the efforts both of you made to resolve the dispute.***'**

Corporate Acquisition

Nationality of parties: Spanish and Italian

Facts: This was a post-acquisition dispute involving the chemical industry. It related to the terms of alleged breaches of a Stock Purchase Agreement (SPA), where Party A acquired shares in a subsidiary of Party B, but then claimed that the seller was in breach of various warranties. Originally five heads of claim were involved in the dispute, although some were dispensed with before the mediation.

Amount in dispute: US $12.8 million

Route to mediation: The dispute was governed by Italian law and the SPA had no mediation provision. However, as a result of an agreement between the Italian and Spanish lawyers, the parties agreed between themselves to refer the matter to CEDR Solve for mediation.

Time between decision to mediate and final outcome: Eight months

Mediator's pre-mediation work: 12 hours of preparation

Length of mediation: Two days

Cost per party (includes preparation work): US $9,000

Conclusion/post mediation work: The parties settled the dispute successfully through the mediation process.

Comments from those involved:

Party A stated '*it was really our pleasure to take full advantage of the mediator's skills in order to find a settlement which in my view is truly satisfactory for both parties. Her understanding of both the case and the parties' psychology, was a key factor in un-locking the negotiations.*'

Party B's legal representative said that the mediator '*was most helpful in moving the parties into a settlement and therefore into reaching a successful resolution at mediation*'. **He went on to comment that the mediator** '*succeeded in building a good rapport with both parties, explaining the reason and clarifying the arguments of each party and convincing them of the reasonable basis of the reached agreement.*'

Corporate Raiding

(a) Nationality of Parties: American and Swiss

Facts: This dispute concerned the Respondent's hiring of numerous members of the Claimant's Geneva, Switzerland, branch office, including the acting branch manager and the three largest producers of business in the office. The Claimant believed that the Respondent's actions constituted a mass hiring of a competitor's salesforce using improper means. The Claimant commenced arbitration proceedings against the Respondent alleging an illegal raid and seeking damages in excess of US $7.5 million. The case was governed by New York law.

Amount in Dispute: US $7.5 million

Route to Mediation: Arbitration in New York was administratively adjourned pending the outcome of this mediation.

Time Between Decision to Mediate and Final Outcome: Two months

Mediators' Pre-mediation Work: Ten hours of preparation

Length of Mediation: Two days

Cost per party (includes preparation): US $9,000

Conclusion/Post-mediation Work: The parties settled their dispute through the mediation process.

Comments from those involved:

The Claimant stated that the main benefits to their organisation of using the mediation process rather than litigation were *'certainty of result, huge time savings, usually huge savings in fees, control [of result]'*. Importantly, the Claimant also felt that the mediation had preserved the relationship between the parties, *'Yes, we left on reasonably good terms.'*

Energy

(a) Nationality of Parties: Spanish and French

Facts: The claimants supply and maintain back-up power generators and other sorts of alternative energy to supplement a variable national supply. Towards this end, they contracted with the defendants for several units of uninterruptible power supplies. Subsequently, they claimed that many of the units failed so they did not pay the remaining invoice and sued for loss of business and repair costs. The defendants counter sued for the remaining invoice, asserting that any unit failure would have been as a result of improper handling on the claimant's part.

Amount in dispute: US $460 million

Route to Mediation: Both parties agreed to put a stay on their respective litigation and enter into mediation.

Time between Decision to Mediate and Final Outcome: Three and a half months

Mediator's Pre-mediation Work: Ten hours of preparation

Length of Mediation: One day

Cost per Party (including preparation): US $8,000

Conclusion/Post-mediation Work: The parties settled with a cooperative agreement

Comments from those involved:

One party commented that both the lawyer and their client were, *'absolutely delighted with the settlement and with the whole process from start to finish.'*

Financial Services

(a) Nationality of Parties: Far Eastern and British

Facts: This dispute arose out of the imposition of exchange controls by the Malaysian monetary authorities and the effect this had on derivatives contracts which were open between the parties at the time.

Amount in Dispute: Approximately US $16 million

Route to Mediation: Proceedings had been commenced in the Commercial Court, London, and CEDR was approached as a result of a direction given by the Court that the parties should attempt to resolve their differences by mediation.

Time Between Decision to Mediate and Final Outcome: Two months

Mediators' Pre-mediation Work: A preliminary meeting was held between the parties' legal representatives and CEDR. Prior to the mediation itself, the Mediators conducted one day's preparation.

Length of Mediation: Two days

Cost per party (includes preparation): US $12,560

Conclusion/Post-mediation Work: After two days of mediation the parties had failed to secure a settlement. However, the mediation process paved the way for a successful settlement agreement, which was reached a few months later.

Comments from those involved:

The legal representative of Party A stated, ' *... we managed to resolve in five months a matter that would probably have led to a couple of years of expensive and management time-intensive litigation ... Following this good experience, I will be suggesting to clients ... that they consider incorporating into their contracts an ADR formula and when disputes arise I shall be able to suggest with some authority that they consider mediation as a possible way of resolving the matter, particularly where there is a long-term relationship at stake.'*

159

(b) Nationality of Parties: French, American, British and Italian

Facts: The Claimant, a French bank, entered into a Global Custody Agreement with the Respondent, a London-based subsidary of a US bank, whereby the Respondent agreed to provide the Claimant with global custody services. The Claimant's claim against the Respondent was for breach of the Agreement and/or breach of a contractual or tortious duty of care and/or breach of fiduciary duty relating to custody services provided in respect of certain shares in an Italian company as a result of which the Claimant had suffered loss. The Respondent denied that it was negligent or in breach of the Agreement and denied that the Claimant had suffered any loss as a result of its conduct.

Amount in Dispute: US $450,000

Route to Mediation: The parties felt it probable that a Court would order that mediation be considered by the parties and so they elected to pre-empt that by voluntary mediation. The Claimant's legal representative proposed the mediation and referred the case to CEDR.

Date Proceedings Commenced: Proceedings had not commenced.

Time Between Decision to Mediate and Final Outcome: Two months

Mediators' Pre-mediation Work: Six hours of preparation

Length of Mediation: One day

Cost per party (includes preparation): US $2,240

Conclusion/Post-mediation Work: The parties settled their dispute through the mediation process. The key turning points were said to be the Respondent's willingness to answer queries raised by the Claimant concerning the factual sequence of events and its internal management structure changes and an apology from the Respondent, face to face, for being non-responsive.

Comments from those involved:

One of the parties stated that the main benefits to their organisation of using the mediation process were, '... *time saving ... [and a] smoother settlement of the argument.'*

Franchise

(a) Nationality of Parties: Canadian and British

Facts: This dispute arose in connection with a commercial arrangement between the parties. The Claimant was a franchise owner, in the UK, of the

160

Canadian Respondent's management system. The allegations in the Claimant's lawsuit included fraudulent or negligent misrepresentations, breach of contract and malicious falsehood and included claims for an injunction and exemplary damages.

Amount in Dispute: In excess of US $640,000

Route to Mediation: The parties themselves agreed to refer the matter to mediation.

Time Between Decision to Mediate and Final Outcome: Four months

Mediators' Pre-mediation Work: Eight hours of preparation

Length of Mediation: One day

Cost per party (includes preparation): US $2,800

Conclusion/Post-mediation Work: Although the mediation was unable to achieve a settlement at the time, the Mediator continued to deal with the parties until a settlement was eventually reached.

Comments from those involved:

The Claimant and lawyers wrote after the mediation to '*express our thanks for the service provided by your organization and the patience and courtesy displayed by the mediator ...*'

Information Technology

(a) *Nationality of Parties: American and British*

Facts: A mortgage and loan company entered into a ten-year agreement with an information technology company to provide the IT services for all its offices. Three years into the contract a dispute occurred over invoicing and payment. The IT company claimed that they had not been paid for their services while the mortgage and loan company claimed that improper invoicing was occurring.

Amount in dispute: US $314.5 million

Route to Mediation: As stipulated in the original outsourcing contract, the two parties agreed to enter into mediation before resorting to litigation.

Time between Decision to Mediate and Final Outcome: Four months

Mediator's Pre-mediation Work: Ten hours of preparation including extensive pre-mediation phone conversations with both parties.

Length of Mediation: Two days

Cost per Party (including preparation): US $10,000

Conclusion/Post-mediation Work: The mediation ended in a settlement, which preserved the cordial working relationship between the two companies and the remaining contract.

(b) Nationality of Parties: British, American and German

Facts: The parties entered into a contract to design, develop and customize an electronic network-based trading system in order for the Claimant, a UK company, to run live auctions on the Internet. The Respondent was also to provide support and maintenance for the System. The Claimant alleged that during a ten-month period the System malfunctioned. They alleged that the System crashed four times during live auctions. The Claimant purported to terminate the Contract for material breach and claimed damages. The Respondent and guarantors alleged that the Claimant was in repudiatory breach of the Contract and counterclaimed damages.

Amount in Dispute: US $3.2 million

Route to Mediation: The parties agreed to refer the matter to mediation.

Time Between Decision to Mediate and Final Outcome: Four months

Mediators' Pre-mediation Work: Eight hours of preparation

Length of Mediation: One day

Cost per party (includes preparation): US $5,200

Conclusion/Post-mediation Work: The parties achieved a settlement through the mediation process.

Comments from those involved:

The senior manager of one of the parties commented *'the mediation allowed a proper airing of the issues and made it possible to find an acceptable settlement figure and the mediator was very good – she kept us talking when it looked impossible.'*

(c) Nationality of parties: British and Swiss

Facts: The dispute arose from an agreement between the parties for the distribution of software. Party A owned the software and entered into a distribution agreement, under which Party B was granted an exclusive licence to market, distribute and support certain defined Licensed Software. Party A sought damages for an alleged breach of the agreement, in that the software was not in accordance with specifications. This was denied by Party B, who then issued a counterclaim for royalties withheld by Party A.

Amount in dispute: US $5 million

Route to mediation: The parties were in the early stages of an ICC arbitration; they then agreed between themselves to refer the matter to mediation.

Time between decision to mediate and final outcome: Three months

Mediator's pre-mediation work: Ten hours of preparation

Length of mediation: One day
Cost per party (includes preparation work): US $10,300
Conclusion/post-mediation work: The parties failed to settle their dispute through the mediation process on the day. However, the case settled shortly after mediation due to the active work of the mediator.
Comments from those involved:
Party A's lawyer thought that the mediation process *'certainly helped in reaching a settlement in principle'*. He also stated that he appreciated the *'tenacity and hard work'* of the mediator and assistant mediator both on the day and afterwards.

Insurance/Reinsurance

(a) Nationality of parties: Central American, American, European

Facts: Party A ran a power plant, which was insured by Party B. The generator at the power plant broke down due to a faulty part and Party A made a claim under its insurance policy for property damage and business interruption losses. Party B and its reinsurers denied liability on a number of accounts, including non-disclosure of a material risk (the defective part), which they claimed had already been brought to Party A's attention following similar incidents. Party A had allegedly failed to take reasonable action to secure new parts and was thus deemed to be grossly negligent, a terminating event under the insurance contract.
Amount in dispute: US $8 million
Route to mediation: The parties agreed between themselves to refer the matter to mediation, pre-issue.
Time between decision to mediate and final outcome: Two months
Mediator's pre-mediation work: Ten hours of preparation
Length of mediation: Two days
Cost per party (includes preparation work): $11,000
Conclusion/post-mediation work: A Memorandum of Understanding was signed and full settlement followed.
Comments from those involved:
The Claimant's lawyer said that *'the mediation was a success'* and that afterwards he could see *'a way forward'*. He thought that the way the mediator handled herself was faultless. The other party's lawyer stated that they achieved exactly what he expected.

163

(*b*) *Nationality of parties: Argentinean and British*

Facts: This dispute involved the obligations of Party A under reinsurance contracts relating to personal accident programmes, written in relation to transport companies in Argentina and reinsured to the Claimant in the UK. The key issue was the effect of devaluation of the currency resulting from legislation in Argentina, which on one interpretation meant that Party A had almost no liability under the reinsurance policy. As a result, they had brought negative declaratory proceedings in England and had secured a positive ruling on jurisdiction.

Amount in dispute: US $45 million

Route to mediation: The matter came to mediation post-issue via a Court Order, after Party B challenged the jurisdiction in English courts.

Time between decision to mediate and final outcome: Three weeks

Mediator's pre-mediation work: Eight hours of preparation

Length of mediation: One day

Cost per party (includes preparation work): US $7,300

Conclusion/post mediation work: The parties settled their dispute through the mediation process and a Tomlin Order was agreed.

Comments from those involved:

The lawyer for Party B stated that the mediation process was as she had expected and that she would use the mediator again in the future.

(*c*) *Nationality of Parties: Spanish and British*

Facts: This dispute arose in connection with an insurance coverage claim. The Claimant was found liable in Spain for damage caused by pollution from a kaolin mine and made a claim against a general liability insurance policy issued by the Respondent. The Respondent denied the claim and relied, inter alia, on exclusion clauses under the policy.

Amount in Dispute: US $4 million

Route to Mediation: The parties were obligated to attempt mediation by Order of the Commercial Court, London.

Time Between Decision to Mediate and Final Outcome: Two months

Mediators' Pre-mediation Work: Eight hours of preparation

Length of Mediation: One day

Cost per party (includes preparation): US $4,400

Conclusion/Post-mediation Work: The parties settled their dispute through the mediation process. The mediation clarified the issues and amounts involved and enabled commercial factors to be introduced, which was the breakthrough. The settlement Agreement was the payment of an agreed sum in four instalments payable over three years. The parties also agreed to take all steps necessary to terminate the litigation simultaneously with the execution of the Agreement.

Comments from those involved:

One of the parties involved stated, ' ... *this mediation was certainly a successful and cost saving exercise ... It achieved a settlement, which the clients were satisfied with. Previously the other side had rejected settlement approaches.'*

(d) Nationality of Parties: Lebanese and British

Facts: This dispute arose in connection with the recovery of claims under a quota share reinsurance treaty. The insurance company, a Lebanese insurer, claimed for an unpaid claim plus interest. The reinsurers, a London company, counterclaimed for fraud in connection with the claims and, alternatively, breach of contract for fraudulent non-disclosure in respect of premium and/or fraudulent inflation of claims.

Amount in Dispute: US $5 million: $2 million claim plus $3 million counterclaim.

Route to Mediation: This dispute was referred to mediation by the Commercial Court, London,

Time Between Decision to Mediate and Final Outcome: Three months

Mediators' Pre-mediation Work: Eight hours of preparation

Length of Mediation: One day

Cost per party (includes preparation): US $3,000

Conclusion/Post-mediation Work: The parties ultimately failed to settle their dispute through the mediation process. Although the parties were quite close at the end of the day they were unable finally to close the gap. The reinsurers asked the Mediator to suggest a non-binding recommendation. About four months later, the insurance company approached the Mediator to comment further on the recommendation because it had become clear that the parties had very different interpretations of what had been said and this was the cause, or one of the causes, of a breakdown in further negotiations. The Mediator offered to clarify the recommendations in order to get them back on track.

Comments from those involved:

One of the parties stated, with regard to the mediation process, that the *'potential benefit is [the] mediator's given opinion of what a good settlement would be – this could be seen as something to work towards.'*

(*e*) *Nationality of Parties: American and European*

Facts: This two-party dispute arose in connection with a series of retrocessional treaties, which governed the retrocession of property and casualty reinsurance by the Respondent, a US company, to the Claimant, the representative of a number of reinsurers from London and Continental Europe. A group of reinsurers initiated a court proceeding seeking rescission of all of the treaties alleging fraud and breach of duty of utmost good faith. They sought repayment of losses previously paid to the Respondent. The Respondent filed a counterclaim requesting payment of its unreimbursed losses.

Amount in Dispute: US $25 million

Route to Mediation: This matter had been ongoing for 12 years. There were 12 to 13 reinsurers involved in long-tail litigation. The idea of mediation was to settle a small number of disputes as well as the main one. The Claimant's legal representative knew the Co-Mediators were involved in a large dispute successfully mediated and approached them to mediate the dispute.

Time Between Decision to Mediate and Final Outcome: Four months

Mediators' Pre-mediation Work A conference call, involving both parties' legal representatives and the Co-Mediators, took place to discuss the mediation procedure. Two days of preparation were conducted by the Co-Mediators prior to the mediation itself.

Length of Mediation: Three days

Cost per party (includes preparation): US $20,800

Conclusion/Post-mediation Work: The parties could not reach a settlement at the mediation but their negotiation continued and developed following the mediation with a number of separate settlements achieved.

(*f*) *Nationality of Parties: American and British*

Facts: This dispute arose in connection with allegations by Party A, a UK insurance company, of fraud in the placement and conduct of reinsurance contracts; alternatively, breaches of reinsurance contracts, and allegations by Party B, a US insurance company, of non-payment of balances due under reinsurance contracts.

Amount in Dispute: US $80 million

Route to Mediation: Proceedings were in process. However, the parties agreed to refer the matter to mediation.

Time Between Decision to Mediate and Final Outcome: Four months

Mediators' Pre-mediation Work: Two preliminary meetings were held involving the Case Manager and the Mediators and all parties' legal representatives by video conference link. Three days of preparation, prior to the mediation itself, were carried out by the mediators.

Length of Mediation: Four days

Cost per party (includes preparation): US $22,400

Conclusion/Post-mediation Work: The parties settled their dispute through the mediation process.

Comments from those involved:

One of the parties involved said that the mediation process helped preserve their business relationship with the other party, *'because the issues we were litigating were particularly corrosive'* and when asked to estimate their cost savings, the same party said that it was *'impossible to say with any accuracy but [savings] could have run to hundreds of thousands of pounds'.*

Intellectual Property

(a) *Nationality of parties: American and British*

Facts: The dispute concerned an allegation by Party A that in founding a company, Party B had breached its fiduciary duties, misappropriated trade secrets and engaged in other torts. Party B denied these allegations.

Amount in dispute: US $200,000

Route to mediation: After the parties had conducted informal settlement discussions and could not arrive at an agreement, they agreed amongst themselves to attempt one last chance through formal mediation.

Time between decision to mediate and final outcome: One month

Mediator's pre-mediation work: Eight hours of preparation

Length of mediation: One day

Cost per party (includes preparation work): US $4,800

Conclusion/post-mediation work: The parties settled the dispute successfully through the mediation process.

Comments from those involved:

One of the parties' legal representatives stated that the mediator's pre-mediation contact was the best that he had ever seen and that the mediation was very efficiently put together by CEDR Solve.

The (American) lawyer for the other party was not familiar with mediation in the UK, and commented that the mediator was very good at dealing with a dispute involving both the British and US legal

systems. She said the mediator was *'prepared, clearly intelligent, experienced and she worked really hard to get it done'*.

(b) Nationality of parties: European and British

Facts: The dispute arose over a promotion run by Party A offering tickets to an international sports match. Party B obtained an interim, prohibiting injunction against the promotion, claiming that it ran contrary to their strict rules on ticket sales and distributions. Party A sought to pursue damages on the cross undertaking given to them at the time of the injunction.

Amount in dispute: US $1.3 million

Route to mediation: After ongoing negotiations proved unsuccessful, the parties sought a stay on a directions hearing that was due, and agreed between themselves to refer the matter to mediation.

Time between decision to mediate and final outcome: Three weeks

Mediator's pre-mediation work: Ten hours of preparation

Length of mediation: One day

Cost per party (includes preparation work): US $5,600

Conclusion/post-mediation work: The parties adjourned the mediation to explore a sponsorship deal as a method of resolution. They failed however to reach agreement. The mediator stayed in telephone contact and brokered a financial settlement of the litigation as an alternative. A joint statement had been agreed.

Comments from those involved:

Party B's lawyer was pleased with the way that the day was handled. He thought the mediator did well to manage the parties in what was an emotional case. He was very pleased with the mediation service and thought that there was nothing further that CEDR Solve could have done. Party A's lawyer agreed that it was an excellent service and stated that it was *'very efficient, organised and helpful'*.

(c) Nationality of Parties: American and British

Facts: The Claimant, UK-based, represented a number of small businesses, which had been producing spare parts for motor vehicles over a period of many years. The Respondent, a European subsidiary of a US parent company, attempted to enforce intellectual property rights over the spare parts.

Amount in Dispute: Approximately US $1.6 million

Route to Mediation: The Respondent Company proposed mediation through CEDR.

Time Between Decision to Mediate and Final Outcome: Eight months

Mediators' Pre-mediation Work: There was a meeting between the Respondent Company, their legal representatives and CEDR. There was a further meeting between the Respondent Company's Patent Agent, their legal representative and the Claimant's legal representative. Prior to the mediation itself, the Mediator conducted eight hours of preparation.

Length of Mediation: One day

Cost per party (includes preparation): US $4,600

Conclusion/Post-mediation Work: The parties achieved a successful settlement through the mediation process.

Comments from those involved:

One party commented *'the mediation was very well conducted and allowed us to make a breakthrough in a difficult situation. We had really not expected to settle this'*.

International Trade and Distribution

(a) Nationality of Parties: American and British

Facts: The Respondent, a UK company, appointed the Claimant, a subsidiary of a US parent company, as distributor of horse feed products first, for Japan, then other Far Eastern Countries, then France and part of the UK. The Respondent later purported to terminate those distributorships.

The Claimant secured a court order that the terminations were unlawful and sought damages, injunctions and compensation for breach.

Amount in Dispute: Between US $1.6 million and $8 million

Route to Mediation: The Commercial Court, London, ordered that the Claimant's application for Summary Judgment be adjourned pending an attempt by the parties to resolve their differences by ADR provided that such was concluded within six weeks.

Time between Decision to Mediate and Final Outcome: Two months

Mediators' Pre-mediation Work: Ten hours of preparation

Length of Mediation: One day

Cost per party (includes preparation): US $3,800

Conclusion/Post-Mediation Work: The Claimant was represented by the Managing Director who indicated from the outset his scepticism of mediation. The Respondent was represented by the Chairman who had not been actively involved in the subject matter but was keenly aware of internal politics within his own organisation. The turning point of the mediation was a joint meeting between the Managing Director and the Chairman, assisted by the Mediator.

One of the most beneficial aspects of the mediation was that the markets for the product were preserved.

Joint Venture

(a) Nationality of Parties: American and British

Facts: This dispute followed the setting up of a joint venture, which had come to an end acrimoniously. One party, UK-based, claimed equity in a holding company and claimed that an agreement to deliver had been breached. The other party, a US company, denied the existence of the Agreement and was suing in the US for damages resulting from the alleged disruption to the business and return of certain funds.

Amount in Dispute: Approximately US $320,000

Route to Mediation: It was agreed between the parties that the subject matter of the proceedings in the UK and other proceedings in the US should be the subject of a mediation in an attempt to resolve the differences of the parties on all issues.

Time between Decision to Mediate and Final Outcome: One month

Mediators' Pre-mediation Work: Eight hours of preparation

Length of Mediation: One day

Cost per party (includes preparation): US $3,500

Conclusion/Post-mediation Work: The parties settled their dispute through the mediation process.

Comments from those involved:

The Respondent's representative stated, 'My clients were very impressed by the effectiveness of the mediation process ...[They] are delighted that the matter has been finally resolved not least so they can now concentrate on their core business without this unwanted distraction.' He further stated that the main benefit to his organization of using the mediation process rather than litigation was 'a satisfied client'.

Manufacturing and Distribution

(a) *Nationality of Parties: Italian*

Facts: This dispute arose between Party A and Party B, both Italian companies, concerning their contractual relations and future development thereof. Party A was a manufacturer of shoes, ski boots and similar products. Party B had been distributing these products for approximately ten years on the basis of merely verbal understandings. Party B had also been involved informally in the development of certain products. The dispute arose between the two companies because of the fact that party A antici-pated their wish to terminate or at least to change the terms of the relationship with Party B. Party B subsequently filed a lawsuit against Party A before a Californian court.

Amount in Dispute: US $800,000

Route to Mediation: Despite the lawsuit being filed, the parties never gave up direct contact because of the fact that they needed reciprocal support. There was, therefore, a substantial interest of both parties in maintaining good relations and finding an acceptable way out of the crisis. For this reason the parties agreed to attempt to solve their dispute through the mediation process.

Time Between Decision to Mediate and Final Outcome: Two months

Mediators' Pre-mediation Work: One day, which included preparation and travel time to Italy.

Length of Mediation: Two days

Cost per party (includes preparation): US $3,600

Conclusion/Post-mediation Work: The parties reached a solution through the mediation process by agreeing a new distribution agreement.

(b) Nationality of Parties: German and American

Facts: This dispute concerned the development of a plastic that was to be capable of withstanding particularly high temperatures. The Respondent, a multinational manufacturer, and the Claimant, a German supplier, through its subsidiary, signed a Memorandum of Understanding regarding this project. The Agreement was governed by Swiss law.

Amount in Dispute: US $3.2 million

Route to Mediation: The parties agreed to attempt a solution using mediation to avoid litigation expense.

Time Between Decision to Mediate and Final Outcome: Four months

Mediators' Pre-mediation Work: 12 hours of preparation

Length of Mediation: Two days

Cost per party (includes preparation): US $7,680

Conclusion/Post-mediation Work: The parties achieved a settlement through the mediation process.

Comments from those involved:

The Respondent's representative stated, 'The matter settled on terms which were favourable to both parties.' He also said that the main benefit to his organisation of using mediation rather that litigation was the 'preservation of the commercial relationship with [the Claimant].' The Claimant's representative stated, 'We would not have used litigation. This was the only way to solve the problem.'

(c) *Nationality of parties: British and Israeli*

Facts: This was a contract dispute between the supplier of garments and a warehousing and distribution company. The parties had entered into an agreement, which foundered in mutual dissatisfaction. This led to a dispute over the warehouse service provided by the distribution company (Party A), who subsequently terminated the agreement and claimed £1.2 million in unpaid invoices and costs of variations to the agreement. Party B counterclaimed for alleged consequential costs of breakdowns in Party A's service.

Amount in Dispute: US $3.7 million

Route to Mediation: A date for arbitration had been set and there was no stay, but the parties agreed between themselves beforehand to refer the matter to mediation.

Time Between Decision to Mediate and Final Outcome: One month

Mediator's Pre-mediation Work: Eight hours of preparation

Length of Mediation: One day

Cost Per Party (includes preparation work): US $7,100

Conclusion/Post if Mediation Work: The parties successfully settled the matter through the mediation process.

Comments from those involved: Party A's lawyer stated of the mediator 'she got to grips with the issues very well and was thoroughly prepared'. He was 'happy that it settled and the process worked'. The lawyer for Party B was very impressed with the mediator and said that his clients were "very happy, incredibly impressed" with the mediator. He said that 'mediation is a great tool and we were ever so pleased overall'.

Maritime

(a) *Nationality of Parties: American and Cypriot*

Facts: The Claimant brought an action against the Respondent under a Bill of Lading. The dispute arose in connection with a claim for breach of contract of carriage of a cargo of soya blend crude by the alleged failure of the Respondent to ensure that their vessel was fit to trade to American Ports and to comply with the requirements of the US Port and Tanker Safety Act 1978. The Claimant alleged that as a consequence the discharge of the vessel was delayed causing spot cargoes to be purchased and the use of disadvantageous blends of crude, which reduced the throughput of the oil refinery receiving the cargo. The oil refinery sought to pass their losses to the company from whom they purchased the cargo. That company in turn sought to pass the loss to the Claimant. The claim was defended on the grounds of title to sue, damages too remote and no basis in US law for the original losses alleged. The Respondent had no assets and security provided originally did not respond to this claim.

Amount in Dispute: US $1.1 million

Route to Mediation: The Commercial Court, London, ordered that an application for security for costs be adjourned pending an attempt by the parties to resolve their differences by mediation.

Time Between Decision to Mediate and Final Outcome: Three weeks

Mediators' Pre-mediation Work: Ten hours of preparation

Length of Mediation: One day

Cost per party (includes preparation): US $2,400

Conclusion/Post-mediation Work: The mediation was scheduled to take place over two consecutive days. However, at the end of day one the parties felt they were unable to settle their dispute through the mediation process. The parties were ultimately US $190,000 apart and no settlement could be reached. The Respondent, nevertheless, requested that the Mediator produce a written recommendation of settlement terms which eventually led to a settlement.

Comments from those involved:
One of the parties involved stated that the Mediator was 'excellent'.

(b) *Nationality of Parties: Chilean and Dutch*

Facts: This dispute arose from a voyage performed under a time charter party. The Claimant was the charterer and the Respondent was the owner. The voyage was from Durban and Cape Town to various South American ports. The Claimant alleged loss of or damage to cargo carried on the voyage and, in particular, for cargo damaged by an explosion on board the vessel whilst at sea en route for her first discharge port. The Respondent counterclaimed for the damage sustained by the vessel in that explosion and miscellaneous expenses relating to the casualty.

Route to Mediation: Following a preliminary meeting held at CEDR, both parties agreed in principle to attempt CEDR mediation subject to agreement on the identity of the mediator and subject to final agreement on procedure.

Amount in Dispute: Between US $4.8 million and $8 million.

Time Between Decision to Mediate and Final Outcome: Two months.

Mediators' Pre-mediation Work: A preliminary meeting was held at CEDR with the parties' legal representatives to discuss nominal procedures and ten hours of preparation work was conducted before the mediation itself.

Length of Mediation: One and a half days.

Cost per party (includes preparation): US $5,400

Conclusion/Post-mediation Work: At the end of a discouraging first day the parties were encouraged, by the Mediator, to continue the mediation process into a second day to which they agreed. Part of the claim was settled before the second day of mediation, the remainder was settled on day two itself. The conclusion of the mediation process resulted in a binding written agreement settling all claims and counterclaims and arbitration in which they were brought.

Comments from those involved:

One of the parties' legal representatives stated that 'I certainly would mediate again ... [the] meeting with [the] opposing solicitor at CEDR was very useful.'

Pharmaceuticals

(a) Nationality of Parties: Chinese and British

Facts: A Chinese pharmaceutical company entered into a distribution agreement with a British firm giving them the exclusive rights to distribute the company's new drug in Europe and the USA. Five years into the agreement, after poor profits for the drug, the British firm pulled the product off the market when safety concerns were raised about the drug. They did this without consulting the Chinese parent company. The Chinese company claimed a breach of contract and demanded compensation for the loss of profit which would be suffered because of the reputation damage done to the drug by the British firm's actions.

Amount in dispute: US $370 million

Route to Mediation: The case was originally taken to arbitration. Potential cost and uncertainty of outcome convinced the parties to seek mediation while the arbitration was pending.

Time between Decision to Mediate and Final Outcome: Four months
Mediator's Pre-mediation Work: 15 hours of preparation
Length of Mediation: Three days
Cost per Party (including preparation): US $18,500
Conclusion/Post-mediation Work: An additional day of mediation was agreed upon to finish the mediation, set three weeks from the second day of mediation. A settlement was reached on that last day of mediation.

Comments from those involved:

Both parties were very impressed with the mediator's style and approach. One party remarked that the way the mediation was conducted was, 'very appropriate considering the cultural differences in terms of doing business.'

(b) Nationality of Parties: American, British and Israeli

Facts: The Claimant, a UK corporation manufacturing pharmaceutical products, appointed the Respondent, a privately-owned company, which imported, marketed and distributed pharmaceutical products in Israel and some neighbouring territories, as exclusive distributor of the Claimant's products. The Distribution Agreement was to last for five years. The Respondent withheld payment of invoices to the Claimant alleging failure to remedy numerous complaints and breaches of contract of which they had been notified. The Claimant terminated the Distribution Agreement based on the Respondent's non-payment of invoices and other alleged deficiencies in the distributor's actions. The Respondent counterclaimed for loss of future business, various supplier failings and unlawful termination.

Amount in Dispute: US $2.2 million

Route to Mediation: The parties agreed to refer the matter to mediation before starting court proceedings.

Time Between Decision to Mediate and Final Outcome: One month

Mediators' Pre-mediation Work: Eight hours of preparation

Length of Mediation: One day

Cost per party (includes preparation): US $3,000

Conclusion/Post-mediation Work: At the conclusion of the mediation, a settlement offer was made and left for negotiation/agreement by telephone. The Co-Mediators monitored the matter, which was settled with some further final bargaining between the lawyers within a week.

Comments from those involved:

The Respondent's legal representative concluded that the success of the mediation resulted in a 'considerable' saving in management time and because the matter could have resulted in litigation, estimated a 'substantial' cost saving.

Professional Services

(a) Nationality of Parties: Luxemburgisch and British

Facts: This dispute concerned a professional negligence claim brought by the Claimant, liquidator of a Luxembourg company, which was the former client of the Respondent. The Respondent acted for the Luxembourg company in connection with the sale of its assets to a company registered in the British Virgin Islands. The Claimant asserted that the Respondent, based in the UK, were negligent in carrying out their original instructions and also in undertaking related transactions in the months following, to the extent of acting as part of a fraudulent conspiracy.

Amount in Dispute: US $10 million

Route to Mediation: The lawyers for the parties advised them to attempt mediation.

Time Between Decision to Mediate and Final Outcome: Two months

Mediators' Pre-mediation Work: Ten hours of preparation

Length of Mediation: Two days

Cost per party (includes preparation): US $6,000

Conclusion/Post-mediation Work: The parties settled their dispute through the mediation process. The outcome of the settlement was a court order that the Respondent pays to the Claimant a sum in full and final settlement of all claims.

Comments from those involved:

The Respondent's legal representative stated that the main benefits to their clients were 'early settlement' and a financial saving of 'approximately $400,000' in legal expenses.

(b) Nationality of Parties: American and British

Facts: This dispute arose from the Respondent's retainer by the Claimant, a US banking firm, in connection with an agreement entered into by the parties. The essence of the claim made against international professional

176

advisers was that they had provided negligent advice in their opinion letter and in general advice concerning the transaction.

Amount in Dispute: Between US $8 million and $16 million

Route to Mediation: The parties were oblige to attempt mediation by order of the Court.

Time Between Decision to Mediate and Final Outcome: One month

Mediators' Pre-mediation Work: 15 hours of preparation

Length of Mediation: One day

Cost per party (includes preparation): US $8,000

Conclusion/Post-mediation Work: The parties settled their dispute through the mediation process. The settlement agreement was one which was acceptable to both parties and which, importantly, preserved the existing relationship between the parties by avoiding a lengthy legal battle.

Comments from those involved:

One of the parties stated, 'I am quite sure that without your mediation the parties would have found it far more difficult to reach a satisfactory settlement and would probably have got to – and possibly through – the court door ... I am a real convert to the advantages of mediation in complex cases and am spreading the word.'

Retail and Design

(a) Nationality of Parties: American and British

Facts: The Claimant, a UK company, specialized in the design, planning and management of promotional games. The Respondent, a UK subsidiary of a US company, frequently used promotional games as a marketing tool and was the Claimant's largest customer. The Claimant submitted to the Respondent, proposals for the promotion of a leading manufacturer's video games as prizes and for a promotion in relation to film-related merchandise. The Respondent ran promotions with the particular manufacturer's video games as a theme and also a motion picture theme. The Claimant contended that the Respondent made use of their original concepts and, thus, misused confidential information belonging to them and by using and adapting their proposals the Respondent acted in breach of contract. The Respondent contended that the general concept of using that particular manufacturer's video games or a motion picture-based theme had been suggested to them before and after the Claimant's proposal and that neither concept was capable of being protected as confidential information.

Amount in Dispute: Approximately US $1.2 million

Route to Mediation: The Claimant initially approached CEDR to discuss proposals to mediate the proceedings between the parties.

Time Between Decision to Mediate and Final Outcome: Two months

Mediators' Pre-mediation Work: The parties had a preliminary meeting with the Mediator at CEDR's offices. Prior to the mediation itself, the Mediator carried out eight hours of preparation.

Length of Mediation: One day

Cost per party (includes preparation): US $7,920

Conclusion/Post-mediation Work: The parties did not reach a settlement at the end of the mediation and the process was adjourned. A settlement agreement was reached the day after mediation to the effect that the parties settled on the terms reached in the mediation.

Supply of Goods

(a) *Nationality of parties: Mauritian and British*

Facts: Party B was Party A's distributor in Mauritius, selling and maintaining back-up power supplies used in the case of power failure from the national power supply. Party B failed to pay for the units supplied, stating that many units had failed. Party A sued for unpaid invoices and Party B issued a counterclaim for lost business.

Amount in dispute: US $370,000

Route to mediation: After unsuccessful attempts at direct negotiation to settle the dispute, the parties obtained a stay on proceedings and agreed between themselves to refer the matter to mediation.

Time between decision to mediate and final outcome: Four and a half months

Mediator's pre-mediation work: Eight hours of preparation

Length of mediation: One day

Cost per party (includes preparation work): US $3,900

Conclusion/post-mediation work: The parties settled the dispute successfully through the mediation.

Comments from those involved:

The representatives of both parties were very pleased with the outcome of the mediation. Party B's lawyer added, 'Your services, mediator and venue were all absolutely superb. Both my client and I were absolutely delighted with the settlement outcome and with the whole process from start to finish. We are a small firm and it was so nice to feel on an equal footing with the larger firm on the other side; it

was great to be on neutral ground. **My client was so pleased that this matter has now come to a conclusion and finality has been reached ... thank you very much, we were all very impressed with everything'.**

(*b*) *Nationality of parties: Chinese and British*

Facts: This dispute concerned a claim for damages following the alleged termination of a two-year-old franchise agreement between the parties, and embraced several issues relating to supply chains and marketing. Party A (the franchisor) terminated the agreement on grounds including relating to failure to pay invoices, damage to Party A's reputation, disclosure of confidential information and failure of Party B to open the requisite number of stores. Party B denied the breaches and claimed lost income as a result of the termination.

Amount in dispute: US $18.2 million

Route to mediation: After direct negotiations failed, the parties agreed between themselves to refer the matter to mediation.

Time between decision to mediate and final outcome: Three months

Mediator's pre-mediation work: Ten hours of preparation

Length of mediation: One day

Cost per party (*includes preparation work*): US $4,400

Conclusion/post-mediation work: A settlement was achieved two days after the mediation took place.

Comments from those involved:

Party B's lawyer thought that the mediator did well and gave credit to the mediator for bridging the large gap between the parties, which ultimately enabled them to settle shortly after the mediation.

Telecommunications

(*a*) *Nationality of Parties: Israeli and American*

Facts: The Claimant was granted a licence to operate a cellular telephone network in Israel. The Respondent, a US company, was the Claimant's main supplier. A malfunction in the Claimant's network was caused by a serious fault in the Respondent's telephones. This dispute involved three principal issues: the Claimant's withholding of payment to the Respondent for the cellular telephones, the extent of the Respondent's liability, if any, for a latent software problem in the telephones and the scope of the Claimant's direct expenses for repairs and the nature and amount of damages the Claimant allegedly suffered as a result of the software problems in the telephones.

Amount in Dispute: Between US $25 million and $30 million

Route to Mediation: The Respondent first suggested mediation as a means of solving the dispute but the Claimant rejected this suggestion. At a later date, the Claimant proposed an attempt at mediation, which the Respondent accepted. A UK mediator was chosen because of the neutrality of the UK, in relation to Israel and the USA, and CEDR was proposed by the Respondent's lawyers in the UK.

Time Between Decision to Mediate and Final Outcome: Four months

Mediators' Pre-mediation Work: There was a preliminary meeting between the Respondent Company's Vice-President, the Claimant's legal representative and CEDR. Prior to the mediation itself, the Mediators conducted eight hours of preparation.

Length of Mediation: Two days

Cost per party (includes preparation): US $10,000

Conclusion/Post-mediation Work: The parties achieved a settlement through the mediation process.

Comments from those involved:

The Respondent Company's Vice-President wrote to 'express my thanks to [your] mediators for a job well done'. She further indicated a 'considerable' management time saving as a result of using the mediation process, '[the] mediation timing was relatively quick as compared to the length of the dispute.'

(b) Nationality of Parties: Danish and American

Facts: This dispute arose in connection with a claim for breach of warranty and misrepresentation arising out of a Stock Purchase Agreement entered into between the Claimant and the Respondent, both Danish companies, in the telecommunications industry. The Claimant maintained breaches of obligations, in essence of the Respondent's failure to make adequate disclosures and/or adequate provision by way of reserves and/or that amounts receivable, including royalties, were grossly overstated.

Amount in Dispute: US $6.6 million

Route to Mediation: In the event of any dispute, the Contract between the parties provided for conciliation under UNCITRAL Rules, to be administered by the LCIA. The conciliator was to be from CEDR. Proceedings had not commenced because of the contractual obligation placed on the parties, which provided for the use of conciliation in the event of any dispute.

Time Between Decision to Mediate and Final Outcome: Two months

Mediators' Pre-mediation Work: 15 hours of preparation

Length of Mediation: One day

Cost per party (includes preparation): US $6,000

Conclusion/Post-mediation Work: The dispute between the parties was settled through the mediation process, albeit not until some weeks following the day of mediation itself.

Comments from those involved:

One of the parties commented, '... we would not have concluded a settlement without your expert intervention and conduct of the mediation proceedings ...I would like to thank [the Mediator and Assistant Mediator] for your excellent services in this matter.'

2   CEDR Model ADR Contract Clauses

1   Why you should consider including an ADR clause in your commercial contract

Including in a contract a clause which requires the parties to attempt to settle any dispute arising out of the contract by some form of ADR should increase the chances of settling any such dispute before, or notwithstanding that, the parties resort to court proceedings or arbitration.

The advantages of inserting an ADR clause include:
- It prompts the parties to consider a process which, unlike negotiation, may not necessarily occur to them.
- It introduces a specific process, which gives the parties a clear framework for exploring settlement.
- The mediation process involves a neutral third party trained to work with parties to facilitate communication which is geared towards an agreed durable settlement.
- The mediation process changes the focus for the parties away from the events of the past towards the realism of the present and the needs of the future.
- Including a contract clause which requires the parties to attempt to settle any dispute arising out of a contract by mediation should increase the chances of settling any such dispute before, or notwithstanding that the parties resort to, court proceedings or arbitration.
- Such a clause may give the parties a chance to pre-empt an order from the court requiring ADR and enable them to conduct any ADR process on their own pre-agreed terms. For example, under the Civil Procedure Rules of England and Wales there is an overriding objective requiring the courts to actively manage cases with Rule 1.4 (i)(e) empowering the court to encourage use of ADR procedures, to prompt an earlier settlement. The Rules are based on a requirement of fairness and proportionality and take into account the large number of cases that have settled without a full hearing. The judges in the English jurisdiction have become increasingly aware of the success of mediation in bringing about an end to what often appeared to be intractable and difficult disputes. A large body of case law has now developed since the new Rules came into effect some years ago – see EDR Law on the

CEDR website (www.cedr.co.uk). An ADR clause will pre-empt the courts and provide for the process to take place on the parties' own pre-agreed terms.

– The potential of achieving a binding solution – over 70 per cent of mediations reach an agreed and binding solution despite earlier impasse.
– Keeping and/or moving the negotiation process out of the public arena.
– An early successful conclusion to the dispute will provide substantial savings in legal and management costs, freeing up the business for more productive endeavours.

How

For a clause to be effective the draftsperson needs to decide firstly whether they wish to use a simple or multi-tiered clause.

The following is a checklist for the draftsperson.

1 Decision makers

Do you want to identify the decision makers engaging in the ADR process, eg managing director, CEO? It is not strictly necessary, you can simply refer to the parties, leaving the decision to the relevant time. They are encouraged to come with full authority under the CEDR Model Mediation Procedure.

2 Pre-litigation

Do you want to attempt the ADR process before any adversarial process begins? In England one cannot oust the jurisdiction of the court, but the court will stay proceedings to allow parties to honour their agreement to mediate. A party's right to seek injunctive or declaratory relief or to avoid a time bar will always be preserved. The prospect of settlement may be higher before the lines of battle have been drawn by a hostile step of commencing court proceedings/arbitration. The CEDR Model Mediation Procedure provides that litigation or arbitration may be commenced or continued unless the parties agree otherwise (Clause 15).

3 Single or multi-step clause

Do you want a single stepped process or a multi-step process? The choice is whether to move straight to mediation or to provide for direct negotiations followed by mediation if the negotiations fail.

4 Time limits/time span

What time frame do you want? To be effective, it is better to provide for a clear process and timetable. The CEDR Model Mediation procedure has a termination provision under Clause 14.

5 Identifying procedural rules

Are you content to refer to the CEDR Model Mediation Procedure? In *Cable & Wireless plc v IBM* [2002] EWHC Ch 2059, Mr Justice Colman said 'Resort to CEDR and participation in its recommended procedure are, in my judgment, engagement of sufficient certainty for a court readily to ascertain whether they have been complied with.' Your clause will be more effective if you refer to a known and accepted model mediation procedure. The CEDR Model Mediation Procedure can be found on CEDR's website at www.cedr.co.uk.

To be effective ensure that you have:
(a) a clear process,
(b) a trigger for the process,
(c) a time frame (beginning and end),
(d) easily identifiable decision makers,
(e) clarity on whether you want the mediation to take place before or during an adversarial procedure or whether you want to leave your options open.

2 Model clauses

1 Simple core mediation clause

Core wording

'If any dispute arises in connection with this agreement, the parties will attempt to settle it by mediation in accordance with the CEDR Model Mediation Procedure. Unless otherwise agreed between the parties, the mediator will be nominated by CEDR.'

Notes

This clause by itself should be sufficient to give the parties the opportunity to attempt to settle any dispute by mediation. The CEDR Model Mediation

Procedure provides clear guidelines on the conduct of the mediation and requires the parties to enter into an agreement based on the Model Mediation Agreement in relation to its conduct. This will deal with points such as the nature of the dispute, the identity of the mediator and where and when the mediation is to take place. If an ADR/mediation clause is sufficiently certain and clear as to the process to be used it should be enforceable. The reference in the clause to a model mediation procedure should give it that necessary certainty: *Cable & Wireless Plc v IBM United Kingdom Ltd* [2002] EWHC Ch 2059.

2   Simple core mediation clause including time and notification

Core wording

'If any dispute arises in connection with this agreement, the parties will attempt to settle it by mediation in accordance with the CEDR Model Mediation Procedure. Unless otherwise agreed between the parties, the mediator will be nominated by CEDR. To initiate the mediation a party must give notice in writing ('ADR notice') to the other party[ies] to the dispute requesting a mediation. A copy of the request should be sent to CEDR.

The mediation will start not later than [ ] days after the date of the ADR notice.'

Notes

This wording is to address the concern that mediation should provide a quick solution rather than delay an outcome. It evidences intention that a mediation should happen quickly and provides a trigger for commencement of the mediation with the service of the notice, including a copy to CEDR so that it can assist the parties to move the process as quickly as possible.

3   Simple core mediation clause including time, plus reference to court proceedings in parallel

Core wording

'If any dispute arises in connection with this agreement, the parties will attempt to settle it by mediation in accordance with the CEDR Model Mediation Procedure. Unless otherwise agreed between the parties, the mediator will be nominated by CEDR. To initiate the mediation a party must give notice in writing ('ADR notice') to the other party[ies] to the dispute requesting a mediation. A copy of the request should be sent to CEDR. The mediation will start not later than [ ] days after the date of the ADR notice. The commencement of a mediation will not prevent the parties commencing or continuing court proceedings/an arbitration.'

Notes

Strictly this wording is not necessary as nothing in the core mediation wording prevents the issuance of court proceedings. Further, CEDR's Model Mediation Procedure, Clause 15, provides that litigation or arbitration may commence or continue unless the parties are otherwise agreed. The inclusion of this wording in the contract clause may, however, allay the concern if a party wishes to retain the ability to resort to court proceedings.

4 Simple core mediation clause including time, plus reference to no court or arbitration proceedings until mediation terminated

Core wording

'If any dispute arises in connection with this agreement, the parties will attempt to settle it by mediation in accordance with the CEDR Model Mediation Procedure. Unless otherwise agreed between the parties, the mediator will be nominated by CEDR. To initiate the mediation a party must give notice in writing ('ADR notice') to the other party [ies] to the dispute requesting a mediation. A copy of the request should be sent to CEDR. The mediation will start not later than [ ] days after the date of the ADR notice. No party may commence any court proceedings/arbitration in relation to any dispute arising out of this agreement until it has attempted to settle the dispute by mediation and either the mediation has terminated or the other party has failed to participate in the mediation, provided that the right to issue proceedings is not prejudiced by a delay.'

Notes

The rationale for this wording is that an ADR contract clause is intended to curtail court proceedings, etc, and that for them to run in parallel may not be conducive to any attempt to settle. The prospects of settlement may be higher before the lines of battle have been drawn by the hostile steps of commencing court proceedings/arbitration. Bear in mind that, under the English jurisdiction, the courts always retain the ability to issue interim relief but they will stay proceedings to allow parties to honour an agreement to mediate.

5 Multi-tiered process

Core wording

'If any dispute arises in connection with this agreement, directors or other senior representatives of the parties with authority to settle the dispute will, within [ ] days of a written request from one party to the other, meet in a good faith effort to resolve the dispute.

If the dispute is not resolved at that meeting, the parties will attempt to settle it by mediation in accordance with the CEDR Model Mediation Procedure. Unless otherwise agreed between the parties, the mediator will be nominated by CEDR. To initiate the mediation a party must give notice in writing ('ADR notice') to the other party(ies) to the dispute requesting a mediation. A copy of the request should be sent to CEDR Solve. The mediation will start not later than [ ] days after the date of the ADR notice.'

[The draftsperson has the choice to add Version 1, referring to court proceedings in parallel, or Version 2, no court proceedings until the mediation is completed.]

Version 1: 'The commencement of a mediation will not prevent the parties commencing or continuing court proceedings/an arbitration.' Version 2: 'No party may commence any court proceedings/arbitration in relation to any dispute arising out of this agreement until it has attempted to settle the dispute by mediation and either the mediation has terminated or the other party has failed to participate in the mediation, provided that the right to issue proceedings is not prejudiced by a delay.'

Notes

This adds an extra step providing for negotiations before mediation and the choice is then to have arbitration or litigation in parallel or deferred until after the mediation has effectively terminated.

6 International core mediation clause

Core wording

'If any dispute arises in connection with this agreement, the parties will attempt to settle it by mediation in accordance with the CEDR Model Mediation Procedure. Unless otherwise agreed between the parties, the mediator will be nominated by CEDR. The mediation will take place in [city/country of neither/none of the parties] and the language of the mediation will be [ ]. The Mediation Agreement referred to in the Model Procedure shall be governed by, and construed and take effect in accordance with [English] law. The courts of [England] shall have exclusive jurisdiction to settle any claim, dispute or matter of difference which may arise out of, or in connection with, the mediation. If the dispute is not settled by mediation within [ ] days of commencement of the mediation or within such further period as the parties may agree in writing, the dispute shall be referred to and finally resolved by arbitration under the [CEDR rules – LCIA rules – UNCITRAL rules – ICC rules – JAMS rules – [other] as at present in force]. In any arbitration commenced pursuant to this clause, the number of arbitrators shall be [1/3] and the seat or legal place of arbitration shall be [London, England].'

Notes

This model clause should be suitable for international contracts, ie contracts between parties in different jurisdictions, but consideration should be given to including provisions relating to the location/language of the mediation, as well as the governing law and jurisdiction applicable to the mediation agreement along the lines of this paragraph. There is a choice of arbitration body or the non-administered UNCITRAL rules.

The clause can be amended to refer to 'CEDR, London' if the draftsperson believes this will specify more clearly where to find CEDR for international parties.

3 CEDR Model Mediation Procedure and Agreement (Edition 9A)

Mediation Agreement

1 The parties ('the Parties') to the dispute in question ('the Dispute'), the Mediator and the Centre for Effective Dispute Resolution ('CEDR Solve') will enter into an agreement ('the Mediation Agreement') based on the CEDR Model Mediation Agreement in relation to the conduct of the Mediation. This procedure ('the Model Procedure') will be incorporated into, form part of, and may be varied by, the Mediation Agreement.

The Mediator

2 CEDR Solve will, subject to the agreement of the Parties or any court order, nominate an independent third party(ies) ('the Mediator'). The Mediator, after consultation with the Parties where appropriate, will:

 – attend any meetings with any or all of the Parties preceding the mediation, if requested or if the Mediator decides this is appropriate and the Parties agree;

 – read before the Mediation each Case Summary and all the Documents sent to him/her (see paragraph 7 below);

 – chair, and determine the procedure for, the Mediation;

 – facilitate the drawing up of any settlement agreement; and

 – abide by the terms of the Model Procedure and the Mediation Agreement.

3 The Mediator (and any member of the Mediator's firm or company) will not act for any of the Parties individually in connection with the Dispute in any capacity either during the currency of this agreement or at any time thereafter. The Parties accept that in relation to the Dispute neither the Mediator nor CEDR Solve is an agent of, or acting in any capacity for, any of the Parties. The Parties and the Mediator accept that the Mediator (unless an employee of CEDR Solve) is acting as an independent contractor and not as an agent or employee of CEDR Solve.

Optional/additional wording

4   CEDR Solve, in conjunction with the Mediator, will make the necessary arrangements for the Mediation including, as necessary:

–   nominating, and obtaining the agreement of the Parties to, the Mediator;

–   drawing up the Mediation Agreement;

–   organising a suitable venue and dates;

–   organising exchange of the Case Summaries and Documents;

–   meeting with any or all of the Parties (and the Mediator if appointed), either together or separately, to discuss any matters or concerns relating to the Mediation; and

–   general administration in relation to the Mediation.

5   If there is any issue about the conduct of the Mediation (including as to the nomination of the Mediator) upon which the Parties cannot agree within a reasonable time, CEDR Solve will, at the request of any Party, decide the issue for the Parties, having consulted with them.

Participants

6   The Lead Negotiators must be sufficiently senior and have the full authority of their respective Parties to settle the Dispute, without having to refer to anybody else. If there is any restriction on that authority, this should be discussed with CEDR Solve and/or the Mediator before the Mediation.

Parties should inform CEDR Solve prior to the date of Mediation of all persons attending the mediation on behalf of each Party.

Exchange of information

7   Each Party will prepare for the other Party(ies), the Mediator and Assistant Mediator sufficient copies of:

–   a concise summary ('the Case Summary') of its case in the Dispute; and

–   all the documents to which the Summary refers and any others to which it may want to refer in the Mediation ('the Documents').

The Parties will exchange the Case Summary and Documents with each other at least two weeks before the Mediation, or such other date as may be agreed between the Parties and CEDR Solve, and send copies directly to the Mediator and Assistant Mediator on the same date. Each Party will send a copy of the Case Summary to CEDR Solve.

In addition, each Party may send to the Mediator (through CEDR Solve) and/or bring to the Mediation further documentation which it wishes to disclose in confidence to the Mediator but not to any other Party, clearly stating in writing that such documentation is confidential to the Mediator and CEDR Solve.

8   The Parties should try to agree:

-   the maximum number of pages of each Case Summary; and

-   a joint set of Documents or the maximum length of each set of Documents.

The mediation

9   The Mediation will take place at the arranged place and time stated in the Mediation Agreement.

10 The Mediator will chair, and determine the procedure at, the Mediation.

11 No recording or transcript of the Mediation will be made.

12 If the Parties are unable to reach a settlement in the negotiations at the Mediation, and only if all the Parties so request and the Mediator agrees, the Mediator will produce for the Parties a non-binding recommendation on terms of settlement. This will not attempt to anticipate what a court might order but will set out what the Mediator suggests are appropriate settlement terms in all of the circumstances.

Settlement agreement

13 Any settlement reached in the Mediation will not be legally binding until it has been reduced to writing and signed by, or on behalf of, the Parties.

Termination

14 Any of the Parties may withdraw from the Mediation at any time and shall immediately inform the Mediator and the other representatives in writing. The Mediation will terminate when:

-   a Party withdraws from the Mediation; or

- the Mediator, at his/her discretion, withdraws from the mediation; or

- a written settlement agreement is concluded.

The mediator may also adjourn the mediation in order to allow parties to consider specific proposals, get further information or for any other reason, which the mediator considers helpful in furthering the mediation process. The mediation will then reconvene with the agreement of the parties.

Stay of proceedings
15 Any litigation or arbitration in relation to the Dispute may be commenced or continued notwithstanding the Mediation unless the Parties agree otherwise or a court so orders.

Confidentiality etc.
16 Every person involved in the Mediation will keep confidential and not use for any collateral or ulterior purpose all information (whether given orally, in writing or otherwise) arising out of, or in connection with, the Mediation, including the fact of any settlement and its terms, save for the fact that the mediation is to take place or has taken place.
17 All information (whether oral, in writing or otherwise) arising out of, or in connection with, the Mediation will be without prejudice, privileged and not admissible as evidence or disclosable in any current or subsequent litigation or other proceedings whatsoever. This does not apply to any information, which would in any event have been admissible or disclosable in any such proceedings.
18 The Mediator will not disclose to any other Party any information given to him by a Party in confidence without the express consent of that Party.
19 Paragraphs 16 –18 shall not apply if, and to the extent that:

- all Parties consent to the disclosure; or

- the Mediator is required under the general law to make disclosure; or

- the Mediator reasonably considers that there is a serious risk of significant harm to the life or safety of any person if the information in question is not disclosed; or

   – the Mediator reasonably considers that there is a serious risk of his/her being subject to criminal proceedings unless the information in question is disclosed.

20 None of the Parties to the Mediation Agreement will call the Mediator or CEDR Solve (or any employee, consultant, officer or representative of CEDR Solve) as a witness, consultant, arbitrator or expert in any litigation or other proceedings whatsoever arising from, or in connection with, the matters in issue in the Mediation. The Mediator and CEDR Solve will not voluntarily act in any such capacity without the written agreement of all the Parties.

Fees, expenses and costs

21 CEDR Solve's fees (which include the Mediator's fees) and the other expenses of the Mediation will be borne equally by the Parties. Payment of these fees and expenses will be made to CEDR Solve in accordance with its fee schedule and terms and conditions of business.

Each Party will bear its own costs and expenses of its participation in the Mediation.

Exclusion of liability

22 Neither the Mediator nor CEDR Solve shall be liable to the Parties for any act or omission in connection with the services provided by them in, or in relation to, the Mediation, unless the act or omission is shown to have been in bad faith.

Guidance notes

The paragraph numbers and headings in these notes refer to the paragraphs and headings in the Model Procedure.

The same terms ('the Parties' etc.) are used in the Model Procedure and the Model Agreement.

Introduction

The essence of mediation is that it:
– involves a neutral third party to facilitate negotiations;
– is quick and inexpensive, without prejudice and confidential;
– enables the Parties to devise solutions which are not possible in an

adjudicative process, such as litigation or arbitration, and which may be to the benefit of both/all Parties, particularly if there is a continuing business relationship;

– involves representatives of the Parties who have sufficient authority to settle. In some cases, there may be an advantage in the representatives being individuals who have not been directly involved in the events leading up to the dispute and in the dispute itself;

– The procedure for the mediation is flexible and this Model Procedure can be adapted (with or without the assistance of CEDR Solve) to suit the Parties.

A mediation can be used:

– in both domestic and international disputes;
– whether or not litigation or arbitration has been commenced; and
– in two-party and multi-party disputes.

Rules or rigid procedures in the context of a consensual and adaptable process, which is the essence of ADR, are generally inappropriate. The Model Procedure and the Model Agreement and this Guidance note should be sufficient to enable parties to conduct a mediation.

In some cases the agreement to conduct a mediation will be as a result of an 'ADR clause' (such as one of the CEDR Model Contract Clauses) to that effect in a commercial agreement between the Parties, or a court order. Where that is the case the Model Procedure and Mediation Agreement may need to be adapted accordingly.

The Model Agreement, which has been kept short and simple, incorporates the Model Procedure (see paragraph 1).

The Mediation Agreement can vary the Model Procedure; the variations can be set out in the body of the Mediation Agreement, or the Mediation Agreement can state that variations made in manuscript (or otherwise) on the Model Procedure are to be incorporated.

Mediation Agreement – paragraph 1

If CEDR Solve is asked to do so by a Party wishing to initiate a mediation, it will approach the other Party(ies) to a Dispute to seek to persuade it/them to participate.

Alternatively, the Party who has taken the initiative in proposing the mediation may wish to send a draft agreement based on the Model Agreement to the other Party(ies).

Representatives of the Parties (and the Mediator if he/she has been nominated) and CEDR Solve may meet to discuss and finalise the terms of the Mediation Agreement.

The Mediator – paragraphs 2–3

The success of the Mediation will, to a considerable extent, depend on the skill of the Mediator. CEDR Solve believes it is very important for the Mediator to have had specific training and experience. CEDR Solve will propose mediators suitable for the particular matter.

In some cases it may be useful to have more than one Mediator, or to have an independent expert who can advise the Mediator on technical issues. All should sign the Mediation Agreement, which should be amended as appropriate.

It is CEDR Solve's practice, as part of its mediator development programme, to have an assistant mediator ('the Assistant Mediator') attend most mediations. The Assistant Mediator signs the Mediation Agreement and falls within the definition 'the Mediator' in the Model Procedure and the Model Agreement.

It is advisable, but not essential, to involve the Mediator in any preliminary meeting between the Parties.

CEDR Solve – paragraphs 4–5

The Model Procedure envisages the involvement of CEDR Solve because in most cases this is likely to benefit the Parties and the Mediator and generally to facilitate the setting up and conduct of the Mediation. The Model Procedure, however, can be amended if CEDR Solve is not to be involved.

Participants – paragraph 6

The lead role in the mediation is usually taken by the Lead Negotiators, because the commercial or other interests of the Parties will often take the negotiations beyond strict legal issues.

The Lead Negotiator must have full authority to settle the Dispute, as detailed in the text of paragraph 6. Full authority means they are able to negotiate freely without restriction or limits on their authority and that the representative does not need to refer to anyone outside the mediation when negotiating and agreeing a settlement. If negotiating authority is less than full, this fact should be disclosed to the other Party and to the Mediator at least two weeks before the Mediation.

The Lead Negotiator should be at the Mediation throughout the whole day. It is easy to forget that the mediation sessions often go well into the evening.

In certain cases, for example claims involving public bodies and class actions, the Lead Negotiator may only have the power to make a recommendation. In these circumstances the following clause should be substituted:

> 'the Lead Negotiator(s) [for Party] will have full authority to make recommendations on terms of settlement on behalf of its Party'.

Professional advisers, particularly lawyers, can, and usually do, attend the Mediation. The advisers play an important role in the exchange of information, in supporting their clients (particularly individuals) in the negotiations, advising their clients on the legal implications of a settlement and in drawing up the settlement agreement.

Exchange of information – paragraphs 7–8

Documentation which a Party wants the Mediator to keep confidential from the other Party(ies) (eg a counsel's opinion, an expert report not yet exchanged) must be clearly marked as such. It can be disclosed confidentially to the Mediator by the Party before or during the Mediation. It will not be disclosed by the Mediator or CEDR Solve without the express consent of the Party.

One of the advantages of ADR is that it can avoid the excessive disclosure process (including witness statements) which often blights litigation and arbitration. The Documents should be kept to the minimum necessary to understand the Party's case and to give the Mediator a good grasp of the issues. The Summaries should be similarly brief.

Should the Parties require CEDR Solve to conduct a simultaneous exchange of Case Summaries and Documents, the following wording is suggested:

> 'Each party will send to CEDR Solve at least two weeks before the Mediation, or such other date as may be agreed between the Parties and CEDR Solve, sufficient copies of:
>
> – a concise summary ('the Case Summary') of its case in the Dispute; and

–   all documents to which the Summary refers and any others to which it may want to refer in the Mediation ('the Documents'), which CEDR Solve will send simultaneously to the other Party(ies), the Mediator and Assistant Mediator.'

The Mediation – paragraphs 9–12

The intention of paragraph 12 is that the Mediator will cease to play an entirely facilitative role only if the negotiations in the Mediation are deadlocked. Giving a settlement recommendation may be perceived by a Party as undermining the Mediator's neutrality and for this reason the Mediator may not agree to this course of action. Any recommendation will be without prejudice and will not be binding unless the Parties agree otherwise.

Settlement agreement – paragraph 13

If no agreement is reached, it is nonetheless open to the Parties to adjourn the Mediation to another time and place. Experience shows that even where no agreement is reached during the Mediation itself, the Parties will often reach a settlement shortly after, as a result of the progress made during that Mediation.

Termination- paragraph 14

A mediator may withdraw from the mediation at any time if, in their view, there is not a reasonable likelihood of the parties achieving a workable settlement; or if in their discretion there is any other reason that it would be inappropriate to continue with the mediation.

Stay of proceedings – paragraph 15

Although a stay may engender a better climate for settlement, it is not essential that any proceedings relating to the Dispute be stayed. If they are stayed, it is the responsibility of the Parties and their legal advisers to consider and, if necessary, deal with the effect of any stay on limitation periods. Suggested wording for a stay, which can be incorporated into the Mediation Agreement, is:

'No litigation or arbitration in relation to the Dispute is to be commenced [Any existing litigation or arbitration in relation to the Dispute is to be stayed] from the date of this agreement until the termination of the Mediation.'

Confidentiality – paragraphs 16–20

Documents which would in any event be disclosable will not become privileged by reason of having been referred to in the Mediation and will therefore still be disclosable. The position on this may depend on the relevant jurisdiction and it is the responsibility of the Parties and their legal advisers to consider and, if necessary, deal with this.

If either Party wishes to keep confidential the fact that Mediation is taking place or has taken place, paragraph 16 can be amended by replacing the wording *'save for the fact that the Mediation is to take place or has taken place'* with the wording *'including the fact that the Mediation is to take place or has taken place'*.

[Paragraph 18 provides an exception to the general requirement for confidentiality where all Parties consent to disclosure or where the Mediator reasonably considers that there are public interest or similar reasons that would require disclosure to be made; this would include any circumstances arising under the Proceeds of Crime Act 2002 or any similar legislation.]

Fees, expenses and costs – paragraphs 21–22

The usual arrangement is for the Parties to share equally the fees and expenses of the procedure, but other arrangements are possible. A Party to a Dispute, which is reluctant to participate in mediation, may be persuaded to participate if the other Party(ies) agree to bear that Party's expenses. Parties may also amend the agreement to identify that the costs of mediation may be taken into account in any court orders if there is no settlement at the Mediation.

International disputes – language and governing law/jurisdiction

The Model Agreement can be easily adapted for international cross-border disputes by the addition in the Mediation Agreement of wording along the following lines:

'Language

The language of the Mediation will be [English]... Any Party producing documents or participating in the Mediation in any other language will provide the necessary translations and interpretation facilities.'

Governing law and jurisdiction

The Mediation Agreement shall be governed by, construed and take effect in accordance with, [English] law.

The courts of [England] shall have exclusive jurisdiction to settle any claim, dispute or matter of difference which may arise out of, or in connection with, the Mediation.'

Where the law is not English or the jurisdiction not England, the Mediation Agreement may need to be amended to ensure the structure, rights and obligations necessary for a mediation are applicable.

Model Mediation Agreement

Parties

_____

('Party A')

_____

('Party B')

[_____

('Party C') etc.]

(jointly 'the Parties')   *Add full names and addresses*

_____ ('the Mediator')

('the Mediator')

Centre for Effective Dispute Resolution Limited, 70 Fleet Street, London EC4Y 1EU ('CEDR Solve')

Dispute ('the Dispute')

Add brief description of the Dispute.

Participation in the Mediation

1   The Parties will attempt to settle the Dispute by mediation ('the Mediation'). The CEDR Model Mediation Procedure ('the Model Procedure') [as varied by this agreement] will determine the conduct of the

Mediation and is incorporated into, and forms part of, this agreement. The definitions in the Model Procedure are used in this agreement.

The Mediator
2   The Mediator[s] will be

_____

If an Assistant Mediator is appointed by CEDR Solve, he/she will be bound by the terms of this agreement. The Mediator and Assistant Mediator will be referred to individually and jointly as 'the Mediator'.

Participants
3   At least one attendee on behalf of each Party at the Mediation will have full authority to settle at the Mediation as set out in paragraph 6 of the Model Procedure ('the Lead Negotiator').
4   Each representative in signing this agreement is deemed to be agreeing to the provisions of this agreement on behalf of the Party he/she represents and all other persons present on that Party's behalf at the Mediation.

Place and time
5   The Mediation will take place on _____

Confidentiality
6   Each Party to the Mediation and all persons attending the Mediation will be bound by the confidentiality provisions of the Model Procedure (paragraphs 16–20).

Mediation fee
7   The person signing this agreement on behalf of the Party he/she represents is agreeing on behalf of that Party, to proceed on the basis of CEDR Solve's standard terms and conditions including the mediation fee as previously agreed by the Parties and CEDR Solve.

Law and jurisdiction
8   This agreement shall be governed by, construed and take effect in

accordance with, English law. The courts of England shall have exclusive jurisdiction to settle any claim, dispute or matter of difference which may arise out of, or in connection with, the Mediation.

Human Rights

9   The referral of the Dispute to mediation does not affect any rights that may exist under Article 6 of the European Convention on Human Rights. If the Dispute is not settled by the Mediation, the Parties' rights to a fair trial remain unaffected.

Model Procedure amendments

10   Set out amendments (if any) to the Model Procedure – see introduction to Model Procedure guidance notes.

If any litigation or arbitration is to be stayed, paragraph 15 of the Model Procedure should be excluded/deleted and wording along the following lines should be added in the agreement: 'No litigation or arbitration in relation to the Dispute is to be commenced [Any existing litigation or arbitration in relation to the Dispute is to be stayed] from the date of this agreement until the termination of the Mediation'.

Signed

On behalf of Party A

_____ Date_____

On behalf of Party B

_____ Date_____

On behalf of Party C

_____Date_____

On behalf of the Mediator

_____ Date_____

On behalf of CEDR Solve

_____ Date_____

4   MEDAL Rules

International Mediation Rules

Application of Rules

1   These Rules apply to the mediation of disputes where the parties seek the amicable settlement of such disputes and where, either by stipulation in a contract or by agreement, they have agreed that these Rules will apply. The parties may agree to vary these Rules in writing at any time.

Initiation of Mediation

2   Any party or parties to a dispute wishing to initiate mediation may do so by filing with a MEDAL Member Organization ('MMO') a submission to mediation or a written request for mediation pursuant to these Rules.

3   A party may request the MMO to invite another party to participate in mediation. Upon receipt of such a request, the MMO will contact the other party involved in the dispute and attempt to obtain an agreement to participate in mediation. Unless otherwise specified within a contract between the parties to the dispute, a period of 30 days from the date of issue shall be regarded as a reasonable time within which a party should respond to an invitation to participate in mediation.

4   A request for mediation should contain a brief statement of the nature of the dispute. It shall also set forth the contact information of all parties to the dispute and the counsel, if any, who will represent them in the mediation.

Appointment of the Mediator

5   Upon receipt of a request for mediation, and if the parties have not jointly notified the MMO of their mutual choice of a mediator, the MMO will provide the parties with a list of no fewer than three persons who would, in the MMO's view, be qualified to mediate the dispute. In compiling the list, the MMO will take into account the nationalities of the parties, the language in which the mediation will be conducted, the place of the mediation, any substantive expertise that may be required or helpful, the availability of the mediator and any known conflict of interests. Each party will number the names in the order of preference.

In light of the parties' expressed preferences, the MMO will appoint the mediator. Normally, a single mediator will be appointed unless the parties agree otherwise.

Disclosures and Replacement of a Mediator

6   Any mediator, whether selected jointly by the parties or appointed by the MMO, will disclose both to the MMO and to the parties whether he or she has any financial or personal interest in the outcome of the mediation or whether there is any other matter of which the mediator is aware which could be regarded as involving a conflict of interest (whether apparent, potential or actual) in the mediation. Upon receiving any such information, or in any other circumstance in which a selected mediator indicates that he or she is unable to act, after soliciting the views of the parties, the MMO may replace the mediator, preferably from the lists of acceptable mediators previously returned by the parties.

Representation

7   Any party may be represented by persons of the party's choice. Representation by counsel is not required but highly recommended. Parties other than natural persons are expected to have present throughout the mediation an officer, partner or other employee with full authority to settle the dispute.

Date, Time and Place of the Mediation

8   The mediator will fix the date and the time of each mediation session. The mediation will be held at the MMO office convenient to the parties, or at such other place as the parties and the mediator agree.

Conduct of the Mediation and Authority of the Mediator

9   The mediator may conduct the mediation in such a manner as he or she considers appropriate, taking into account the circumstances of the case, the wishes of the parties, and the need for a speedy settlement of the dispute. The mediator does not have the authority to impose a settlement on the parties. The mediator is authorized to conduct both joint and separate meetings with the parties. If requested by all parties in writing, the mediator may make oral or written recommendations concerning an appropriate resolution of the dispute.

Privacy

10 Mediation sessions are private. Persons other than the parties and their representatives may attend only with the permission of the parties and with the consent of the mediator.

Confidentiality

11 All information, records, reports or other documents provided to any MMO in connection with the initiation of the mediation or produced in the mediation will be confidential. The mediator and every officer or employee of the MMO will not be compelled to divulge such records or to testify or give evidence in regard to the mediation in any adversary proceeding or judicial forum. The parties and everyone present at the mediation – including counsel and experts – will maintain the confidentiality of the mediation and will not rely upon, or introduce as evidence in any arbitral, judicial or other proceeding:

   (i)   views expressed or suggestions or offers made by another party or the mediator in the course of the mediation proceedings;

  (ii)   admissions made by another party in the course of the mediation proceedings; or

 (iii)   the fact that another party had or had not indicated a willingness to accept a proposal for settlement made by another party or by the mediator.

The requirement to confidentiality shall not apply if, and to the extent that:

   (i)   all parties consent to the disclosure; or

  (ii)   the mediator is required under the general law to make disclosure; or

 (iii)   the mediator reasonably considers that there is a serious risk of significant harm to the life or safety of any person if the information in question is not disclosed; or

 (iv)   the mediator reasonably considers that there is a serious risk of his/her being subject to criminal proceedings unless the information in question is disclosed.

Facts, documents or other things otherwise admissible in evidence in any arbitral, judicial or other proceeding, will not be rendered inadmissible by reason of their use in the mediation.

Exclusion of Liability
12 Neither the mediator, nor the MMO or any employee or consultant engaged by it will be liable to any party for any act or omission alleged in connection with any mediation conducted under these Rules.

Interpretation and Application of the Rules
13 The mediator will interpret and apply these Rules insofar as they relate to the mediator's duties and responsibilities. All other procedures will be interpreted and applied by the MMO administering the mediation.

Administrative Fees
14 Unless otherwise agreed by the parties to the mediation, all of the MMO's administrative fees and expenses, including, without limitation, the fees and expenses of the mediator, will be divided equally between or among the parties to the mediation.

Role of Mediator in Other Proceedings
15 Unless all parties agree in writing, the mediator may not act as an arbitrator or as a representative of, or counsel to, a party in any arbitral or judicial proceedings relating to the dispute that was the subject of the mediation.

Resort to Arbitral or Judicial Proceedings
16 The parties undertake not to initiate, during the mediation, any arbitral or judicial proceedings in respect of a dispute that is the subject of the mediation, except that a party may initiate arbitral or judicial proceedings when, in its opinion, such proceedings are either necessary to toll a limitations period, including a statute of limitations that may be applicable, or are necessary otherwise to preserve its rights in the event that the mediation is unsuccessful.

Referral to another MMO
17 In the event the parties express a preference to mediate in another

MEDAL Member country, the MMO may transfer responsibility for administering the mediation to the MMO requested by the parties.

Governing Law and Jurisdiction

18 The mediation shall be governed by, construed and take effect in accordance with the laws of the MMO administering the mediation. The courts of such MMO shall have exclusive jurisdiction to settle any claim, dispute or matter of difference which may arise out of or in connection with the mediation.

Termination of the mediation

19 Any of the Parties may withdraw from the Mediation at any time and shall immediately inform the Mediator and the other representatives in writing. The Mediation will terminate when:

- a Party withdraws from the Mediation; or

- the Mediator, at his/her discretion, withdraws from the mediation; or

- a written settlement agreement is concluded.

The mediator may also adjourn the mediation in order to allow parties to consider specific proposals, get further information or for any other reason, which the mediator considers helpful in furthering the mediation process. The mediation will then reconvene with the agreement of the parties.

Settlement agreements

20 Any settlement reached in the Mediation will not be legally binding until it has been reduced to writing and signed by, or on behalf of, the Parties.

MEDAL Partners

The addresses of the five MEDAL partners are:

ACB Mediation (Netherlands)
Bezuidenhoutseweg 12, 2594 AV Den Haag
Tel. +31 70 34 90 493

Fax +31 70 34 90 295
E-mail ACB@vno-ncw.nl
Website http://www.mediation-bedrijfsleven.nl/
    ADR Center (Italy)
Via del Babuino, 114 – 00187 Roma
Tel. +39 06 693.800.04
Fax +39 06 691.904.08
E-mail info@adrcenter.it
Website http://www.adrcenter.com/adrcenter/index.php
    CEDR Solve (UK)
International Dispute Resolution Centre, 70 Fleet St, London, EC4Y 1EU
Tel. +44 (0)20 7536 6060
Fax +44 (0)20 7536 6061
Email info@cedr-solve.com
Website http://www.cedrsolve.com//index.php?location=/default.htm
    CMAP (France)
39, Avenue Franklin D. Roosevelt, 75008 Paris
Tel. +33 1 44 95 11 40
Fax +33 1 44 95 11 49
Email blasserre@cmap.fr
Website http://www.cmap.fr/
    JAMS (USA) New York
Downtown, 45 Broadway, 28th Floor, New York, NY 10006
Tel. 001- 212-751-2700
Fax 001- 212-751-4099
Website http://www.jamsadr.com/index.asp
    JAMS (USA) San Francisco
Two Embacadero Center, Suite 1100, San Francisco, CA 94111, USA
Tel. 001-415-982-5267
Fax 001-415-982-5287
Website http://www.jamsadr.com/index.asp

5   UNCITRAL Model Law

Resolution adopted by the General Assembly

[on the report of the Sixth Committee (A/57/562 and Corr.1)]

57/18.   Model Law on International Commercial Conciliation of the United Nations Commission on International Trade Law

The General Assembly,

Recognizing the value for international trade of methods for settling commercial disputes in which the parties in dispute request a third person or persons to assist them in their attempt to settle the dispute amicably,

Noting that such dispute settlement methods, referred to by expressions such as conciliation and mediation and expressions of similar import, are increasingly used in international and domestic commercial practice as an alternative to litigation,

Considering that the use of such dispute settlement methods results in significant benefits, such as reducing the instances where a dispute leads to the termination of a commercial relationship, facilitating the administration of international transactions by commercial parties and producing savings in the administration of justice by States,

Convinced that the establishment of model legislation on these methods that is acceptable to States with different legal, social and economic systems would contribute to the development of harmonious international economic relations,

Noting with satisfaction the completion and adoption by the United Nations Commission on International Trade Law of the Model Law on International Commercial Conciliation,*

Believing that the Model Law will significantly assist States in enhancing their legislation governing the use of modern conciliation or mediation techniques and in formulating such legislation where none currently exists,

Noting that the preparation of the Model Law was the subject of due deliberation and extensive consultations with Governments and interested circles,

Convinced that the Model Law, together with the Conciliation Rules recommended by the General Assembly in its resolution 35/52 of 4 December 1980,

---

Official Records of the Genreal Assembly, Fifty-seventh Session, Supplement No. 17 (A/57/17), annex I.

contributes significantly to the establishment of a harmonized legal framework for the fair and efficient settlement of disputes arising in international commercial relations,

1. *Expresses its appreciation* to the United Nations Commission on International Trade Law for completing and adopting the Model Law on International Commercial Conciliation, the text of which is contained in the annex to the present resolution, and for preparing the Guide to Enactment and Use of the Model Law;

2. *Requests* the Secretary-General to make all efforts to ensure that the Model Law, together with its Guide to Enactment, becomes generally known and available;

3. *Recommends* that all States give due consideration to the enactment of the Model Law, in view of the desirability of uniformity of the law of dispute settlement procedures and the specific needs of international commercial conciliation practice.

52nd plenary meeting
19 November 2002

Part One

UNCITRAL Model Law on International Commercial Conciliation (2002)

Article 1. Scope of application and definitions

1. This Law applies to international[1] commercial[2] conciliation.

2. For the purposes of this Law, "conciliator" means a sole conciliator or two or more conciliators, as the case may be.

3. For the purposes of this Law, "conciliation" means a process, whether referred to by the expression conciliation, mediation or an expression of similar import, whereby parties request a third person or persons ("the conciliator") to assist them in their attempt to reach an amicable settlement of their dispute arising out of or relating to a contractual or other legal relationship. The conciliator does not have the authority to impose upon the parties a solution to the dispute.

4. A conciliation is international if:

(a) The parties to an agreement to conciliate have, at the time of the conclusion of that agreement, their places of business in different States; or

(b) The State in which the parties have their places of business is different from either:

(i) The State in which a substantial part of the obligations of the commercial relationship is to be performed; or

---

[1]States wishing to enact this Model Law to apply to domestic as well as international conciliation may wish to consider the following changes to the text:
— Delete the word "international" in paragraph 1 of article 1; and
— Delete paragraphs 4, 5 and 6 of article 1.

[2]The term "commercial" should be given a wide interpretation so as to cover matters arising from all relationships of a commercial nature, whether contractual or not. Relationships of a commercial nature include, but are not limited to, the following transactions: any trade transaction for the supply or exchange of goods or services; distribution agreement; commercial representation or agency; factoring; leasing; construction of works; consulting; engineering; licensing; investment; financing; banking; insurance; exploitation agreement or concession; joint venture and other forms of industrial or business cooperation; carriage of goods or passengers by air, sea, rail or road.

(ii) The State with which the subject matter of the dispute is most closely connected.

5. For the purposes of this article:

(a) If a party has more than one place of business, the place of business is that which has the closest relationship to the agreement to conciliate;

(b) If a party does not have a place of business, reference is to be made to the party's habitual residence.

6. This Law also applies to a commercial conciliation when the parties agree that the conciliation is international or agree to the applicability of this Law.

7. The parties are free to agree to exclude the applicability of this Law.

8. Subject to the provisions of paragraph 9 of this article, this Law applies irrespective of the basis upon which the conciliation is carried out, including agreement between the parties whether reached before or after a dispute has arisen, an obligation established by law, or a direction or suggestion of a court, arbitral tribunal or competent governmental entity.

9. This Law does not apply to:

(a) Cases where a judge or an arbitrator, in the course of judicial or arbitral proceedings, attempts to facilitate a settlement; and

(b) [. . .]

Article 2. Interpretation

1. In the interpretation of this Law, regard is to be had to its international origin and to the need to promote uniformity in its application and the observance of good faith.

2. Questions concerning matters governed by this Law which are not expressly settled in it are to be settled in conformity with the general principles on which this Law is based.

Article 3. Variation by agreement

Except for the provisions of article 2 and article 6, paragraph 3, the parties may agree to exclude or vary any of the provisions of this Law.

Article 4.   Commencement of conciliation proceedings[3]

1.   Conciliation proceedings in respect of a dispute that has arisen commence on the day on which the parties to that dispute agree to engage in conciliation proceedings.

2.   If a party that invited another party to conciliate does not receive an acceptance of the invitation within thirty days from the day on which the invitation was sent, or within such other period of time as specified in the invitation, the party may elect to treat this as a rejection of the invitation to conciliate.

Article 5.   Number and appointment of conciliators

1.   There shall be one conciliator, unless the parties agree that there shall be two or more conciliators.

2.   The parties shall endeavour to reach agreement on a conciliator or conciliators, unless a different procedure for their appointment has been agreed upon.

3.   Parties may seek the assistance of an institution or person in connection with the appointment of conciliators. In particular:

(a) A party may request such an institution or person to recommend suitable persons to act as conciliator; or

(b) The parties may agree that the appointment of one or more conciliators be made directly by such an institution or person.

4.   In recommending or appointing individuals to act as conciliator, the institution or person shall have regard to such considerations as are likely to secure the appointment of an independent and impartial conciliator and, where appropriate, shall take into account the advisability of appointing a conciliator of a nationality other than the nationalities of the parties.

---

[3]The following text is suggested for States that might wish to adopt a provision on the suspension of the limitation period:

Article X.   Suspension of limitation period

1.   When the conciliation proceedings commence, the running of the limitation period regarding the claim that is the subject matter of the conciliation is suspended.

2.   Where the conciliation proceedings have terminated without a settlement agreement, the limitation period resumes running from the time the conciliation ended without a settlement agreement.

5.   When a person is approached in connection with his or her possible appointment as conciliator, he or she shall disclose any circumstances likely to give rise to justifiable doubts as to his or her impartiality or independence. A conciliator, from the time of his or her appointment and throughout the conciliation proceedings, shall without delay disclose any such circumstances to the parties unless they have already been informed of them by him or her.

Article 6.   Conduct of conciliation

1.   The parties are free to agree, by reference to a set of rules or otherwise, on the manner in which the conciliation is to be conducted.

2.   Failing agreement on the manner in which the conciliation is to be conducted, the conciliator may conduct the conciliation proceedings in such a manner as the conciliator considers appropriate, taking into account the circumstances of the case, any wishes that the parties may express and the need for a speedy settlement of the dispute.

3.   In any case, in conducting the proceedings, the conciliator shall seek to maintain fair treatment of the parties and, in so doing, shall take into account the circumstances of the case.

4.   The conciliator may, at any stage of the conciliation proceedings, make proposals for a settlement of the dispute.

Article 7.   Communication between conciliator and parties

The conciliator may meet or communicate with the parties together or with each of them separately.

Article 8.   Disclosure of information

When the conciliator receives information concerning the dispute from a party, the conciliator may disclose the substance of that information to any other party to the conciliation. However, when a party gives any information to the conciliator, subject to a specific condition that it be kept confidential, that information shall not be disclosed to any other party to the conciliation.

Article 9.   Confidentiality

Unless otherwise agreed by the parties, all information relating to the conciliation proceedings shall be kept confidential, except where disclosure is required under the law or for the purposes of implementation or enforcement of a settlement agreement.

Article 10.   Admissibility of evidence in other proceedings

1.   A party to the conciliation proceedings, the conciliator and any third person, including those involved in the administration of the conciliation proceedings, shall not in arbitral, judicial or similar proceedings rely on, introduce as evidence or give testimony or evidence regarding any of the following:

(a) An invitation by a party to engage in conciliation proceedings or the fact that a party was willing to participate in conciliation proceedings;

(b) Views expressed or suggestions made by a party in the conciliation in respect of a possible settlement of the dispute;

(c) Statements or admissions made by a party in the course of the conciliation proceedings;

(d) Proposals made by the conciliator;

(e) The fact that a party had indicated its willingness to accept a proposal for settlement made by the conciliator;

(f) A document prepared solely for purposes of the conciliation proceedings.

2.   Paragraph 1 of this article applies irrespective of the form of the information or evidence referred to therein.

3.   The disclosure of the information referred to in paragraph 1 of this article shall not be ordered by an arbitral tribunal, court or other competent governmental authority and, if such information is offered as evidence in contravention of paragraph 1 of this article, that evidence shall be treated as inadmissible. Nevertheless, such information may be disclosed or admitted in evidence to the extent required under the law or for the purposes of implementation or enforcement of a settlement agreement.

4.   The provisions of paragraphs 1, 2 and 3 of this article apply whether or not the arbitral, judicial or similar proceedings relate to the dispute that is or was the subject matter of the conciliation proceedings.

5.   Subject to the limitations of paragraph 1 of this article, evidence that is otherwise admissible in arbitral or judicial or similar proceedings does not become inadmissible as a consequence of having been used in a conciliation.

Article 11.   Termination of conciliation proceedings

The conciliation proceedings are terminated:

(a) By the conclusion of a settlement agreement by the parties, on the date of the agreement;

(b) By a declaration of the conciliator, after consultation with the parties, to the effect that further efforts at conciliation are no longer justified, on the date of the declaration;

(c) By a declaration of the parties addressed to the conciliator to the effect that the conciliation proceedings are terminated, on the date of the declaration; or

(d) By a declaration of a party to the other party or parties and the conciliator, if appointed, to the effect that the conciliation proceedings are terminated, on the date of the declaration.

Article 12.   Conciliator acting as arbitrator

Unless otherwise agreed by the parties, the conciliator shall not act as an arbitrator in respect of a dispute that was or is the subject of the conciliation proceedings or in respect of another dispute that has arisen from the same contract or legal relationship or any related contract or legal relationship.

Article 13.   Resort to arbitral or judicial proceedings

Where the parties have agreed to conciliate and have expressly undertaken not to initiate during a specified period of time or until a specified event has occurred arbitral or judicial proceedings with respect to an existing or future dispute, such an undertaking shall be given effect by the arbitral tribunal or the court until the terms of the undertaking have been complied with, except to the extent necessary for a party, in its opinion, to preserve its rights. Initiation of such proceedings is not of itself to be regarded as a waiver of the agreement to conciliate or as a termination of the conciliation proceedings.

Article 14.   Enforceability of settlement agreement[4]

If the parties conclude an agreement settling a dispute, that settlement agreement is binding and enforceable . . . [*the enacting State may insert a description of the method of enforcing settlement agreements or refer to provisions governing such enforcement*].

---

[4]When implementing the procedure for enforcement of settlement agreements, an enacting State may consider the possibility of such a procedure being mandatory.

6   European Code of Conduct for Mediators

EUROPEAN CODE OF CONDUCT FOR MEDIATORS

This code of conduct sets out a number of principles to which individual mediators can voluntarily decide to commit, under their own responsibility. It is intended to be applicable to all kinds of mediation in civil and commercial matters.

Organisations providing mediation services can also make such a commitment, by asking mediators acting under the auspices of their organisation to respect the code. Organisations have the opportunity to make available information on the measures they are taking to support the respect of the code by individual mediators through, for example, training, evaluation and monitoring.

For the purposes of the code mediation is defined as any process where two or more parties agree to the appointment of a third-party – hereinafter "the mediator" - to help the parties to solve a dispute by reaching an agreement without adjudication and regardless of how that process may be called or commonly referred to in each Member State.

Adherence to the code is without prejudice to national legislation or rules regulating individual professions.

Organisations providing mediation services may wish to develop more detailed codes adapted to their specific context or the types of mediation services they offer, as well as with regard to specific areas such as family mediation or consumer mediation.

European Code of Conduct for Mediators

European Code of Conduct for Mediators

1. COMPETENCE AND APPOINTMENT OF MEDIATORS

1.1 Competence

Mediators shall be competent and knowledgeable in the process of mediation. Relevant factors shall include proper training and continuous updating of their education and practice in mediation skills, having regard to any relevant standards or accreditation schemes.

1.2 Appointment

The mediator will confer with the parties regarding suitable dates on which the mediation may take place. The mediator shall satisfy him/herself as to his/her background and competence to conduct the mediation before accepting the appointment and, upon request, disclose information concerning his/her background and experience to the parties.

1.3 Advertising/promotion of the mediator's services

Mediators may promote their practice, in a professional, truthful and dignified way.

2. INDEPENDENCE AND IMPARTIALITY

2.1 Independence and neutrality

The mediator must not act, or, having started to do so, continue to act, before having disclosed any circumstances that may, or may be seen to, affect his or her independence or conflict of interests. The duty to disclose is a continuing obligation throughout the process.

Such circumstances shall include
- any personal or business relationship with one of the parties,
- any financial or other interest, direct or indirect, in the outcome of the mediation, or
- the mediator, or a member of his or her firm, having acted in any capacity other than mediator for one of the parties.

In such cases the mediator may only accept or continue the mediation provided that he/she is certain of being able to carry out the mediation with full independence and neutrality in order to guarantee full impartiality and that the parties explicitly consent.

2.2 Impartiality

The mediator shall at all times act, and endeavour to be seen to act, with impartiality towards the parties and be committed to serve all parties equally with respect to the process of mediation.

European Code of Conduct for Mediators

European Code of Conduct for Mediators

3. THE MEDIATION AGREEMENT, PROCESS, SETTLEMENT AND FEES

3.1   Procedure

The mediator shall satisfy himself/herself that the parties to the mediation understand the characteristics of the mediation process and the role of the mediator and the parties in it.

The mediator shall in particular ensure that prior to commencement of the mediation the parties have understood and expressly agreed the terms and conditions of the mediation agreement including in particular any applicable provisions relating to obligations of confidentiality on the mediator and on the parties.

The mediation agreement shall, upon request of the parties, be drawn up in writing.

The mediator shall conduct the proceedings in an appropriate manner, taking into account the circumstances of the case, including possible power imbalances and the rule of law, any wishes the parties may express and the need for a prompt settlement of the dispute. The parties shall be free to agree with the mediator, by reference to a set of rules or otherwise, on the manner in which the mediation is to be conducted.

The mediator, if he/she deems it useful, may hear the parties separately.

3.2   Fairness of the process

The mediator shall ensure that all parties have adequate opportunities to be involved in the process.

The mediator if appropriate shall inform the parties, and may terminate the mediation, if:
- a settlement is being reached that for the mediator appears unenforceable or illegal, having regard to the circumstances of the case and the competence of the mediator for making such an assessment, or
- the mediator considers that continuing the mediation is unlikely to result in a settlement.

3.3   The end of the process

The mediator shall take all appropriate measures to ensure that any understanding is reached by all parties through knowing and informed consent, and that all parties understand the terms of the agreement.

The parties may withdraw from the mediation at any time without giving any justification.

The mediator may, upon request of the parties and within the limits of his or her competence, inform the parties as to how they may formalise the agreement and as to the possibilities for making the agreement enforceable.

European Code of Conduct for Mediators

European Code of Conduct for Mediators

3.4 Fees

Where not already provided, the mediator must always supply the parties with complete information on the mode of remuneration which he intends to apply. He/she shall not accept a mediation before the principles of his/her remuneration have been accepted by all parties concerned.

4. CONFIDENTIALITY

The mediator shall keep confidential all information, arising out of or in connection with the mediation, including the fact that the mediation is to take place or has taken place, unless compelled by law or public policy grounds. Any information disclosed in confidence to mediators by one of the parties shall not be disclosed to the other parties without permission or unless compelled by law.

Further Reading

M Albright, *Madam Secretary* (Macmillan, 2003)

R Axelrod, *The Evolution of Co-operation* (Penguin Books Ltd, 2004)

J Bercovitch & J Z Rubin, *Mediation in International Relations: Multiple Approaches to Conflict Management* (Macmillan, 1994)

M Nesic & L Boulle, *Mediation – Principles, Process, Practice* (Tottel Publishing, 2001)

H Brown & A Marriott, *ADR Practices and Principles* (Sweet & Maxwell, 1999)

C Bühring-Uhle, *Arbitration and Mediation in International Business* (Kluwer, 1996)

J Corbin, *Gaza First* (Bloomsbury, 1994)

T F Crum, *The Magic of Conflict* (Pocket Books, 1999)

EA Dauer (Ed), *Manual of Dispute Resolution: ADR Law and Practice*, Vols I & II (McGraw-Hill, 1994)

R Fisher & Scott Brown, *Getting Together: Building a Relationship that gets to Yes* (Penguin, 1989)

R Fisher & D Shapiro, *Beyond reason: Using Emotions as You Negotiate* (Random House Business Books, 2006)

R Fisher & W Ury, *Getting to Yes: The Secret to Successful Negotiation* (Random House Business Books, 2003)

JC Freund, *The Neutral Negotiator* (Prentice Hall, 1994)

E Galton, *Representing Clients in Mediation* (Texas Lawyer Press, 1994)

J Gresser, *Piloting through Chaos* (Five Rings press, 1996)

TJ Griffin & WR Daggatt, *The Global Negotiator: Building Strong Business Relationships Anywhere in the World* (Harper Business, 1992)

DW Hendon & R A Hendon, *How to Negotiate Worldwide: A Practical Handbook* (Gower, 1994)

JF Henry & J K Lieberman, *The Manager's Guide to Resolving Legal Disputes* (Harper & Row, 1985)

M Hunter *et al*, *The Freshfields Guide to Arbitration and ADR Clauses in International Contracts* (Kluwer, 1999)

J Krivis, *Lessons from the Lion's Den: A Mediator's Stories of Conflict About Love, Money, Anger and the Strategies That Resolved Them* (Jossey Bass Wiley, 2006)

D A Lax & JK Sebenius, *The Manager as Negotiator: Bargaining for Co-operation and Competitive Gain* (Free Press, 1987)

Further Reading

JD Lewis, *The Connected Corporation: How Leading Companies Win through Customer-Supplier Alliances* (Simon & Schuster Ltd, 1996)

KJ Mackie & E P Carroll, *ADR Route Map, 2nd Ed.* (CEDR, 1998)

KJ Mackie (Ed), *A Handbook of Dispute Resolution – ADR in Action* (Routledge, 1991)

KJ Mackie, D Miles, W Marsh & T Allen,*The ADR Practice Guide: Commercial Dispute Resolution* (Tottel Publishing, 2000)

BS Mayer, *Beyond Neutrality – Confronting the Crisis in Conflict Resolution* (Jossey Bass Whiley, 2004)

JB McCall, & M B Warrington, *Marketing by Agreement: A Cross-Cultural Approach to Business Negotiations,* 2nd Ed. (John Wiley and Sons, 1984)

Senator George Mitchell, *Making Peace* (William Heinemann, London, 1999)

C Newmark & A Monaghan, *Butterworths Mediators on Mediation: Leading Mediator Perspectives on the Practice of Commercial Mediation* (Tottel Publishing, 2005)

OECD Guidelines for Multinational Enterprises (OECD,2000)

M Parker Follett, *The Creative Experience* (The Thoemmes Libraries, 2003)

H Raiffa, *The Art and Science of Negotiation* (Harvard University Press, 1985)

JW Salacuse, *Making Global Deals: what every Executive should know about negotiating abroad* (Times Books, 1992)

Jane Singer et al, *The EU Mediation Atlas: Practice and Regulation* (Lexis Nexis, 2004)

L Susskind & J Cruikshank, *Breaking the Impasse: Consensual Approaches to Resolving Public Disputes* (Basic Books, 1989)

William Ury, *Getting Past No* (Bantam Books, 1993)

William Ury, *The Third Side* (Penguin, 2005)

Lord Woolf, *Review of the Working Methods of the European Court of Human Rights* (Strasbourg, 2005)

S York, *Practical ADR Handbook (Dispute Resolution)* (Sweet & Maxwell, 1996)

About the Authors

Eileen Carroll has a distinguished record in international dispute resolution both as a lawyer and a mediator. She co-founded CEDR in 1990, and is seen as one of the top mediators in Europe, receiving an award for her pioneering work from the New York based CPR Institute of Dispute Resolution. Her career began in international chemical and industrial consultancy, moving to Law in 1981 and became a partner in a major London firm in 1987. In over 20 years of practice she has worked with multinational corporations in Europe, the Far East, India and the United States. She spent 10 years working intensively with an American client, spending time with a US firm in San Francisco. She has written and lectured extensively on international negotiation and settlement techniques including at Harvard and the OECD, and founded the Mary Parker Follett group of leading international women mediators. In 2005 she received an Entrepreneurial Award from the European Union of Women.

Dr Karl Mackie has received international acknowledgment as being one of Europe's best practitioners and experts in negotiation, mediation and conflict management and has written widely on the subject. Engaged in dispute resolution practice since 1980, he became founding Chief Executive of CEDR in 1990. A barrister and psychologist by training, he has been a partner in a business strategy consultancy, an academic at leading UK universities and an arbitrator as well as a commercial mediator. Uniquely qualified in law, psychology, education and management, his clients comment on the diplomacy and good humour he brings to conflict resolution, alongside a toughness and determination to break through apparently intractable deadlocks. His work has taken him into virtually every sector of business and legal practice, mediating cases with parties from over 30 countries. He helped take CEDR from a £12,000 start-up to be one of the world's largest and best known non-profit centres of excellence in dispute and conflict management services.

Alison Carroll has a distinguished record of
international service. Resident both as a teacher and a scholar. She co-authored a Clerk in Town
Hall as co-author, one of the top managers in
Human Relations ... within the industry. She
worked at the *New York Times* based CPR in charge of
public relations. Her educational ... she
earned chemical and industrial University,
earning her degree in 1984 and became a teacher in
English Literature later in 1987. In over 20 years of
practice she has worked different parts of the
centre of England, the Far East and the United States. She spent 10
years abroad and she works independently spending her time with a US
medical firm ... She has worked and trained consultancies. International software and different companies including ... She worked on the
SCRUD and founded the MIPV Forward role in a group of helping the research of
various consultants in 2005 over 20 over 20 Computational Award from the
Harrison House of Service.

Dr. Karl Mueller has received international
acknowledgment for being one of Europe's best
practitioners and foremost negotiation mediation ... and led the management call ... senior
executive in the Shmidt-Freeman in Stuttgart, Germany a practice since 1985. He became a leading
travel executive to CoEDE in GPR. A position
and has climbed his way up the industry
practice in business, practice, executive theory, for
academic management leading UK universities and an individual there. He was ... as a recognized of the higher
European certified in leading technology education
and management centre clients report in the marketplace by one great account
Pre in presses conflict's future strategic ... toughness and determination to
drive through, apparently inside deadlines. He is co-author when he writes
simultaneously over ... of training and legal profile ... media and society with
experience from over 20 companies. The helped take CPDR from over a decade
... up to being one of the world's largest and best known not-for-profit service of
its class in negotiate and certified management services.

224